D1246786

Gay Liberation to Campus Assimilation

"Patrick Dilley's new historical study based on universities in the Midwest since 1969 helps transform the study and understanding of the diversity and complexity of both student life and student organizations on the American campus. In analyzing the trends from Gay Liberation to Campus Assimilation, he simultaneously provides a sorely needed study of previously overlooked students and their organizations. By bringing this story into the mainstream of higher education scholarship, he has expanded our understanding of the entire American college and university structures and cultures."
— John R. Thelin, *Professor of Higher Education and Public Policy,*
University of Kentucky, USA

"In this meticulously researched book, Patrick Dilley not only gives us the first comprehensive history of LGBT organizing on college campuses, he also provides a framework for understanding how these student groups formed, did their work, and ultimately changed their politics with the world around them. This is required reading for historians of education, activism, and sexuality."
— Nicholas L. Syrett, *Professor of Women, Gender, and Sexuality Studies,*
University of Kansas, USA

"In this book, Dilley articulates the evolution of non-heterosexual student movements and, at the same time, provides powerfully moving stories of individual student leaders of the time period. He presents nuanced evidence of the inherent tensions caused by local, regional, and historical contexts, as students struggle to define the purposes of these early activist groups and as these purposes evolve to meet contemporary needs of students. This comprehensive and well-sourced history is an excellent contribution to our understanding of social movements on college campuses."
— Robert D. Reason, *Professor of Student Affairs and Higher Education,*
Iowa State University, USA

"The explosive rise of queer university student organizations is one of the most important stories in the history of higher education during the 1960s–70s, yet it is shockingly understudied largely because of how difficult it is to unearth sources for these ephemeral groups. Patrick Dilley has broken ground for this research by compiling an impressive collection of accounts describing the surge of activism during these years at a variety of large Midwestern institutions."
— Jackie Blount, *Professor of Philosophy and History of Education,*
Ohio State University, USA

"Once again, Patrick Dilley has applied his considerable talent to bring forward important stories in the history of higher education and of what some scholars now call queer history. Through painstaking archival research, he focuses on students who were then–as queer students are now–engaged in the project of liberation. Dilley's newest project connects past to present, honors student organizers and activists, and illuminates enduring themes in the evolution of student engagement with and against their own institutions. This book will be a key resource for understanding queer campus life in the second half of the 20th century."
—Kristen A. Renn, *Professor of Higher, Adult, and Lifelong Education, Michigan State University, USA*

Patrick Dilley

Gay Liberation to Campus Assimilation

Early Non-Heterosexual Student Organizing at
Midwestern Universities

palgrave
macmillan

Patrick Dilley
Educational Administration and Higher Education
Southern Illinois University
Carbondale, IL, USA

ISBN 978-3-030-04644-6 ISBN 978-3-030-04645-3 (eBook)
https://doi.org/10.1007/978-3-030-04645-3

Library of Congress Control Number: 2019931006

This Palgrave Macmillan imprint is published by the registered company Springer Nature Switzerland AG
The registered company address is: Gewerbestrasse 11, 6330 Cham, Switzerland

Also by Patrick Dilley
Queer Man on Campus: A History of Non-Heterosexual Men in College, 1945–2000
The Transformation of Women's Higher Education: The Legacy of Virginia Gildersleeve

ACKNOWLEDGMENTS

Historians are indebted to those who save and cull pieces of the past for future use. Of note in this project are the unnamed folks who scanned and made searchable the student newspapers at the University of Illinois, the University of Michigan, the Ohio State University, Michigan State University, and others. When I began this project, I was dependent upon what report-age and clippings others had found and saved; I never thought I would be able to read, at my leisure, far from their campus of origin, those student newspapers. A part of me is glad I did not finish this project "on schedule," so that I was able to learn—and to cite—from those sources.

Similarly, I am thankful to institutional archivists and administrators from across the Midwest, including Ellen Swain, Anna Trammell, Chris Pram, Monica Burney, Katie Nichols, and Curt McKay at the University of Illinois; Frederick Honhart, Jennie Russell, Megan Malone, and Ruth Ann Jones at Michigan State University; Bradley D. Cook, Carol Fischer, Dale Mitchell, Eric Groves, and Doug Bauder at Indiana University; Jean-Nicholas Tretter, Rachel Mattson, and Lisa Vecoli of the Tretter Collection at the University of Minnesota; Beth Zemsky, Peter Berg, and Erik Moore, also at the University of Minnesota; David McCartney at the University of Iowa; Gerald Peterson at the University of Northern Iowa; Jill Rosenshield at the University of Wisconsin at Madison; Anselm M. Huelsbergen, Julie Herada, and Debbie Landi at the University of Missouri; Kathy A. Lafferty, Emily Beran, and Becky Schulez at the Spencer Research Library at the University of Kansas (KU); Michelle Drobik at the Ohio State University; Stephen Kerber at the Louisa H. Bowman University Archives at Southern Illinois University Edwardsville; Tanya Zanish-Belcher, Jerry P. Hayes, and Michele Christian at Iowa State University; Karen L. Jania at the Bentley Historical Library at the University of Michigan; and Lois Henrickson, also at the University of Michigan. A queer kudos to Dr. Leah Reinert for doing the legwork for me at the University of Minnesota. Thanks, too, to Jim Morrow and the late Stuart Timmons, for their assistance at the ONE Archives/National Gay & Lesbian Archives at the University of Southern California (USC) Libraries. Hats off to Tim Bradlee for keeping (and printing) a chronology of events at KU in 1990, and to KU's Julia Gilmore Gaughan for tracking down Student Senate Bill 1998-093. Special thanks to Amy Cantu at the Ann Arbor District Library.

In addition, other librarians and archivists at a number of institutions assisted me in locating and accessing information about gay and lesbian students and organizing at their campuses. Thank you to the staffs of the Bentley Historical Library at the University of Michigan, the University of Kansas, the University of Illinois, the Ohio State University, the University of Northern Iowa, Iowa State University, the University of Iowa, the University of Missouri, Michigan State University, the University of Minnesota–Twin Cities, Southern Illinois University Edwardsville, the University of Missouri at St. Louis, the University of Wisconsin, Indiana University, and the Kinsey Institute at Indiana University.

Working with student newspaper editorial staffs, which changed, of course, during the 16 years I worked on this project, was very rewarding. I thank the editorial staff at the *Iowa State Daily*, *Daily Illini*, *The Michigan Daily*, and the *Ohio State Lantern* for assistance obtaining permission for photographs for this book. James Andres and Dennis Brumm must be congratulated and thanked for publishing their memories, photographs, and transcriptions covering the early history of gay organizing at Southern Illinois University Edwardsville and Iowa State University, respectively. I appreciate the assistance of the *Minneapolis Star Tribune* and Barcroft Media for allowing me to license images they each owned. In addition, thanks to Stephen Behrens, Brian Smith, Carol Wayman, and Dan Jones for use of their photographs.

I am immensely grateful to the former college student activists who spoke with me over the course of this project. Thank you to Jim Toy, Jerry De Grieck, Dan Jones, Leonard Graaf, Ruth Lichtwardt, David Hardy, Carol Wayman, Michael Blake, Kristina Boerger, and Steve Carlson. I wish I could have included more of our conversations within this text. I also wish I could have profiled all of the institutions I researched.

I was fortunate enough to present portions of the data and my thinking about this project at a number of academic conferences, including the History of Education Society, the Organization of Educational Historians, the American College Personnel Society, the Association for the Study of Higher Education, the Midwest Educational Research Association, and the American Educational Research Association. I thank the conference proposal reviewers for their feedback. Additionally, in conference sessions, Jackie Blount, Karen Graves, and Ellen Broido gave comments that helped my thinking and my writing.

I would particularly like to thank my colleagues in the History of Education Society: Michael Havel, Jackie Blount, Lucy Bailey, Karen Graves, Margaret Nash, Linda Eisenman, and Andrea Walton. Their encouragement and joviality have sustained me through this project. Also essential to me for the past 16 years were my friends Eric Moore, Kristen Renn, Jim Antony, Karl Woelz, William Harris, Tamara Yakobowski, Judith Green, and Saran Donahoo.

The editorial staff at Palgrave Macmillan was supportive, encouraging, and insistent when necessary. I want to thank the original commissioning editor, Mara Berkoff, for her continued belief in my research projects. Milana Vernikova, who provided much assistance during my first Palgrave book, maintained her excellent oversight of the project. Linda Braus, the editorial coordinator, was prompt and understanding, as well as having an excellent editorial eye.

This project was funded in part through a Faculty Seed Grant Award and research funding from Southern Illinois University Carbondale, as well as a grant from the Association of College Personnel Administration. I thank both institutions for their support, although neither have any responsibility for what I write in this book.

Finally, this book is dedicated to someone I only met once. At the first meeting of the History of Education Society I attended, I knew few other people. For the open business meeting lunch, I hid on the side, at a large, round table. There were a few newbies, and across the table were two senior colleagues, heads close, involved in a conversation that did not concern us. At one point, I mentioned to one of my lunch-mates that my main line of research had been gay and lesbian college students. "But I'm not sure I will ever do anything with it," I said. "I think the interest in the subject is gone."

After the lunch session ended, I gathered my bag to leave. One of the senior colleagues came up to me and said, out of nowhere, "You have to continue your work. I use your work in my classes, and what you do is too important not to finish." When I saw his name tag, I realized I knew his work, had read and admired it in graduate school. I thanked him, and he walked away.

Unfortunately, I was unable to complete the project before his untimely passing. Professor Harold Wechsler, I hope this book is close to what you had in mind.

CONTENTS

1 An Introduction to Early Gay and Lesbian Campus
   Organizing   1

2 Student Groups' Formulation of Gay Liberation Identity
   in the 1970s: Part I   13

3 Student Groups' Formulation of Gay Liberation Identity
   in the 1970s: Part II   75

4 Gay and Lesbian Student Groups Struggle to Serve
   Campus in the 1980s   119

5 Student Groups Assimilate Despite Campus Resistance in
   the Early 1990s   181

6 How Non-heterosexual Student Groups Utilized
   Liberation to Achieve Campus Assimilation   233

Bibliography   253

Index   257

List of Figures

Fig. 1.1   Jack Baker, University of Minnesota–Twin Cities initial student
            body president campaign photo, 1970. (From the Michael
            McConnell Files. Used courtesy of the Jean-Nickolaus Tretter
            Collection in GLBT Studies, University of Minnesota Libraries)
            Jack Baker's initial campaign poster for his first campaign to
            be student body president of the University of Minnesota–Twin
            Cities. In this image, Baker consciously wearing high heels. The
            queering of his image was not reflective of Baker's disposition
            or his campaign.   2
Fig. 2.1   University of Minnesota–Twin Cities FREE picket, 1970.
            (Powell Kruger, copyright 1970, *Star Tribune*)
            Members of FREE at the University of Minnesota picket at
            the Minnesota State Services for the Blind building, February
            10, 1970. The picket was an opportunity for activism for equity
            of rights as well as for visibility of the FREE and its issues. FREE
            co-founder Koreen Philips, the woman with glasses, is the fourth
            person from the left in the photograph; the other co-founder,
            Stephen Ihrig, is the man behind her, holding the poster that
            says "Homos Are Human."   26
Fig. 2.2   Jack Baker, University of Minnesota–Twin Cities second student
            body president campaign poster, 1970. (From the Michael
            McConnell Files. Used courtesy of the Jean-Nickolaus Tretter
            Collection in GLBT Studies, University of Minnesota Libraries)
            Jack Baker's second campaign poster for his 1970 student
            body president campaign at the University of Minnesota–Twin
            Cities. This one more accurately represents Baker's ideology of

gay assimilation into straight society. The image plays on all of
the traditional political tropes—flag, Lincoln, the Bible, apple pie,
babies, and a kindly grandmother (local pizza maven Mama Dee).   27

Fig. 2.3   Jim Toy, University of Michigan, 1973. (*The Michigan Daily*,
The Michigan Daily Digital Archives, Bentley Historical
Library, The University of Michigan)
Jim Toy in 1973. One of the founders of Gay Liberation at
the University and in the state of Michigan, Toy was the first
man appointed by a university as an advocate for non-
heterosexual students. The framed photo over his left hand is a
desecrated portrait of Richard Nixon.   28

Fig. 2.4   Jerry De Grieck and Nancy Wechsler, 1972. (*Ann Arbor News*,
courtesy of Ann Arbor District Library, copyright Barcroft
Media; used with permission)
Jerry De Grieck and Nancy Wechsler, 1972. De Grieck was
the University of Michigan student government officer who
defied the administration by unlocking the Student Activities
Building to allow a gay conference to be held on campus. De
Grieck and Wechsler, who were also students at Michigan, were
elected to the East Lansing City Council in 1971. Both publicly
came out as non-heterosexual while on the city council.   42

Fig. 2.5   Gay Liberation at the Indiana University, 1973. (Indiana
University Archives (P0066957))
Members of the Gay Lib at the Indiana University. In this
image from the 1974 *Arbutus* yearbook shows them smiling
while raising their fists as a sign of political resistance and
solidarity. The group was far less militant than it was fun-loving.   43

Fig. 2.6   Gay Liberation Halloween Dance, Indiana University, 1974.
(Indiana University Archives (P0066955))   44

Fig. 2.7   Gay Liberation Halloween Dance, Indiana University, 1974.
(Indiana University Archives (P0066956))
Gay Lib's Halloween Dances at Indiana University rose to
campus legend in the 1970s. These two photos, from the 1975
Arbutus yearbook, demonstrate the gender-bending, sexualized
outlandishness and cross-gendered attendance that
characterized the events.   45

Fig. 2.8   Gay Liberation Front in homecoming parade, University of
Iowa, 1970. (*Hawkeye Yearbook*, 1971, University Archives,
The University of Iowa Libraries)
Iowa University crowned no homecoming queen in 1970,
but the homecoming parade did feature the first public
demonstration of the campus' GLF.   50

Fig. 3.1   Michigan State Gay Liberation participates in the march at
Vietnam Veterans Against the War, Washington, D.C., 1971.
(Copyright Steve Behrens; used with permission)
Members of Gay Liberation at Michigan State University
traveled to Washington, D.C., to participate in the Vietnam
Veterans Against the War march, April 24, 1971. In this photo,
they are joined by members of the DC Gay Liberation Front.   81

Fig. 3.2   Dan Jones, Michigan State University student body president
campaign poster, 1978. (Courtesy of Daniel P. Jones)
Dan Jones ran for student body president at Michigan State
University in 1978. His campaign poster traded on implicit
male sexuality (a strategy gaining prevalence in the 1970s) as
well as the notion of a gay person cleaning up the traditionally
heterosexual student government.   85

Fig. 3.3   University of Missouri Gay Liberation march to first on-campus
meeting, April 20, 1978. (Copyright Brian Smith; courtesy of
University Archives, the University of Missouri)
Glenda Dilley, strumming her guitar and singing, leads Gay
Liberation at the University of Missouri to its first on-campus
meeting, date. Soon after this photo was taken, the Mizzou
students—along with the journalists covering their march—
would be subjected to verbal harassment and physical violence.   110

Fig. 4.1   Masked protesters occupy president's office, University of
Michigan, 1984. (*Ann Arbor News*, courtesy of Ann Arbor
District Library; copyright Barcroft Media; used with permission)
The "Unknown Comic" was a short-lived celebrity in the
mid-1970s; he wore a paper bag over his head when he
performed, to save him from public ridicule. These protesters at
the University of Michigan in 1984 used that concept to
demonstrate both the ubiquitous ubiquity of non-heterosexuals
on campus along with the fear of coming out on campus that
many felt. These protesters had just marched across the campus,
ending at the office of the university president, to bring
attention to the University's lack of attention to their calls for
codifications of campus rights and protections.   129

Fig. 4.2   Ruth Lichtwardt of Gay and Lesbian Services of Kansas, circa
1985. (Kenneth Spencer Research Library, University of Kansas
Libraries, The University of Kansas)
Ruth Lichtwardt being interviewed by KJHK radio, mid-
1980s. Lichtwardt was the longest-serving leader of the
non-heterosexual student group at the University of Kansas.
She was at the center of one of the most controversial eras of
discrimination and harassment of gays and lesbians at KU, one
much more insidious than was generally known to the public.   132

Fig. 4.3   Protesters at the University of Illinois, 1986. (Jean Lachat, copyright *Daily Illini*, courtesy of University of Illinois Archives, the University of Illinois)
            Student supporters of gay rights march in protest of the University's continued refusal to codify gay and lesbian protections on campus, January 30, 1987.   150

Fig. 4.4   Carol Wayman of the University of Michigan's LaGROC, circa 1985. (Courtesy of Carol Wayman)
            Carol Wayman was the founder of the second iteration of LaGROC at the University of Michigan. Wayman's political style utilized brazen public confrontations to draw awareness to issues non-heterosexual students faced, which often served to shame the administration.   156

Fig. 4.5   LaGROC occupies Virginia Nordby's office at the University of Michigan, 1984. (*The Michigan Daily*, The Michigan Daily Digital Archives, Bentley Historical Library, The University of Michigan)
            LaGROC occupies the office of the University of Michigan's director of Affirmative Action, Virginia Nordby, whose back is to the viewer in this photo. Nordby and LaGROC had publicly contradicted each other over the understood outcomes of a meeting about enacting protections for non-heterosexuals on campus. To ensure a greater understanding, LaGROC decided to visit Nordby, bringing along the press, to ensure a record of the conversation. Carol Wayman is on the left side of the photo, second from the top.   161

Fig. 5.1   Tom Fletcher leads a protest against ROTC's discrimination policy, Ohio State University, 1990. (*Ohio State Lantern*, courtesy of Ohio State University Libraries University Archives, The Ohio State University)
            Tom Fletcher, in military drag, leads protesters in a campus march against OSU ROTC's policy of not allowing gay or lesbian students to join its campus-based programs, May 7, 1990. Fletcher had been elected president of the Gay and Lesbian Alliance at OSU the previous fall.   190

Fig. 5.2   Protest at Ohio State University after gay threats, 1990. (*Ohio State Lantern*, courtesy of Ohio State University Libraries University Archives, The Ohio State University)
            Tom Fletcher and Mike Scarce were roommates at OSU, as well as officers in GALA. After months of enduring harassment and threats of violence, they forced the University to respond. OSU's housing director shut down the floor they lived on, separating the perpetrators by transferring all of the men to other residence halls.

Students supporting Fletcher and Scarce, and those supporting
their tormentors, held opposing protests, May 25, 1990.   194

Fig. 5.3   Suzanne Denevan, University of Minnesota–Twin Cities, ACT
UP Minnesota protest, 1990. (*Minnesota Daily*, courtesy of
University of Minnesota Archives, University of Minnesota–
Twin Cities)
Suzanne Denevan was elected student body president at the
University of Minnesota–Twin Cities in 1990. Although not
publicly out when elected, she soon declared her lesbianism at
this protest in June, 1990, speaking out against ROTC and
DOD policies at a demonstration sponsored by ACT UP
Minnesota. She wears one of their T-shirts.   204

Fig. 5.4   Queer Nation kiss-in against ROTC discrimination, Armory
Building at University of Minnesota, November 12, 1990.
(*Minnesota Daily*, courtesy of University of Minnesota Archives,
University of Minnesota–Twin Cities)
Held in conjunction with the National Gay and Lesbian Task
Force's "Creating Change" conference in Minneapolis that year,
this kiss-in was the first public action of Queer Nation, which had
just formed a campus chapter. Some critics of the time wondered
how public displays of affection related to issues of gay and lesbian
service in the military; the public displays were to demonstrate how
unquestioning the straight population was of its own social
entitlement and privilege in all aspects of U.S. society.   205

Fig. 5.5   Protesting students occupy Strong Hall Rotunda at University
of Kansas, 1990. (Kenneth Spencer Research Library, University
of Kansas Libraries, The University of Kansas)
A coalition of student minority groups and their supporters
occupy the Rotunda in the administration building, Strong
Hall, April 13, 1990.   209

Fig. 5.6   Protest in front of Watson Library, University of Kansas,
1990. (Kenneth Spencer Research Library, University of Kansas
Libraries, The University of Kansas)
From one of several campus protests at the University of Kansas
over lack of attention to minority student issues, July 18, 1990.
Members of GLSOK are prominent in this photograph, including
those holding the banner reading "No Bigots on My Campus," as
well as those directly behind, in front of, and aside them.   211

Fig. 5.7   Amy Myers, Gay and Lesbian Services of Kansas, Gay and
Lesbian Pride March, 1989. (Kenneth Spencer Research
Library, University of Kansas Libraries, The University of Kansas)

Gay Pride Week march, Summer 1990. Amy Myers, recently elected as director of Gay and Lesbian Services of Kansas, holds the sign reading "Save the Gay Whales."   213

Fig. 5.8   Aaron Andes speaks at rally for minority student issues, University of Kansas, 1990. (Kenneth Spencer Research Library, University of Kansas Libraries, The University of Kansas)

Aaron Andes, KU student and former GLSOK director, speaking from the steps of Watson Library at the Rally Against Discrimination and Sexism, September 28, 1990.   217

CHAPTER 1

An Introduction to Early Gay and Lesbian Campus Organizing

In the spring of 1971, Jack Baker was elected president of the student government of the University of Minnesota (Fig. 1.1). Baker's campaign was structured around his being an outsider; specifically, he presented himself in a fashion that activists and scholars would later label "queer." One of Baker's campaign posters depicted him in a coy pose, sitting, knees drawn up to his chest, his feet in brightly colored women's high heels, the caption: "Put yourself in Jack Baker's shoes."

Baker's impetus to run for student office stemmed from his desire to challenge campus and societal rules of acceptance of gays and lesbians, to promote gay visibility while advocating for inclusion into the structures of campus and society.

> He offered a platform based on student and minority rights... call[ing] for students to take an active role in policy decisions... [and advocating] equal roles for women and black on and off campus.[1]

Utilizing the nascent gay and lesbian organizing in Minneapolis and the UM Twin Cities campus, which he had helped form and foster, Baker became the first openly gay elected student body president in the United States, perhaps the most visible symbol of inclusion into a campus culture possible.

Baker, however, was non-traditional beyond being gay. For one thing, he was older, a graduate student in the University of Minnesota Law School, living off campus. He and his partner, Michael McConnell, were

© The Author(s) 2019
P. Dilley, *Gay Liberation to Campus Assimilation,*
https://doi.org/10.1007/978-3-030-04645-3_1

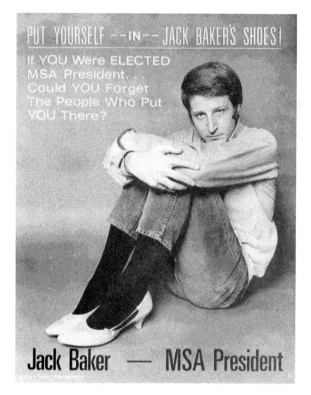

Fig. 1.1 Jack Baker, University of Minnesota–Twin Cities initial student body president campaign photo, 1970. (From the Michael McConnell Files. Used courtesy of the Jean-Nickolaus Tretter Collection in GLBT Studies, University of Minnesota Libraries)

Jack Baker's initial campaign poster for his first campaign to be student body president of the University of Minnesota–Twin Cities. In this image, Baker consciously wearing high heels. The queering of his image was not reflective of Baker's disposition or his campaign.

in the midst of ongoing struggles to marry legally and to force the University to extend to them benefits offered to married employees. For Baker, then, one freedom of being gay seemed to be epitomized by inclusion into "straight" culture, albeit it on openly gay and equitable terms.

This ironic stance—a desire to be recognized on campus for being different from other student cultures, yet also to be included in the orthodox campus culture—epitomized early gay and lesbian student organizing on college campuses (although, oddly enough, not Jack Baker). The campus and social structures that formed the basics of membership into campus culture and society needed to allow non-heterosexual students a proverbial place at the table.

Such a desire for recognition and integration into campus was a central goal of many non-heterosexual college students, and college student organizations, in the twentieth century, but it was not the only goal expressed by such students. Indeed, the earliest gay and lesbian campus organizations sprung from a liberation ethos rooted in eliminating the very structures that favored normative behavior. As historian and 1970s gay activist Martin Duberman recalled,

> Most of the radical young recruits to GLF had previously been in the closet in regard to their sexuality; they felt that now, in "speaking truth" about their own lives, they would forthwith be welcomed and would link arms with those telling truth about racism, sexism, and unjust war — with the result of creating a powerful political coalition that would refashion society as a whole.[2]

The desire to unchain aspects of identity from social and political control linked campus-based social activists, from black power to women's liberation to the initial gay liberation organizations.

To "liberation" students, at least those initial organizers of campus gay and lesbian organizations, efforts such as Baker's—attempting to effect change from within a social/organizational structure—were difficult to reconcile with their attempts to overthrow that structure; the systems of power that formed those structures would always necessitate a class (or classes) of excluded and exploited people.

> Most of GLF's members in the early seventies were militantly anti-authority, whether that authority was embodied in the church, the state, or the medical profession. They denied the right of the courts, the clergy, or the psychiatric profession to pass judgment on their behavior or to "guide" it into the mainstream; they wanted their differentness acknowledged, not suppressed, wanted harassment and violence against them to cease.[3]

The leaders of the liberation groups desired, it would seem, not a place at the table but rather to overturn the table. Gay Liberation was necessary specifically to dismantle those structures that relegated non-normative sexuality to the status of social pariah.[4]

And yet, many students who were part of the initial non-heterosexual campus organizations held less lofty goals. For them, having a Gay Liberation Front (GLF; or other group for homosexuals without an objective purpose on campus) meant they might find friends, romance, levels of community that seemed impossible with "straight" students. Some members wanted to help others "come out of the closet," to have if not positive then at least less debilitating and derogatory images of themselves. A few, like Jack Baker, expressed a desire not to dismantle the American social order but to extend its ideals (and understandings) to a population newly identifying as a part of the body politic. Disagreements over the philosophies and identities of the gay liberation groups persisted; between the late 1960s and the early 1970s, members were divided between an approach calling for tolerance and/or inclusion into campus life and for efforts to deconstruct society as a whole, akin to the social liberation espoused by other student radical groups.

Eventually, by the mid-1970s, the cry for political and social liberation for the most vocal activists on campuses subsided.[5] Nonetheless, non-heterosexual students' desires for connection, for socialization, and, indeed, for political change (albeit for inclusion, not destruction) remained. One way of understanding gay and lesbian campus organizing, then, can be viewed as a transformation from a policy of Gay Liberation to one of campus assimilation.

To understand that story, though, one needs to hear the voices of the people involved in the actions and ideations of non-heterosexual identity that made that transformation occur. Each campus has its own story: the efforts of non-heterosexual members of campus finding each other, expressing shared goals, and establishing the foundations of community (whether extant or ephemeral) were important to those students, to their campuses, and to our collective cultural understanding of democratic citizenry; those stories should be discovered and remembered, and, indeed, several fine, local histories of the beginnings of gay and lesbian student organizations have been produced in the past two decades.[6] That historiography, however, is not my purpose here.

In this book, I trace this change as it occurred over roughly 25 years. *Gay Liberation to Campus Assimilation* is a history, not *the* history, of non-heterosexual students organizing at Midwestern institutions of higher education. It is comprehensive in scope (from the earliest beginnings in the heady late 1960s) but not exhaustively inclusive of all campuses, either in the Midwest or across the United States.[7] The campus histories I present here are themselves partial snapshots of those campus non-heterosexual organizations. I chose these organizations, these institutions, in part because of the extant data available for a historical study but also because the vignettes I present from these campuses combine for a generalizable history beyond just what happened at those particular institutions. Together, these vignettes form a bricolage of the history of non-heterosexual campus organizing (at least in the Midwest).

The campuses I studied were, for the most part, removed from metro-politan areas. Being apart from larger organized gay and lesbian communi-ties seems to have forced the campus organizations to become self-sufficient and more encompassing than they might have in large cities; the early gay and lesbian college organizations served not just the campus but also the entire community beyond the campus gates. The graduation of students resulted in regular membership turnover for the campus organizations; at least through the late 1980s, it also fostered a sense of students recreating many of the earlier organization(s)'s services and projects.

Gay Liberation to Campus Assimilation provides a structure for under-standing the development of these particular non-heterosexual or "queer" collegiate communities. (Note: The nomenclature of the campus groups is rife for contemporary misunderstanding. Initially, "homosexual" was the term used by non-heterosexuals to describe or to identify themselves. That term was replaced by the late 1960s by the gender-inclusive "gay," which by the mid-1970s became used primarily [although not exclusively] to refer to males, while "lesbian" became the appellation of choice for most non-heterosexual females. "Bisexual" and "transgender," as identi-ties, became more commonly differentiated in the late 1980s and early 1990s, and the inclusion of members identifying as such prompted much debate and discussion within the campus organizations, if for no other reason than to determine how to denote inclusion. The term "queer" was still anathema to many non-heterosexuals into the 1990s, particularly those who were born before 1970.) In this work, I attempt to use the contemporaneous names for the campus organizations and members, but when speaking collectively or analytically, I tend to use the term "non-heterosexual," which I hope connotes distinction from heterosexu-als without engendering or politicizing the individual people I discuss.

The scaffolding for this history is built from understanding events on individual campuses, in relation to contemporaneous cultural events play-ing out on those campuses. The ideas of the communities—the ideals, the ideology, the specific identities—were sometimes adopted, sometimes adapted, sometimes recreated seemingly ad nauseam to fit the desires and needs of each campus. By the late 1970s, student activists on those campuses drew from other gay organizations' prior work in collegiate settings; such knowledge sometimes facilitated (and often hurried) the structuring of non-heterosexual organizing, so that by the early 1990s (the end of this book's story), a set of institutional responses, "best practices," organizational services, and campus politic solidified.

I base my narrative and analysis on research I conducted at university archives at 16 postsecondary institutions (University of Illinois, Indiana University, University of Kansas, University of Michigan, University of Minnesota, University of Missouri at Columbia, University of Minnesota–Twin Cities, University of Iowa, University of Wisconsin, Iowa State University, Michigan State University, Ohio State University, University of Northern Iowa, University of Missouri at Saint Louis, Southern Illinois University Carbondale, and Southern Illinois University Edwardsville), two national gay and lesbian archives (the ONE/International Gay and Lesbian Archives, housed at the University of Southern California, and the Jean-Nickolaus Tretter Collection in Gay, Lesbian, Bisexual and Transgender (GLBT) Studies, located at the University of Minnesota), and materials from the Bentley Historical Library at the University of Michigan and the Kenneth Spencer Research Library at the University of Kansas. In addition, I draw from a number of institutional and personal websites concerning the history of gay student activities and organizing on college campuses. Further, I conducted oral history interviews with members of early gay groups from the University of Kansas, the University of Michigan, and the University of Wisconsin. From these sources, I culled a variety of materials, including photographs; local and campus newspaper clippings; organizational newsletters, meeting minutes, correspondence, and publicity materials; and official institutional documents and correspondence.

I focus on a limited number of these 16 universities in presenting the narrative of this history, primarily the University of Kansas, the University of Illinois, the University of Michigan, the University of Minnesota, Ohio State University, and Indiana University. All are extensive state universities with large student enrollments, along with well-documented non-heterosexual student activism and organizing. Additionally, I include briefer accounts of other state institutions, to compare and contrast non-heterosexual student organizing on those campuses, as well as to give a fuller portrait of campus issues facing non-heterosexual students. Some institutions have more than one entry per chapter, so that the reader might have a sense of the development of issues across campuses over time.

Losing sight of individual campus activities, individual people, is a risk for a historical overview. Including some people or incidents as examples excludes both confirmatory and contradictory pieces of history. My intention for *Gay Liberation to Campus Assimilation* was to provide one form of analysis, one way to make sense of the (all too few) histories of non-heterosexual students in the United States; I certainly hope the reader will forgive the sifting of stories, the trimming of tales, that I did to compose this one.

For the analysis necessary for this project, I concentrate most upon two factors: the ideology expressed by the membership of the organizations and the activities the members conducted. Both of those factors developed in relation to the dominant campus cultures. I attempt to reflect the motivations and intentions declared by the members and their organizations (from interviews with me or journalists of the times, or in position papers or publicity materials), in order to understand the personal impetus and cultural climates behind the actions and declarations of identity (of both the individual students and their organizations), as well as the effects of the campus activities.

I present this story mainly chronologically, starting in 1969 and ending in 1993, covering events on campuses that exemplify points of transition in the development of campus gay and lesbian organizations. Chapters 2 and 3 cover roughly 1969 to 1979. In those chapters, I present the "origin stories" of some of the non-heterosexual student organizations I studied. I depict the initial disagreement over identity that played out among the students' philosophies and language: was non-heterosexual organizing to be based upon notions of tolerance (i.e., the homophile movement of the 1950s and early 1960s) or upon more radical, liberation-focused philosophies (i.e., Students for a Democratic Society)? The students founding these initial campus groups were influenced profoundly by the spirit of liberation, and consequently, the first groups were constructed as "Gay Liberation Front" organizations. Between 1969 and 1973, most of the student organizations modeled themselves on the GLF (itself based upon other movements, such as the anti-war movement and the Black Power movement), which espoused an ongoing principle of revolution from the dominant, oppressive, heterosexual culture. Visibility was key to most of their efforts, from individual "coming out" to physical coming out for group activities and campus functions. Consequently, the alignment with minority-identity movements led to the second theme: the formulation of a gay liberation identity.

From their inception, the earliest groups were beset by administrators, legislators, and other students who did not wish non-heterosexuals to be allowed on campus; consequently, the membership found itself advocating both for inclusion into and reform (if not outright destruction) of their university campus. Early Gay Liberation campus members were torn between destroying the system and helping other non-heterosexual people to be able to be self-respecting participants, by reforming the system to allow full participation of non-heterosexuals.

Chapter 4 covers the 1980s. A new cohort of non-heterosexual activists came to campus and came of age, and building communities with a common culture became the groups' focus. This period is notable for an expansion of on-campus services for non-heterosexual students (and community members) begun in the earlier years. The non-heterosexual groups began to expand their efforts beyond simply accommodating non-heterosexuals into a hostile campus culture, toward structural and legal protections for non-heterosexuals to be able to come out and participate in campus activities and institutional endeavors.

AIDS took its toll on a generation of non-heterosexual alumni who came of age through organizing their campus student organization. The lack of cultural and institutional responses to AIDS prompted increased attention to legal on-campus protections, as well as a return to questioning the ethos of a heteronormative campus culture. Overt discrimination and harassment, even violence, marred the experiences of many non-heterosexual students during this decade, forging in some of the members of the groups a more militant spirit, similar to the early gay liberation but wiser, less naïve, of their limited abilities to enact large-scale social change; instead, they focused on their immediate camps lives. Most groups worked toward formal ratification of rights and protections for non-heterosexuals on campus. In order to achieve this, many gay and lesbian students—both those "out" and those in some process of becoming "out"—expanded the numbers of non-heterosexual students openly involved in elected campus governance structures. The 1980s also saw a renewed—and mostly successful—connection with other student minorities on campuses; indeed, non-heterosexual came to be seen as a comparable minority.

In the early 1990s, the period covered in Chap. 5, non-heterosexual students returned to the public, political action events popular with many of the early Gay Liberation Movement (GLM) students. While such actions had not disappeared in the late 1970s and the 1980s, the influence of national gay action movements ACT UP and Queer Nation gave campus non-heterosexual organizations renewed belief in the power of public demonstrations to prompt questions of equality and equity, to shame administrators into supporting campus reforms, and to demand the rights of non-heterosexuals to be a part of, not apart from, all aspects of U.S. life. That included, ironically, the ability to serve as open non-heterosexuals in the U.S. military—something the early GLF campus leaders would have found antithetical to "being" gay. The non-heterosexual moved an ethos of total liberation to complete assimilation.

In the final chapter, Chap. 6, I analyze the history of non-heterosexual collegiate organizing from a more general viewpoint. Initially, I provide a framework of three areas on which to understand the distinctions over time of the differing actions undertaken and beliefs expressed by the student groups. Drawing from theories of gay and lesbian organizing around politics and identities, I structure the components of the framework chronologically: first, providing opportunities and structures for non-heterosexual students to engage with the University; next, striving for formal, public recognition, both of the organization by the institution but, perhaps more importantly, of one's non-heterosexual identity by oneself. The final component of the frame centers on how to make sense of the changing ideologies, from liberation to assimilation, as expressed by the words and deeds of the non-heterosexual student collegians and their organizations.

After the framework, I present a short history of non-heterosexual collegiate organizing. Utilizing the framework I presented earlier in Chap. 6, I analyze the organizations' histories. I posit four themes reflective of the internal changes within the groups over time within the organizations, followed by four themes of changes within the groups prompted by external factors. Finally, in conclusion, I pose questions of my analysis. These questions come from recent scholarship on identity of non-heterosexual college-aged youth, and from historicism of the consequence or effectiveness of the GLM.

The history of gay and lesbian students on college campuses is, of course, more than just a schema of themes, a recitation of events, even a listing of people noted at the time as being "involved." History is rarely so neat, and the historiography of non-heterosexuals never so clear. In reviewing documents for this project, I came across names—sometimes once, perhaps more frequently—of people I could not pinpoint in time; I read words, heard "voices," of people whose moment on the stage of this history was fleeting. I saw them in newspaper photographs, holding picket signs, marching in parades, dining at picnics, rallying at protests. And those were just the students who were there, at that time on that day.

For every photo of a gay dance, there were many more students who were not photographed, whose wish was to attend a dance, not change the world; just beyond every photo of a gay event is a number of faces of those who wished to support but did not lead. For every document in archives, there are those who kept those copies, who perhaps were parts of conversations and actions not reported by newspapers or recorded in memos. Gay and lesbian student organizations were not, are not, made just of leaders; they include "those who also serve": those who aided in the grunt work, who supervised the support groups, who trained the peer counselors, who staffed the hotlines, who raised funds for the programs. Of course, there are also students whom those organizations hosted, briefly, students who would drop in and out, who attended to meet other gay people, who were looking for friends in a new environment. Their history, a more personal one, I did not tell, but the campus organizing the pioneering gay students achieved was for those students as well as themselves.

NOTES

1. McConnell, Michael, with Jack Baker, and Gail Langer Karwoski. *The Wedding Heard 'Round the World: America's First Gay Marriage* (Minneapolis, MN: University of Minnesota Press, 2016), 109.
2. Martin Duberman, *Has the Gay Movement Failed?* (Oakland, CA: University of California Press, 2018), p. xvii.
3. Duberman, *Has the Gay Movement Failed?*, 13.
4. I draw my understanding of the early gay and lesbian movement from a number of contemporaneous sources (primarily print journalism), along with memoirs and, particularly, historical examinations of the times. Memoirs I studied include Arthur Bell, *Dancing the Gay Lib Blues: A Year in the Homosexual Liberation Movement* (New York: Simon & Schuster, 1971); Arnie Kantrowitz, *Under the Rainbow: Growing Up Gay* (New York: William Morrow and Co., 1977); Karla Jay, *Tales of the Lavender Menace: A Memoir of Liberation* (New York: Basic Books, 1999); and Allen Young, *Left, Gay & Green: A Writer's Life* (North Charleston, SC: CreateSpace, 2018). The historical analyses and depictions most influential on my understanding include Mary Bernstein, "Celebration and Suppression: The Strategic Uses of Identity by the Lesbian and Gay Movement," *American Journal of Sociology*, 103, no. 3 (November, 1977), 531–565; Mary Bernstein, "Identities and Politics: Toward a Historical

Understanding of the Lesbian and Gay Movement," *Social Science History*, 26, no. 3 (Fall, 2002), 531–581; David Carter, *Stonewall: The Riots That Sparked the Gay Revolution* (New York: St. Martin's Press, 2004); Dudley Clendinen and Adam Nagourney, *Out for Good: The Struggle to Build a Gay Rights Movement in America* (New York: Simon & Schuster, 1999); Margaret Cruikshank, *The Gay and Lesbian Liberation Movement* (New York: Routledge, 1992); Jim Downs, *Stand By Me: The Forgotten History of Gay Liberation* (New York: Basic Books, 2016); Martin Duberman, *Stonewall* (New York: Dutton, 1993); David Eisenbach, *Gay Power: An American Revolution* (New York: Carroll & Graf, 2006); Lillian Faderman, *The Gay Revolution: The Story of a Struggle* (New York: Simon & Schuster, 2015); Eric Marcus, *Making History: The Struggle for Gay and Lesbian Equal Rights, 1945–1990* (New York: Harper Collins, 1992); Toby Marotta, *The Politics of Homosexuality* (Boston: Houghton Mifflin, 1981); Tommi Avicolli Mecca (Ed.), *Smash the Church, Smash the State: The Early Years of Gay Liberation* (San Francisco: City Lights Books, 20009); and Donn Teal, *The Gay Militants: How Gay Liberation Began in America, 1969–1971* (New York: St. Martin's Press, 1995).

5. See Beth Bailey, *Sex in the Heartland* (Cambridge, MA: Harvard University Press, 1999); Helen Lefkowitz Horowitz, *Campus Life: Undergraduate Cultures from the End of the Eighteenth Century to the Present* (New York: Alfred A. Knopf Books, 1987); Robert A. Rhoads, *Freedom's Web: Student Activism in an Age of Cultural Diversity* (Baltimore, MD: Johns Hopkins University Press, 1998); and Tony Vella, *New Voices: Student Activism in the '80s and '90s* (Boston: South End Press, 1988).

6. Brett Beemyn, "The Silence is Broken: A History of the First Lesbian, Gay, and Bisexual College Student Groups," *Journal of the History of Sexuality*, 12, no. 2, April 2003, 205–223; Jessica Clawson, "Coming Out of the Campus Closet: The Emerging Visibility of Queer Students at the University of Florida, 1970–1982," *Educational Studies: Journal of the American Educational Studies Association*, 50 no. 3, 2014, 209–230; T. Evan Faulkenbury and Aaron Hayworth, "The Carolina Gay Association, Oral History, and Coming Out at the University of North Carolina," *Oral History Review*, 43, No. 4 (2016), 115–137; David A. Reichard, "Behind the Scenes at the *Gayzette*: The Gay Student Union and Queer World Making at UCLA in the 1970s," *Oral History Review*, 43, No. 1 (2016), 98–114; David A. Reichard, "'We Can't Hide and They Are Wrong:' The Society for Homosexual Freedom and the Struggle for Recognition at Sacrament State College, 1969–1971," *Law and History Review*, 28, No. 3 (August 2010), 629–674; John D. Wrathall, "What are you after?": A History of Lesbians, Gay Men, Bisexuals and Transgender People at the Twin Cities Campus of the University of Minnesota, 1969–1993, in

Breaking the Silence: Final Report of the Select Committee on Lesbian, Gay, and Bisexual Concerns, University of Minnesota, November 1, 1993, 48–58; and Oberlin College Alumni Office, *Into the Pink: An Oral History of Lesbian, Gay, and Bisexual Students at Oberlin College from 1937 to 1991* (Oberlin, OH: Amherst College Library, 1996).

7. Determining what campus community hosted the first gay student organization is problematic: does "first" refer to the earliest "unnamed" gatherings, or the earliest group that publicly named itself and designated itself as aligned to a particular campus, or the earliest group that received recognition of doing so, either through the press or, more officially, campus administration? It appears, so far as researchers have been able to establish, that the groups that could claim at least two of those distinctions are the Student Homophile League (SHL) at Columbia University in 1967, followed by SHL chapters at Cornell University and New York University in 1969. In addition, Homosexuals Intransigent! formed at the City University of New York in 1969. For more on the history of those organizations, see Beemyn, "The Silence is Broken."

CHAPTER 2

Student Groups' Formulation of Gay Liberation Identity in the 1970s: Part I

The early campus gay student organizations attempted two related but different goals. One was to provide a space for non-heterosexuals to "come out," to forge relationships with others, and to develop a sense of self-esteem and pride; this approach was more "radical" in the sense that such actions were not generally accepted in U.S. society at the time. This goal was not that of the earlier "homophile" pleas for tolerance of a silent population; early gay student activists wanted visibility and recognition for their members and their organizations, as component elements of campus and society.

The other goal was "revolutionary": activists supporting this goal desired a deconstruction of the social and cultural order that crafted such negative images of homosexuality, in both gays and straights. The desire of many of these student activists was to eliminate the power structure at colleges and universities that kept gays—and other oppressed groups of people—suppressed and subservient to a dominant (white, male, straight) system.

Funding for gay and lesbian student groups at state institutions—from the 1970s through the 1990s—was always a target for public citizens and state lawmakers. One memorable example is from Illinois State University (ISU) in 1973. Webber Borchers, an arch-conservative Republican state representative from Decatur, argued against the use of student fees to fund ISU's Gay People's Alliance. The funding came not from state sources but rather from student fees. Nonetheless, Borchers ranted:

© The Author(s) 2019
P. Dilley, *Gay Liberation to Campus Assimilation*,
https://doi.org/10.1007/978-3-030-04645-3_2

The appropriations were against the wishes of a large number of students....
I don't condemn them (Gay Alliance) for their actions, but if funds from a
state university go towards their promotion, we are recognizing them. It's
just not normal to suck another man's cock.[1]

University of Wisconsin–Madison, 1970–1971

The Statement of Purpose and Principle from the University of Wisconsin's
(UW's) Gay Liberation Organization (GLO) conveys this dichotomy facing the early campus gay student organizations. The document, received
in UW-Madison's Office of Student Activities on June 23, 1970, first provided a preamble declaring the need for such an organization.

> In this era of social, economic and moral revolution, the growing awareness
> of the suppression of the Gay community has prompted the organization of
> this community for the purpose of securing their rights through positive
> courses of action. These rights include equal protections under the laws in
> all areas....
>   The development of a sense of self-pride in the Gay community is an
> essential part of the liberation movement. The engrained feelings of guilt
> must be torn apart and replaced with the realization that GAY IS GOOD!

With new determination, the gay community must now realize that
their oppression is not unique and is part of a generalized suppression of
minorities who deviate from the norms of any established society. It is with
firm commitment that we declare our solidarity with other oppressed
minority groups. Outstanding in the struggle for complete freedom are
the liberation movements of the blacks, Mexican-Americans, and Indians;
the women's liberation movement; and the people's liberation movements around the world. United, we declare WE ARE NOT AFRAID
ANYMORE! ALL POWER TO THE PEOPLE![2]

The GLO at Madison began, briefly, as the Homosexual Freedom
League.[3] A dozen men initiated the group, staffing an information booth in
the lobby of the Union to share information about their organizational
meeting. That meeting was also held in the Union, on March 5, 1970. At the
organizational meeting, approximately 75 people decided upon the moniker
GLO. Rifts between the two approaches to organizational mission—the radical (who sought reforms of current social structures) and the revolutionary
(who sought to dismantle current social structures)—splintered the group.[4]

The more revolutionary members removed themselves to actions centered in Milwaukee, banding together at the Gay Liberation Front (GLF); the radicals remaining on the Madison morphed into a new organization, the Gay People's Union. By the fall of 1971, Gay People's Union had ceased operating as a student organization on the Madison campus. Those members, too, centered their actions in Milwaukee, where the Gay People's Union would operate as a community-based organization throughout the 1970s.[5]

University of Minnesota–Twin Cities

Koreen Phelps was a freshman at the Twin Cities campus of the University of Minnesota in 1968–1969. When she was 15, Phelps had first told someone else—a teacher—that she was attracted to girls. That teacher told her parents, and they had Phelps committed to a hospital for three months, to "teach her a lesson."[6] After her release, at age 16, Phelps stole her mother's car and credit card, and she drove from Minnesota to San Francisco, where, by her account, she started doing drugs and almost died from an overdose of speed.

The totality of the experience had a profound effect upon Phelps' view of individual agency and personal autonomy. Those ideals, in turn, helped craft the first non-heterosexual-themed campus organization in the Midwest.

> I was only nineteen when I started FREE. It was a short period of time when all this turmoil and misery really set me up to start something or be angry enough to take that big a risk. I don't know, that's not to say in order to do something political you have to be locked in a cell. Being locked in a cell really taught me something about being free and not being free. I was very angry about that.[7]

Phelps had already come out, very publicly, in an article in the *Minnesota Daily* in the winter quarter of 1968. In the spring of 1969, she discovered the liberal, even radical, community that congregated in the bars and shops in the West Bank area of the University.[8] Phelps enjoyed the Extempore Coffee House, which attracted a diverse crowd and "where you could be a hippie and get high."[9]

It was at the Extempore that Phelps met Stephen Ihrig. Ihrig was also enrolled at the time at the University; more important, he and Phelps shared a near-instantaneous sense of connection about ideas, questions, and values. In Ihrig's words, "We became intensely involved with each other, and at the same time – almost simultaneously – caught up with trying to create a world, I guess, for ourselves, that was open and decent."[10]

Ihrig said in July of 2007 that the idea behind what would eventually become FREE (Fighting Repression of Erotic Expression) was Phelps' idea. "She created the gay liberation community in Minneapolis, maybe even in the Midwest."[11] Phelps credited Ihrig for her inspiration, telling him in a joint interview in 1989, "I always thought of Stephen as the spirit of the movement. You were very emotional and you were inspired... you didn't want to have much to do with the organizational business... the in-fighting and that... you and I sat late that night thinking and talking philosophy and what the future could bring and what we needed to do...."[12]

They decided to craft a course on homosexuality and arranged to offer it under the auspices of the Free University in Minneapolis.[13] Reflecting on their choice to organize as a curricular course, Phelps said,

> I don't know how we thought we could teach people about being gay because we didn't know hardly anybody else who was. We really didn't know very much and, [sic] we were really sort of educating ourselves by starting this class.[14]

In May of 1969, Phelps and Ihrig advertised their "course," "The Homosexual Revolution," in the *Minnesota Daily*, the campus newspaper.[15]

The first meeting of six Sunday night meetings was held on May 18, 1969—six weeks before the Stonewall riots began. Despite Phelps' and Ihrig's inexperience, over 100 people showed up, a mixture of students and young people, radical to conservative.[16] "About 15 people of many ages made up the core of the discussion group at the first meeting. About 30 per cent were homosexual, about 30 per cent were bi-sexual, and the rest were open-minded, concerned people...."[17]

In 1993, Phelps recalled the decision she and Ihrig made to extend their efforts beyond the short course they intended to teach. "We thought, 'Oh, well, if this many people showed up maybe we should do something with this.'"[18] The first meeting "...was an incredible mixture of people, all of us trying to go in some direction, so the debate and discussion was really interesting and important too."[19] She had to stand on a table and call for order.

From that conversation, the need for an ongoing group was decided. Its name would echo Phelps' desire for freedom. "We are not saving people from being gay.... This is not a therapy session. We just want people to accept themselves for what they are."[20] In an interview in the *Minnesota Daily* the week after the first coffeehouse meeting, Ihrig suggested the benefit of coming out personally and publicly.

> We wanted to reach the hip, young gay people here in Minneapolis. Many young, gay men and women are alienated and frustrated because they feel so separated, not only from society, but from their friends and family as well. We want to reach these people on a social level as well as a political one.... We are at the mercy of the power structure. At the moment things are pretty loose in Minneapolis and the police leave us alone.... But things could change.[21]

Again, Ihrig's vision for FREE's efforts was one of ideal acceptance and connection.

> The main difference between a gay person and a hip gay person is self acceptance.... A hip gay person is not ashamed of what he is.[22]

The process of making a gay person "hip" was coming out as not heterosexual, whether that be lesbian, gay, or bisexual. Nevertheless, being "hip" was not only the providence of non-heterosexuals; straight people had their own issues and "hang-ups" about sexuality that could be improved. The act of personal acceptance within public action would foster a person's sense of self-worth.

FREE was intended to be open to people of all sexual persuasion. "It wasn't supposed to be exclusively just a gay group. We wanted to include everyone."[23] FREE wanted to do so in order that everyone might exercise:

> ... the freedom to be sexual, and [FREE's] stated goal was to overturn the sodomy laws which made gay people into criminals. For those who were coming to FREE's meetings, the freedom to dance, date, fall in love and have sex were the paramount goals. Getting married was the furthest thing from their minds.[24]

FREE on Campus

Still, FREE's primary focus—and its primary audience—was campus-aged non-heterosexuals, who perhaps were most stymied and crippled by the repressive anti-sexual society. As Ihrig said, "One of our main functions as a group is to acclimate the straight public to our existence – to our reality."[25] As such, as historian Kevin P. Murphy noted, the ideology of FREE was more aligned with the "Gay Power" espoused by the GLF in New York City.[26]

Consequently, Ihrig and Phelps, still nominally students at the University of Minnesota (although not for much longer), along with Robert Halfhill, an undergraduate who attended his first FREE meeting on July 13, applied to register their efforts as FREE: Fighting Repression of Erotic Expression. FREE declared itself a political and social action organization on its official registration form, submitted to the Student Affairs Bureau on August 8, 1969. FREE's purpose was:

> To educate the U community about erotic minorities and their place in society; to defend the rights of erotic minorities and protest legislation of sexual morality; to establish and coordinate meeting among erotic minorities for communication of information.

As part of this education, FREE limited voting rights to those who contributed "six hours of non-public work or two hours of public work." In FREE's definition, "public" meant settings in which it would be necessary for the member to come of out the closet, either on campus or in the broader community.[27]

At its outset, FREE recognized the interrelated issues that are called "otherness" now. FREE declared as one of its purposes in its constitution that the organization opposed represented "all discrimination on the basis of race, sex, creed, nationality, political persuasion, or sexual preference.... FREE is willing to support the efforts of any political groups fighting against such discrimination if said group is in turn willing to defend the rights of gay people."[28]

The group was "recognized" by the University's Senate Committee on Student Affairs (SCSA) on October 24, 1969, and secured a mailbox in the Coffman Memorial Union. By being a registered student organization, FREE had access to University facilities and services for students. One of the advantages of being registered was permission to staff an information table. Lyn Miller, an undergraduate at the University in 1970, wrote of first learning about the group—and the concept of joining others who had emotional and sexual feelings as she had—through FREE members she spoke with at that table.

> A booth was setup in the basement of Coffman Union, in the long row of political booths that promoted civil rights, socialism, fundamentalist Christianity, an end to the Vietnam War. The basement of Coffman was a better-attended classroom than many in those days of ferment.[29]

Another outreach effort was the FREE newsletter, which commenced publication in 1969. The first issue was a one-sheet, typed, mimeograph on goldenrod-colored paper. Entitled "a manifesto," the sheet defined FREE as:

> ...an organization that is part of a nation-wide movement to free people from outdated, damaging moral restrictions. Every state in the Union, with the exception of Illinois, prohibits homosexual activity....
>   Our long range goals are to abolish any law or prejudice that prohibits any sexual activity between consenting persons. The common interest of all Gay people is freedom: freedom to walk hand in hand down the street, to embrace in public, to dance together; to live in peace with our lovers without feeling the guilt that this straight, sick society has forced upon us.

The newsletter also lists their activities in "creative education," which "builds pride in ourselves by teaching misinformed straights about sexuality. We use literature tables, lectures, debate, television, radio, theatre, art, guerrilla theatre." In addition, FREE fostered "social activity" ("A happy homosexual is a Gay person and an effective one."), including "dances, parties, happenings, [and] dinners"; "political activity," through "petitions, peaceful demonstrations, [the] ACLU, Peace and Freedom Party, legislators, and the church." Finally, FREE sponsored actions they termed "Encounter," intended "for Gay people who want to know more about themselves and others."

FREE Dances

At least initially, the most public—and perhaps the most transformative for FREE's members—were the dances. FREE sponsored the first non-heterosexual dance on the University of Minnesota campus in November of 1969, on a Tuesday, at "The Whole," a coffeehouse located in the

Coffman Memorial Union. One of Minneapolis' daily newspapers, the *Minneapolis Star*, sent a reporter, Mike Wolff, to cover the event; the resulting article named several attendees (including Phil Graham, a university employee and vice president of FREE) and conveyed positively their experiences.

Nick Lenarz, a sophomore, was one of 60 people attending the dance. Lenarz extolled the joy of being able to dance with someone who might hold more emotional possibility than a platonic friendship.

> These dances are really something – they really release me.... I feel just like a 'straight' person who had never danced before.... I've been to school dances and things, but now I'm really dancing for the first time.[30]

University of Minnesota senior Tim Peterson was Lenarz's dance partner. He expressed to Wolff that going to FREE meetings was his introduction to "the gay society." Peterson said he knew since childhood he was gay, "but I felt terribly guilty about it." In FREE meetings, however, Peterson's guilt was absolved. "We learned to accept each other as people, not as queers or faggots or whatever else people call us."[31]

Koreen Phelps, who had dropped out of the University by November of 1969, was listed in the article as a 20-year-old "adviser." She told Wolff that part of what FREE helped students do is to come out to their parents, "not to lash out at them, but to help their parents understand them."[32] Phelps reiterated her personal goals, which had formed FREE: "We want to educate people.... Gay is good, and we should be free to take the rights of the 'straight' society."[33] Her choice of words—"take the rights"—is clearly more active, more forceful than simply requesting those rights. While part of the work of FREE was to educate for reform, a stronger part of its impetus—at least in the philosophies of Phelps and Ihrig—was to change the dominant, heterodoxy.

Still, much of the dismantling of the personal shackles of the heterosexual paradigm happened through dancing. Terry Hanson, a pre-med freshman who was FREE's entertainment director, noted that the "Gay Tuesday" dances would continue, perhaps with a live band and not just a jukebox. "We'll have go-go boys," he said, as he took suggestions and sold tickets.[34]

Lyn Miller, who later became a leader in FREE's community, recalled attending her first FREE dance in late January, 1970.

That night I went to the dance. There were about forty men and five women. It was very dark. For some reason, I was not afraid. I strode through the darkness and climbed up and sat down on a table, knees apart, leaning forward on them with my elbows, in a gesture I had been stifling since my stomach first fell at the sight of another girl. These were my people. I had been inching, inching, all my life, through a narrow, lightless passage I thought would never end. Here, I could expand, I could breathe. The room felt miles wide and the darkness friendly.[35]

Under new leadership, FREE's dances would become weekly events, drawing "several hundred people."[36] That new leadership was centered in Jack Baker.[37]

FREE Divisions

By the summer of 1969, the initial interest in FREE had dwindled. Robert Halfhill noted that "attendance at the meetings had declined to about a dozen when I attended my first meeting on July 13."[38] Halfhill recalled that "Koreen and Stephen said that most of the people involved had not been ready for any sort of militant action and had been scared away when they kept pushing for public demonstrations."[39]

Lyn Miller was an undergraduate who joined FREE in the late January, 1970; she noted, "Early on, there was a split in the group between conservatives and the more flagrant hippies and drag queens."[40] In 1993, Phelps noted that early in the organization's history, "Factions started to develop. One of the motives was, 'Let's have social activities,' and the other was, 'Let's go picket and raise hell and demonstrate.'"[41]

In 1989, Phelps reflected on her experiences in the 1960s that had shaped what she envisioned for FREE and the fissures between her vision and the desires of the many of FREE's membership.

I wanted FREE to be a political militant organization, along the lines of what was around us at that time – the Anti-War Movement, the Feminist Movement, the Civil Rights Movement. I thought it should be like that. Because we didn't have any rights. There were a lot of people who wanted it to be a social organization. And there's nothing wrong with that. But I always felt that I had to defend the political position, or else it would just become only a social group.[42]

In Miller's estimation, "Conservatism largely prevailed."[43]

FREE's relative "conservatism" was embodied and expressed by Jack Baker. Rather than social revolution or even interpersonal consciousness raising, Baker desired equal rights for homosexuals under the law. He preferred traditional protest actions, such as picketing and lobbying, instead of "zaps" or sit-ins. In the words of FREE officer Robert Halfhill, "Jack Baker probably did more to change the focus, and the image, of FREE than anyone else."[44]

As spring turned into summer, FREE had begun to host Sunday afternoon picnics in 1969 in Riverside Park, along the Mississippi River. Robert Halfhill recalled Jack Baker first "showing up" at one such picnic on September 28, 1969.[45] Phelps remembered,

> When [Baker] came into town, FREE had only met maybe three times or so as an official campus student group. Jack came to a meeting[;] he seemed very excited and interested and wanted to out to coffee with us [Phelps and Ihrig]. We did that.[46]

Baker became an officer, eventually president, of FREE. "He obtained Phelps and Ihrig's initial support for his plans to expand the organization."[47] Under Baker's skill for organizing and obtaining publicity, FREE initiated a speakers bureau on campus and accepted regular opportunities for FREE (and Baker) to appear in journalistic accounts of their efforts.

For their increasing media appearances, Phelps noted, "At the time we wanted to look, in appearance, as non-threatening as we could. We were so desperate."[48] For their first television appearance, a debate on a local station, the notion of the image of those representing FREE came to debate.

> One of the big [issues] very early on was how we were going to present ourselves to the public. Are we going to be like all heterosexual people? Are we going to look straight or should we just not pay attention to that?[49]

While everyone felt Phelps was "feminine" enough, they questioned what now scholars might call "gender presentation."

> Jack looked the straightest.... We did have a debate on whether to have Stephen or Jack. It all came down to appearance, and it was Jack because he had a crew cut at the time. Looking back at it now that seems unfortunate that we made a decision that way.[50]

After that televised debate, Baker became the face of FREE. "Jack was chosen to be the spokesperson because he looked like the boy next door."[51] Ideologically, however, Baker's vision for FREE did not match that of Ihrig or Phelps. Ihrig went so far as to amending FREE's constitution to abolish the office of president, in order to demote Baker's status to no higher than other "coordinators."[52] During the winter quarter of 1970, the rancor between the founders and Baker intensified, leaving the direction of the organization in question.[53]

Public Picketing

The distance between the two factions of FREE's leadership came into question during what would turn out to be Ihrig's and Phelps' final significant involvement with FREE. Nineteen-year-old Thom Higgins was the chief on-air announcer and program manager for Radio Talking Book Network, a project under the auspices of the State Services for the Blind.[54] On February 4, 1970, Higgins informed his supervisor that he was a member of FREE and going to be publicly identified soon as the group's publicity director. He was summarily fired, although his supervisor claimed it was for his irregular work habits, not his sexuality. In protest, 30 members of FREE picketed the St. Paul office of the State Services for the Blind, trudging through snow. Higgins told the *Minneapolis Tribune* that the picket was not just for him but also for "all the other discriminated against gay people in Minnesota."[55]

Robert Halfhill wrote at some length about the disagreement within FREE about how to respond. In a rare moment, Phelps, Ihrig, and Baker all sided against a public protest.

> Baker, who in marked contrast to his later political evolution, was at this time still politically conservative, had opposed the demonstration arguing that he hoped we wouldn't picket since there were so many other alternative actions we could do. Phelps and Ihrig had opposed the demonstration because of their past negative experience with scaring people off with their demands for militant action. Despite this opposition, the organization voted to go ahead and held a successful picket....[56]

The picket was on February 10, 1970. Phelps recalled the event in 1993: "Steve [Ihrig] had this picket sign which said, 'homos are human.'... We all looked like drown[ed] rats out there in the wintertime."[57]

Baker used the press coverage of the picket to increase the group's—and his own, as FREE's spokesperson—contacts with the media. In the spring quarter of 1970, Baker was elected to coordinating committee of FREE, a new structure replacing the initial presidential line of authority.[58] Baker issued a press release on March 11, 1970, stating a new *raison d'etre* for the organization: "FREE is comprised of homosexuals wishing to secure equal rights with the heterosexuals in society."

Baker became the face as well as the voice behind FREE. As Dudley Clendinen and Adam Nagourney observed, "On campus, Jack Baker had attracted broad student support and an aura of New Left celebrity as an openly gay law student-politician...."[59] In addition to representing FREE, Baker was becoming involved in student governance on campus, as well as eventually challenging Minnesota's laws allowing for gays or lesbians to be fired for being gay, and the restriction of marriage to only a man and woman.

> ...Jack seemed to be developing his own agenda.... I thought he took a real paternalistic attitude about the Movement.... I was really angry.... and felt that Jack was an opportunist and really in it for himself.[60]

One year to the day of the founding of FREE, Jack Baker and Mike McConnell applied for a marriage license on May 18, 1970. The couple's action was widely publicized as an attempt to force equal rights under the law for homosexuals.[61] Petitioning for marriage, however, was in many ways the antithesis of what Ihrig and Phelps had intended through founding FREE.

> By then [Baker] had pretty much taken over FREE. He was also doing this [marriage] with Mike McConnell.... the right to get married as a publicity stunt.... I was really angry about that and felt that Jack was an opportunist and really in it for himself. After that I didn't have too much to do with him.[62]

No Longer FREE

With more of Baker's energies turned toward utilizing FREE as an advocacy group against restrictive laws that also provided social support for gays on campus, Phelps and Ihrig left behind the group they founded.

After the initial public political things we did, I think the group was moving in a direction of being more just a social organization and moving toward the Democratic party, with Jack being this sort of benevolent dictator. The whole thing was just not what I liked to be a part of.[63]

Phelps remained involved in campus- and city-based gay and feminist organizations; Ihrig moved to New York City. In an interview in 1989, Phelps and Ihrig reflected upon their year of creating gay activism at the University of Minnesota.

Phelps: Well.... it was a lot of pressure. A lot of pressure. It was very intense....

Ihrig: It's happened in other situations that were—for lack of a better term—revolutionary.... Something rather extraordinary happens in a very brief period of time. And it did.... It was very, very brief; it was very intense. And we were the fuel.[64]

In the spring of 1971, Jack Baker ran for student body president at the University of Minnesota. He was the first openly non-heterosexual to do so. His campaign slogan was "Student Control Over Student Concerns," but his initial campaign posters were decidedly queer; in addition to the first (Fig. 2.1), the second poster depicted Baker holding a Bible, standing next to a grandmotherly woman, holding a baby, in front of an American flag and a portrait of Abraham Lincoln (Fig. 2.2). The poster's tagline: "Jack Baker Comes Out – For Things That Count." While "coming out" was certainly something Baker would no doubt say "counted," everything else in the poster proffered images supporting many of the heterosexist institutions that the founders of FREE—and other early campus gay and lesbian groups that adhered to the concept of "Gay Power"—would certainly say curtailed freedom.

Baker received 2766 out of a then-record total of 5049 votes cast. He initiated a student-run bookstore, the implementation of a University-owned FM radio station to publicize the University, and the creation of a corporation owned by the Minnesota Student Assembly (the student government body at Minnesota) to build student housing. Baker was elected to a second term in 1972, receiving 3035 out of 7441 votes.[65] He was removed from office in February of 1973, for not meeting the University's required minimum credit-hour enrollment to be involved on campus.[66]

Fig. 2.1   University of Minnesota–Twin Cities FREE picket, 1970. (Powell Kruger, copyright 1970, *Star Tribune*)
Members of FREE at the University of Minnesota picket at the Minnesota State Services for the Blind building, February 10, 1970. The picket was an opportunity for activism for equity of rights as well as for visibility of the FREE and its issues. FREE co-founder Koreen Philips, the woman with glasses, is the fourth person from the left in the photograph; the other co-founder, Stephen Ihrig, is the man behind her, holding the poster that says "Homos Are Human."

UNIVERSITY OF MICHIGAN, 1970–1971

On March 17, 1970, inspired by the formation of similar organizing, particularly in Detroit, activists in Ann Arbor founded the Ann Arbor GLF.[67] The Ann Arbor GLF (AAGLF, also referred to as GLF) was composed not just of Michigan students but also members from the larger local and campus community. On March 30, at a house located at 300 East Washington, members of the AAGLF considered a proposal for a formal constitution. "Any concerned person shall be considered a member of the AAGLF," it proclaimed, but only those who paid dues were given voting rights, and Robert's Rules of Order were to be utilized.[68] This is a far cry from the decentralized, often unregulated democracy that characterized the early GLF meetings in New York City.

Fig. 2.2 Jack Baker, University of Minnesota–Twin Cities second student body president campaign poster, 1970. (From the Michael McConnell Files. Used courtesy of the Jean-Nickolaus Tretter Collection in GLBT Studies, University of Minnesota Libraries)

Jack Baker's second campaign poster for his 1970 student body president campaign at the University of Minnesota–Twin Cities. This one more accurately represents Baker's ideology of gay assimilation into straight society. The image plays on all of the traditional political tropes—flag, Lincoln, the Bible, apple pie, babies, and a kindly grandmother (local pizza maven Mama Dee).

Historian Tim Retzloff has noted that "Prior to 1970 gay life in Michigan center around a handful of bars which were often targets of police harassment."[69] Jim Toy, a Michigan graduate student who would become a central figure in the struggle for inclusion of non-heterosexuals into the University, reflected on the social climate of the time (Fig. 2.3).

Fig. 2.3 Jim Toy, University of Michigan, 1973. (*The Michigan Daily*, The Michigan Daily Digital Archives, Bentley Historical Library, The University of Michigan)

Jim Toy in 1973. One of the founders of Gay Liberation at the University and in the state of Michigan, Toy was the first man appointed by a university as an advocate for non-heterosexual students. The framed photo over his left hand is a desecrated portrait of Richard Nixon.

> The campus climate here at the end of the so-called "radical years," in Ann Arbor, was still radical. Students, and some faculty and staff, [still] protested against the Vietnam War.... Until we started here... in 1970, there was still no resource for us except for the quote "gay bar." Given the still "radical" temper of the campus, when we decided to attempt to form a group here, some of us felt – and it turned out that we were correct – that we would receive some support from students who did not identify as gay, [including] SDS [Students for a Democratic Society] and Women's Liberation.[70]

Toy had been involved in the formation of an even earlier group, Gay Liberation Movement, in Detroit in January of 1970. Although initially not intended to be associated with other, revolutionary "Front" organizations, the organization—and its philosophies—nonetheless soon aligned with other GLF organizations. In the words of one member, the Detroit group's actions were a "fight against overblown virility in our western culture."[71]

Toy helped organize the March 30 meeting in Ann Arbor. That night, a "PROPOSED CONSTITUTIONAL FORM" was distributed at such a meeting. The language of its preamble explicates the group's perceived needs for the campus community.

> We, who are concerned about the problems of the homosexual and the community, seeking to improve the self-concept of homosexuals and their relationships with each other and with the community at large, endeavoring to provide counseling to homosexuals and intending to serve as a source of information to the academic community concerned with studies of socio-logical and psychological behavior, do hereby establish this constitution of the Ann Arbor Gay Liberation Front.[72]

The proposal included enumeration of officers and executive committee, the use of Robert's Rules of Order, and constitutional amendments. While this document would seem to indicate a rather formal, conventional organization, the Ann Arbor GLF soon espoused positions and engaged in practices that at the time were deemed revolutionary.

Toy and his campus cohorts utilized tactics they had observed had success with forcing institutional change, specifically guerrilla theater actions and public protests. In addition, the protesting students echoed the needs and demands expressed by black students on campus, as a model of analysis for campus climate and culture; they proposed in their demands a system of services modeled after those proposed by activists protesting for women's services. Toy noted the influence of the administrative secretarial staff in assisting the protesting gay and lesbian students conceive of specific needs.

> We talked with several secretaries. One of them said, "There an office here for Black students and an office for women students; don't you think you should have one?" So we wrote a request for a staffed office, submitted it to the Vice-President for Student Services, and in a few months the University gave us a small room, funding for two quarter-time positions, and a few dollars for operating expenses.[73]

While social change was important to Jim Toy, he preferred practical, immediate reforms over deferred revolution.

Such reform was hastened by publicity. *The Michigan Daily*'s Sunday, April 12, 1970, edition boasted an above-the-banner headline article: "Gay Lib: Resisting repression of the homosexual." The article's authors reported that the Ann Arbor Gay and Lesbian Front [AAGLF, also collo-quially called GLF] was a "newly established SGC-approved [Student Government Council] student organization" was a "coalition of homo-sexuals, lesbians, bi-sexuals [sic] and straights who say NO to sexual repression." They quote "the writers of the Ann Arbor GLF constitution" as stating the reason for the organization was because they were "con-cerned about the problems of the homosexual and the community seeking to improve the self-concept of homosexuals and their relationships with each other and the community at large."[74]

The GLF was characterized as operating through committees, including ones on "improving conditions in a local bar patronized by many of the gay people," research and analysis (with goal of establishing counseling and telephone aid services), legal committee, and public relations (which planned to publish a weekly newsletter). Regarding GLF's publications, *The Michigan Daily* reporters wrote, "Since the group has no uniform ide-ology yet, at this juncture, it only hopes to make the community aware of gay people as human beings through its distribution of literature."[75]

Coming Together

The April 12 feature story in *The Michigan Daily* also indicated that the AAGLF was "currently arranging" for a "Midwest Gay Liberation Conference" for the summer of 1970. This was AAGLF's first attempt at focused activity as a student group on the University campus itself. The idea sounds very innocuous today: a drive-in regional set of workshops on homosexuality, intended for all of the Midwest gay organizations and gay individuals. In a letter to Will Smith, assistant to the vice president for student affairs, the GLF stated they sought to rectify "the problems of the homosexual and seek to improve the self-concept of homosexuals and their relationships with each other and with the community at large," through "workshops on homosexuality, public lectures and panel discus-sions by such outside specialists as jurists, doctors, and religious leaders, who would speak to homosexuals and to the public at large on legal, medical and religious aspects of homosexuality." Michigan's president, Robben Fleming, denied Ann Arbor GLF's request, citing the school's regulation that "in order to qualify for the use of University facilities, any conference on the subject of homosexuality ought, in the view of the law, to be clearly educational in nature and directed primarily towards those people who have a professional interest in the field."[76]

Members of the GLF protested Fleming's decision outside the president's house on campus. Chanting, carrying signs, and walking a picket line in front of attending guests, the GLF attempted to bring greater pressure on the president. Two members went inside, publicly appealing in person to Fleming, who still refused. Larry Glover, an AAGLF member, responded, "We don't want to continue the profissional [sic] exploitation of homosexuals – we are not case studies.... We are asserting our humanity and our right to assemble."[77] Jim Toy, who was at the meeting with Fleming, stated that the president feared that "we would attract adverse public reactions and publicity and that we would bring police to the campus."[78] When that appeal did not succeed, members of the AAGLF, "joined by other student groups and several alumni,"[79] protested in front of Fleming's home, during a formal tea party and reception.

The demonstrators chanted and marched a picket line, carrying signs advocating for gay inclusion on campus. Two men "zapped" the president by appearing in drag.[80] Fleming recalled the event in his memoir:

> As we stood in the receiving line, two males dressed in evening gowns suddenly approached. One looked like a football lineman, and sported a great hairy chest made even more evident by his low-cut gown. The other was slender, wore earrings in both ears and lipstick just below his mustache and was dressed in a white gown. The big man said his name was Kitty, so that is what we called him.... Was it simply an act, drummed up for the fun of it?[81]

While it was indeed an act, and the men probably had fun, the act was to disturb the accepted, unquestioned "normalcy," of the tea, of the administration's decorum, of the legality of state statutes regarding sexual expression and activity. Robben Fleming seemed to be a man unable to accept the changes in the cultures he inhabited. In his State of the University address for 1970, he decried that the revolution spoken of by radical activists was "'a figment of their imagination,'" while the threat of repression by social and state authorities "'is a reality.'"[82] To no one's surprise, the tea zap did not change Fleming's mind. According to GLF member Mike Jones, however, "some of the faculty and one of the Regents expressed sympathy and support for us."[83]

On May 27, the Ann Arbor Gay and Lesbian Front distributed flyers on the campus Diag, proclaiming "THE MILITARY IS OUR ENEMY." The flyer, which drew connections between the anti-Vietnam War protests, women's liberation, anti-racism protests, and gay liberation, began,

"THE U.S. MILITARY IS INTRINSICALLY MALE CHAUVINIST." Three points of how the military oppressed gays were listed, the first two of which resulted in economic oppression of gays. Black gays were highlighted as "special victims of pressure" from the military in the third point: "RACISM, ALSO, IS INHERENT IN THE U.S. ARMY."

The flyer also postulated that the military perverted love (although the example given was sexual, not romantic) through a systemic sexual abuse. "The master gratifies himself by abusing sexually those whom he has power over. This power-sex syndrome, which is basic to the military, is a perversion against homosexuality, and as such is anti-Gay." The flyer concluded,

> COME OUT! OUT OF YOUR UNIFORMS, OUT OF YOUR CLOSETS, AND INTO THE STREETS! THE WAY TO STOP SUCKING UP TO THE BRASS IS REVOLUTION! COME – AND JOIN THE BROTHERS AND SISTERS IN THE STRUGGLE AGAINST MALE CHAUVINISM AT THE R.O.T.C. BUILDING, WEDNESDAY, MAY 27, 11:00 to 1:00

The flyer was signed "Gay Liberation Front" and included an upraised fist between conjoined male symbols (representing gay men) and female symbols (representing lesbians).[84]

Ann Arbor GLF member Rich Stanford submitted an undated document (sometime after office space was allotted to GLF) outlining his thinking on the "Goals of the Ann Arbor GLF and Organizing Toward Those Goals," a seven-page treatise on the values, directions, and operations (via a draft constitution) for the organization as it transitioned from an outside group of agitators to a campus organization.[85]

> It seems to me that the overall goal of the GLF in Ann Arbor should be to make being gay a comfortable, enjoyable and enriching experience… to rearrange society in such a way as to make it possible for all homosexuals in Ann Arbor to live openly–without fear of oppression–to associate openly with other homosexuals–without fear of social ridicule–and to lead an intellectually and physically productive life–without fear of senseless repression….
>
> …we are not a political group. Our common bond is not one of political orientation, but rather one of sexual orientation. There are those who firmly believe that gay liberation cannot take place under the existing system, and they feel that all gay political activity should be limited to changing America's political system. And there are those who feel that our system is here to stay, and that we should work within the framework

of that system to liberate the homosexual. In order to legally eradicate homosexual oppression, we cannot limit ourselves to any one political philosophy – radical or reactionary. Rather, we must work within the framework of all political movements.... This means being in touch with political life on all levels. It means being politically aware. It also means getting out and fighting, when necessary.[86]

Summer Strife

The battle over the proposed gay conference at Michigan continued into the summer of 1970. Members of the SGC held a meeting with members of GLF to demand that the administration permit the statewide gay organizations' conference. Jim Toy called for more public attention to the issue: "Right now we're just playing into Fleming's hand by being quiet and obscure.... He's afraid of publicity – and that's where we should direct our efforts."[87]

The Michigan Daily on June 11 also published on its editorial page the entirety of a letter sent to President Fleming, jointly signed by the Student Government Council and the GLF. In the letter, the two groups demanded Fleming reverse his decision, pointing out, among other arguments, that the University seemed selective in its application of popularity as a basis for allowing conferences on campus, as the University had the previous year hosted a conference on "Topics in Military Operations."[88] Nonetheless, the editorial board of the campus newspaper was clearly in support of GLF, as expressed in its editorial of June 10.[89]

The Michigan Daily also reported that the GLF would proceed with the conference, scheduled for the fall semester, despite a second veto that had been issued by President Fleming. The issue had transformed itself from whether the University could (or would) approve a gay-themed event on campus, into a larger struggle between the authority and independent agency of student government against the oversight of the administration. Jerry De Grieck was an undergraduate and executive vice president of the SGC. De Grieck had assisted in SGC's approving of GLF's status as a recognized student organization. Jerry De Grieck was also, secretly, gay.[90]

De Grieck believed that the University president did not have the statutory authority to deny the conference, arguing that a 1965 decision by the

University's Board of Regents transferred the authority to recognize to the SGC the authority "to recognize, approve and schedule events of student organizations"; the matter was as much one of student power and agency as it was of equality.

> "The GLF regional conference will be held as an official University function," De Grieck declared....[91] "Fleming has no right to approve or disapprove any student organizations [sic] event. He has over-stepped his authority."[92]

Fleming contradicted De Grieck's assertion. "I don't agree with their interpretation of the Regents' decision.... The bylaw dealt with the eligibility of University facilities, not with their assignment."[93] Further, Fleming feared legislative reprisal and public disapproval to the University's appropriations: "unless one wishes to totally alienate public support he cannot ignore public reaction to events at the University."[94] An unnamed GLF member critiqued Fleming's decision:

> The Legislature is blackmailing radical groups on campus by withholding funds.... And Fleming is saying we are expendable – our conference is a luxury the University can't afford this year.[95]

The GLF had built alliances with more than other student protest groups, including student government of the University, the Student Government Council (SGC). The SGC and GLF sent a joint letter to Fleming on June 10, 1970, calling on him to reverse his April decision about the conference, accompanied by a unanimously approved SGC resolution condemning Fleming's refusal, as well as endorsing peaceful demonstrations to "call attention to the oppression of homosexuals by the University and by society."[96] De Grieck, the author of the resolution, was fast becoming a central player in the actions of the GLF to gain access, both physical and structural, to the University of Michigan.

On June 11, *The Michigan Daily* printed a photograph on the front page of GLF, SDS, and Women's Liberation practicing their "guerrilla theatre" skits; in it, a man holds a rifle over a man and a woman, ready to strike them. The imagery is shocking and clearly demonstrating an act of violence—both goals of such skits—and no doubt troubling to many University of Michigan community members and administrators. The accompanying article reported that the Student Government had unanimously approved a resolution condemning President Fleming's continuing refusal to approve the GLF conference. In response, the GLF released a statement that read, in part,

> It is necessary that the University recognize and admit that gay people have the right to assemble and define the reality of their own existence, for we reject society's definition of the gay existence.[97]

At least for that meeting, GLF members promoted revolution over reform. It did not seem to move the administration.

The next day, Fleming reiterated that a conference of homosexuals at the University of Michigan would not be advantageous for the institution. "Unless one wishes to totally alienate public support," he wrote, "he cannot ignore public reaction to events at the University."[98] Will Smith, assistant to the vice president for student affairs and acting director of the Michigan's Office of Student Organizations, who would soon leave the University to become dean of students at the University of California, San Diego, publicly disagreed with Fleming's decision. "We made it clear to the administration that Student Government Coalition has certain prerogatives.... Fleming is undercutting the students' established role."[99]

At a time when collegiate leadership across the country was struggling with issues involving the rights and freedoms of students—and concurrent responses from governmental and cultural institutions—the University of Michigan found itself unable to satisfy either constituency. Leaders such as Fleming also often struggled with society's changing mores. Will Smith, in an exit interview with the campus newspaper, summarized the importance of Michigan's responses to the GLF: "The Gay Lib movement brings out the question to what extent the University should be responsive to the needs of interests outside the university, as opposed to students."[100]

Guerrillas in the Michigan Jungle

On July 7, the combination of members from AAGLF, SDS, and Women's Liberation performed their guerrilla theater skits on the steps of the Michigan Union. An estimated 250 spectators watched the students in an anti-war protest. In one skit, "soldiers" enacted a gun drill, but at the call of "About face and present arms," the "soldiers" turned "to each other and fell into one another's arms. The commanding officer then 'shot' all of his men."[101] Mocking contemporary Vietnam War atrocities, the final skit ended with a Cambodian woman being raped by American military members and President Richard Nixon.

The amalgamated protest group produced "guerrilla theater" at several locations on the Michigan campus that day. Ten performers first enacted skits protesting the "University's ROTC program and other military institutions" at North Hall (where the Reserve Officer Training Corps [ROTC] programs were located).[102] Such skits were intended to exaggerate and to pantomime social or governmental regulations, to create an emotional response to issues often considered only cognitively or judicially. The protesters, which also included members from SDS,[103] then marched—"chanting, leafleting, and carrying signs"—to repeat the performances at the Diag and then in front of the Student Union.[104]

The performances, particularly those in front of the Student Union, infuriated Stanfield Wells, the Union's general manager. Wells apparently did not view the acts but did hear of them; he blamed the GLF, saying the group "put on some sort of unpleasant performance which was inappropriate".[105] In response, Wells barred the GLF from using the facilities of the Union; he claimed not to know that SDS and Women's Liberation had participated.[106]

Jim Toy met with Wells that day, asking what would be required for AAGLF to utilize the Union for meetings; Wells "reportedly said that GLF's standards would have to fit 'normal and decent behavior,'" which would certainly not include a conference to advocate for the people to violate state laws outlawing homosexual behaviors.[107] At that point, Wells indicated to Toy that the AAGLF was permanently banned from the Union.[108] A number of campus administrators later indicated they doubted the permanence of Well's ban, including the acting vice president for student affairs and the president of the Union Activities Center.[109]

In response to Wells' ban, GLF held a sit-in of sorts on July 9. They meet—informally, neither scheduled nor in a meeting room—in the first-floor lounge in the Student Union. A photograph on the first page of July 10's *The Michigan Daily* publicized the GLF's flouting of Wells' ban. In the uncharacteristically extensive caption, the paper noted:

> At the meeting it was decided to hold a protest Tuesday in front of the Union. Plans call for leafletting, picketing and a guerrilla theatre performance. The Union Board is scheduled to meet some time in the near future and review Wells' actions. Until then GLF will probably continue to use the Union lounge.[110]

In addition to the photograph, an article within the paper repeated much of the information from the first-page photo. An estimated 40 to 50 attendees set a protest for the next week—peaceful protest—by consensus of the group.[111]

Wells' decision outraged Jerry De Grieck. De Grieck, quoted in *The Michigan Daily*, contended Well's claim that "he alone through the Union has the power to determine the use of Union facilities. SCG claims that his power does not include discriminating against a recognized student organization."[112] Members of the AAGLF noted in a flyer handed out on July 14, on State Street in Ann Arbor, conjectured on Wells' rationale:

WELLS HAS BEEN CASTING ABOUT FOR SOME KIND OF EXCUSE TO TAKE AN ACTION TO SHOW HE IS A MEMBER OF THE UNIVERSITY ADMINISTRATIVE TEAM. WE ASSUME THAT HE THINKS THAT HE HAS BROUGHT HIMSELF IN STEP WITH FLEMING BY EXCLUDING <u>GLF</u> FROM ANY FURTHER USE OF THE UNION FACILITIES.[113]

The GLF had announced its desire to meet with the Board of Regents, "to explain... the nature and purpose of the GLF and its relation to the University" and to advocate for their use of campus facilities in general and for their proposed conference in specific.[114] The Regents were less interested in meeting the GLF, so the GLF picketed the Regent's meeting.

Radical Lesbians

An extension of the conversations at the drive-in conference, the question of focus for the gay liberation groups influenced the creation of a new group on campus. During the fall of 1970, a gender-based split in the GLF students prompted the formation of the Radical Lesbians (sometimes referred to as "Radicalesbians"). In a lengthy editorial in *The Michigan Daily*, the Radical Lesbians presented their political stance, in relation to women's liberation and to gay liberation, declaring the "radical" nature of their existence.

We are radical in that we refuse to accept and internalize society's hatred and fear of homosexuality: we are radical in that we refuse to be blinded by a repressive society to the total beauty – and this includes sexuality – of the members of our own sex.[115]

In the group's spring 1971 publication, *Purple Star*, the Radical Lesbians espoused a goal of "a strong revolutionary women's movement that will fight for women's freedom."[116] More extreme in its aims was a spin-off group, the Revolutionary Lesbians; they published *Spectre*, a separatist publication, in which they proclaimed lesbianism "a basic threat to the foundations of society."[117]

Such identity-based changes in student affiliation occurred, at Michigan as at other campuses across the country, as coalitions of radical activists began to unravel. Taken to the extreme, the ideologies of black liberation, gay liberation, women's liberation, and so on were deemed incompatible with compromise made for liberating other oppression. To the activists, the choice was simple, if personally messy: In which arena would one spend time and energy for change? The core question: Which group represents my personal and political needs best?

Given the generative energy of the times, the heady nature of personal political action, such divisions seemed necessary. Self-expression of one's own life and needs was often sung in a cacophony, rather than in harmony. Nonetheless, the departure of the Radical Lesbians from the GLF was amicable, and the two organizations continued a unified non-heterosexual voice to the campus.

Fall 1970

Martin Hirschman, the editor of *The Michigan Daily*, personally reported upon the ongoing struggle between student government and the Michigan administration that was prompted by GLF's request for a conference. On August 15, Hirschman's front-page headline indicated that Fleming was "backing down" on his resistance to the conference; for his part, Fleming said he was not "backing down" but rather seeking a "resolution to the controversy" by referring the matter to the Union Board.[118] Jerry De Grieck cast a warning tinged by the power felt by student activists: "Hopefully, Fleming has learned not to meddle in the affairs of SGC and the Office of Student Services."[119] Jim Toy stated that "Fleming's attempt to weasel out of the situation is typical of the whole mismanaged affair."[120]

On Saturday, August 15, the Ann Arbor GLF did convene a "drive-in" conference on campus, albeit not at the Union. Jerry De Grieck used his keys to the Student Activities Building to allow GLF access. In 2005, De Grieck reflected on his actions.

It was a no-brainer to me, even though I was closeted at the time and had not dealt with my own sexuality.... It was pretty much of a principled stand that was consistent with my politics and the politics of many of the day.... It was not a difficult decision to make. We, as student government leaders, saw that was our right to do that. We felt we had jurisdiction over all or part of the building.[121]

Given the favorable weather, many of the conference events were held outside; nevertheless, De Grieck took a substantial risk—of his position in the student government, of expulsion, and of criminal charges—in order to facilitate equal access to University resources for the GLF.

According to coverage in *The Michigan Daily*, "approximately 35 people from Lansing, Kalamazoo and Detroit in addition to the Ann Arbor area attended the conference."[122] The attendees spent much of their time debating the purpose and "nature" of GLOs.

Several of the Ann Arbor members felt GLF is a group within a radical movement and should therefore work with other radical organizations such as Students for a Democratic Society.

Members of the Lansing Gay Lib organization, however, argued Gay Lib organizations should be primarily concerned with the specific problems of homosexuals.[123]

In addition to such conversations, the attendees proceeded to march to President Fleming's house; unsurprisingly, no one answered their knocks. According to the newspaper account, the attendees (presumably the ones from GLF) repeated the guerrilla theater skits that had incensed Wells, before proceeding to the Diag for a picnic lunch. Later that evening, members attended the Washtenaw County Democratic Convention in the Union ballroom; the Party allowed the AAGLF members five minutes to speak to the Democrat delegates.[124]

While the drive-in conference was held over the summer, the campus struggle between the Michigan administration and the coalition built around AAGLF's attempts to use the Michigan Union persisted. Jerry De Grieck made that point clear in his comments to *The Michigan Daily*: "This time it was necessary (to give up the Union location) because it was summer. But in the fall we (SCG) plan to back GLF in its effort to hold the Midwest conference in the Michigan Union.... Saturday's conference shows that the only adverse reaction (to a homosexual conference) comes from the fact that Fleming decided to make an issue of the conference."[125] A point was made to the administration: with or without its approval, Gay Liberation would persist at the University of Michigan.

In September, the Michigan regents unanimously concurred with President Fleming's refusal for allowing a gay-centric conference that was not directly educational in nature.[126] Fleming ceded the decision of "educational in nature" to the newly installed Vice President for Student Services, Robert Knauss. Knauss, who had been an assistant professor in the Law School, just into the administrative position, appeared less rigid about the issues surrounding the request. "Asked [after the Regent's meeting] whether a question of academic freedom and freedom of speech is involved in the GLF issue, Knauss said, 'Yes, there may be.'"[127] Fleming made it known that he still retained veto power over the conference.[128]

GLF and the Radical Lesbians bristled at the administration's requirement to submit to Knauss a rationale and a program for their proposed conference. No other student organization was being required to have the vice president approve the content and purpose of their activities. Jim Toy told the press the GLF was not going to jump through those hoops; a member of the Radical Lesbians pointed out the inequality of such a requirement: "We should be treated like any other student organization and we're not going to present any program to Knauss."[129]

When pressed by student reporters, Knauss admitted that approval procedure was "unusual" and that who had jurisdiction over scheduling such activities was "cloudy."[130] Jim Toy sent a letter to Knauss, asking for "proof of educational value" for any student organization's activities would, going forward, be applied to all student organizations. Knauss indicated that he could not answer that question.[131]

A week later, the Policy Board of the Office of Student Services—an advisory group to Knauss that included Jerry De Grieck, among other student leaders—unanimously called for the administration not to prevent the GLF conference.[132] *The Michigan Daily* declared its approval.

> Clearly, a gathering of homosexuals from all parts of the Midwest to discuss their sad social plight cannot help but be productive, refreshing, and educational, even if only to serve notice to straight society that this subject matter is no longer taboo for public discussion.[133]

Knauss accepted the OSS recommendation.[134] Fleming did not veto Knauss' decision. The authority of student organizations—including gay and lesbian organizations—had been upheld.

1971

In February of 1971, the GLF held its first meeting of the term. About 30 people attended. They decided to postpone planning the conference until later in the year.[135] That is the last mention of the proposed Midwest gay conference at Michigan that year.

In December 1971, Jim Toy and Cynthia Gair were appointed as program assistants in the Office of Special Services and Programs, which was a division of Knauss' Office of Student Services. Their role was "to aid the homosexual community on campus.... counseling and working with the local homosexual community."[136] Theirs were the first such positions on a college or university campus in the United States.

Ann Arbor's Human Rights Party
The Human Rights Party (HRP) was a third-party, radical socialist coalition in the state of Michigan during the early 1970s. The HRP was active in Ann Arbor politics, electing some members to local offices. Jerry De Grieck, 21, and Nancy Wechsler, 22, had both been students at Michigan and were both elected on the HRP ticket to the Ann Arbor City Council in 1971. De Grieck, the former student body vice president, was a senior, while Wechsler had only recently graduated and was working in the student-owned university bookstore. HRP ran five candidates for the City Council in 1971, but only De Grieck and Wechsler won; they served from 1972 to 1974. Coincidentally, both were coming to terms with their sexual identity at the time, and both came out at an April 3, 1972, press conference protesting anti-gay discrimination in East Lansing (Fig. 2.4).

INDIANA UNIVERSITY, 1971–1976

GLF at Indiana University started in the early 1970s, at least before 1972. In the estimation of a later gay activist at Indiana, the GLF at Indiana was initiated by "People with anti-war experience... hoping for a radical political organization"; the initial GLF was a "leftist group... but the group became social and never was radical."[137] Wilson Allen was one of the founders.

Fig. 2.4 Jerry De Grieck and Nancy Wechsler, 1972. (*Ann Arbor News*, courtesy of Ann Arbor District Library, copyright Barcroft Media; used with permission)

Jerry De Grieck and Nancy Wechsler, 1972. De Grieck was the University of Michigan student government officer who defied the administration by unlocking the Student Activities Building to allow a gay conference to be held on campus. De Grieck and Wechsler, who were also students at Michigan, were elected to the East Lansing City Council in 1971. Both publicly came out as non-heterosexual while on the city council.

> There were three women and three men… we pulled together the "Bloomington Gay Liberation Front." Our first open activity was a litera-ture table at the SR Activities Fair for the fall semester. We made our big, big splash with the Gay Halloween Dance… and it got better from there.[138]

The organization's name was changed to Gay Lib in 1972, a "year that also saw the departure of some of the more radical people…."[139]

Unlike some newspapers on some campuses, Indiana's provides little insight into the history of this organization. What little media coverage there is comes from the pages of the University's yearbook, the *Arbutus*. In the pages of the 1972 *Arbutus*, the Indiana University yearbook, the group provided photographs and information about itself (Fig. 2.5).

Fig. 2.5 Gay Liberation at the Indiana University, 1973. (Indiana University Archives (P0066957))
Members of the Gay Lib at the Indiana University. In this image from the 1974 *Arbutus* yearbook shows them smiling while raising their fists as a sign of political resistance and solidarity. The group was far less militant than it was fun-loving.

Gay Lib is a group of individuals who have banded together to help their gay brothers and sisters accept and be proud of their gayness so they won't hide in a false front defined by society but will be themselves 24 hours a day.

The people in the pictures are not "rape-'em-in-the-streets" faggots; they are individuals, human beings that care about people enough to face today's society and admit they are gay so that others will be able to do the same without fear. They are revolutionaries, but the means of the revolution is not violence. "An army of lovers cannot be conquered.[140]

As at other Midwestern universities, dances for non-heterosexual students were important, well attended, and paramount for socialization.

Eric Wilson noted it in the passage I quoted above; in 1978, the dances were still going strong.

"There are usually about 700 to 900 people who attend the dance and we get a lot of out-of-town people. A lot of straight people also attend," said Lewis Kyker, BGA chairperson.[141]

Fig. 2.6 Gay Liberation Halloween Dance, Indiana University, 1974. (Indiana University Archives (P0066955))

Fig. 2.7 Gay
Liberation Halloween
Dance, Indiana
University, 1974.
(Indiana University
Archives (P0066956))
    Gay Lib's Halloween
Dances at Indiana
University rose to
campus legend in the
1970s. These two
photos, from the 1975
Arbutus yearbook,
demonstrate the
gender-bending,
sexualized outlandish-
ness and cross-gendered
attendance that
characterized the events.

As shown in Figs. 2.6 and 2.7, from the Gay Alliance's 1974 Halloween
Dance, the dances became a site of what later became known as "gender-
fuck": the purposeful adoption of some aspects of the opposite gender's
dress and appearance. At times, this was often called "skag drag," often
allowing men with facial hair to dress in women's clothing, but not necessarily made up in cosmetics. If this seems somewhat confusing, even
questionable, that was the point: to challenge the social norms, in this
instance, of dress and comportment.
    The appropriation of and revelry in aspects of women's attire and bod-
ies offended the sensibilities of some, particularly feminist, lesbians. They
sometimes wondered if the act by the gay men were not making fun of the

constraints placed upon women by American society; they also sometimes objected to the sexuality emphasized by many of the costumes, particularly the sexualizing of women for men's amusement, as well as the concept that men in general take social license to be sexual in public, often at the expense of women.

Indiana University's Lesbian Liberation Organization identified itself to the campus via the *Indiana Daily Student* in February of 1976.[142] "The organization is not new. It's been active on and off for several years at least. We're just getting started again." While seeking some publicity for their group, the members still felt the need to conceal their family names.

They were more forthcoming, though, about the separation of genders in the gay campus organizations.

> It was just a conflict with some of the men there. They didn't seem to be interested in any kind of change or feminism. They seemed happy with their "piece of the pie" so to speak and they didn't want to do anything about their sexism. They weren't meeting my needs as a woman. I felt oppressed.[143]

The men in the Gay Alliance attempted to reconcile with the lesbians in 1978. The men voted to change the name of the group to the Bloomington Gay/Lesbian Alliance. Out of deference to the women, however, they did not want to change it, for fear of speaking on behalf of the lesbians without their agreement. The vice-chairperson "encourages lesbians to come to the group meetings and request the name change be added to the agenda and that a lesbian caucus form to discuss the matter".[144]

One instance of the campus newspaper giving coverage to gay and lesbian issues on campus during the 1970s was the full-page "Gay Guide" in the *Indiana Daily Student*.[145] In my experience researching campus newspapers, I never saw anything else like it. It was a comprehensive list of local and national resources, along with descriptions of each; the campus resources included quotations from leaders in those efforts about each. The editors wrote:

> This page is meant to give some guidance to the gay person or interested straight person in Bloomington. We are not espousing homosexuality or any sexual propensity by presenting this guide. Instead, it is meant as a service to the gay community and to those people interested in the lifestyle.[146]

Among the listed local and campus organizations and services available were Men and Women's Literary Circle, a gay coffeehouse ("an alternative to bars"), a switchboard service (8 p.m. to 1 a.m.; staffed by women, Wednesday, Thursday, and Friday, and by men Saturday, Sunday, and Monday), a speakers bureau (noted as having eight to ten gay male members), and gay-friendly Bloomington bars, including the "gay disco," the Omni, which boasted a game room, pool table, pinball machines, and a wide-screen television.[147]

Indiana Gay Awareness Conferences

By the mid-1970s, non-heterosexual activism on Indiana's campus created two academic "drive-in" conferences. The first Indiana Gay Awareness Conference was held March 29 through March 31, 1974. In addition to panel discussions and, of course, a dance "in the classic tradition of Bloomington flings," the conference featured speakers that included long-time gay activist Frank Kameny, Peter Fisher (author of *The Gay Mystique*), and the founder of the Metropolitan Community Church, Troy Perry.

Dan Strang, chairperson for the Bloomington Gay Alliance (BGA) Gay Awareness Conference Committee, mailed letters of invitation across the state, primarily, it seems, targeted to a straight audience of Indiana jurists and lawmakers.[148] John Struble, the chairman of the BGA, sent letters of invitation to other gay and lesbian organizations in Indiana. Struble wrote of one of the goals he had for the conference.

> One of the hoped-for aims of this conference will be to establish a state-wide network of communications among all the groups in Indiana, to facilitate more organized political action, social communication, and out-of-town counselling [sic] referral, in addition to the solidarity such a move might bring to our communities.[149]

In addition to mailing the letters, the Conference Committee appears to have placed advertisements in classified columns in campus newspapers, such as the *Sycamore* at Indiana University-Purdue University in Indianapolis.[150]

The first conference was a success, and in the fall of 1975, the Bloomington Gay Alliance, in cooperation with the Indiana Memorial Union Board, planned a second gay conference on campus in 1976. The 1976 conference brought to campus lesbian poet Elaine Noble, Vito

Russo's traveling presentation of *The Celluloid Closet* (as well as Russo's workshop "How Can I Be Liberated and Still Like Judy Garland?"), Alan Bell from the Kinsey Institute for Sex Research, and discharged gay serviceman Leonard Matlovich.

Indiana University's president, John W. Ryan, did not bother to disguise his antipathy toward homosexuals. His attitude is perhaps reflective of many higher education administrators of his era. Ryan had received a letter of:

> ...protest as an Indiana taxpayer and a Christian that such depraved activity should be permitted to openly carry on their activities on state supported property with apparently the blessings of the school's authorities... [unless Ryan were] ...aware of this activity on the school campus.[151]

Responding, Ryan wrote:

> I sympathize completely with your point of view about the Gay Awareness Conference held recently on the Bloomington Campus.
> There is no doubt that such groups utilize University facilities in order to achieve some propaganda objective advancing their cause, or perhaps just to hurt the reputations of thousands of students in the University....
> I find such groups as the Gay Liberation Front undesirable and do not attend any of their functions but the law and recent court decisions do not permit the University to deny their access....[152]

John E. Scott, an attorney in Anderson, Indiana, also wrote to Ryan to complain of non-heterosexual students on the Indiana University campus. In his letter, sent by special delivery, Scott complained to his friend Ryan about having non-heterosexuals—and lesbians, in particular—on campus.

> As a devoted I.U. Alumnus it this bit upsets me more than the Knight fiasco.[153] I suppose you can't get rid of the lesbians, but it doesn't seem you should furnish their facilities. I'm mighty glad I don't have your job.[154]

President Ryan replied with candor and rancor.

> You know I feel the same way you do about the clipping you sent me, but our discretion in space assignment is gone. Under the rule of the courts we can refuse only that which is illegal. What I try to do is see to it that we have wholesome programs in recreation, arts, culture, drama, etc. to provide plenty of alternatives to the bizarre.[155]

Despite progress to public awareness, educational opportunities for the region, and increased access to campus facilities, non-heterosexual students at Indiana were stymied by the moralistic attitudes of the University's senior administration.

University of Iowa, 1970–1975

In late 1970, the campus newspaper, *The Daily Iowan*, ran a five-part "in-depth analysis" of gay student life. The premier article focused on the GLF's first meeting as a registered student organization. On September 23, 1970, 50 students elected Paul Hutson and Gretchen Parker as co-chairs of the GLF.[156]

Early GLF member Gary Smith summarized the radical and militant nature of the gay liberation founders at the University of Iowa. "We had to be.... Visibility and confrontation were our primary aims. We had to let people know we were here."[157] Paul Hutson defined the Iowa City GLF as a:

militant organization with the goal of overturning the views of homosexuals held both by the public and by the homosexual himself, which have been imposed by the oppressive process of sexual socialization of this country.[158]

Perhaps the "oppressive process" on campus, at least in terms of dealing with the administration, was best represented by the attitude of the University's vice provost, who told the newspaper that gay and lesbian students needed psychological counseling (Fig. 2.8). "Other than this counseling, the university has taken no stand on homosexuals."[159]

The impetus for their organizing, however, was not so much radical politics as it was traditional student festivity. October 16, 1970, was the date of the homecoming parade for the University.

On that Friday afternoon, 12 members of the newly formed Gay Liberation Front (GLF) decked out a late model Cadillac and rode in the homecoming parade. They chanted political slogans, threw candy kisses to the crowd, and made the "NBC Evening News."[160]

Early GLF member Terry Adamson recalled their efforts in the fall of 1970.

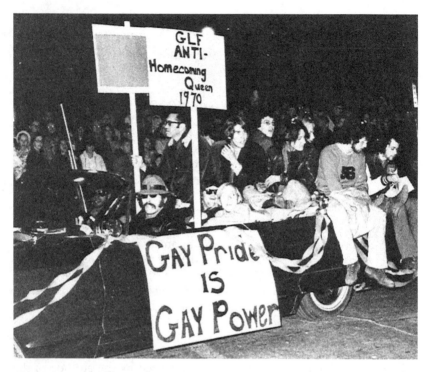

Fig. 2.8   Gay Liberation Front in homecoming parade, University of Iowa, 1970. (*Hawkeye Yearbook*, 1971, University Archives, The University of Iowa Libraries)

Iowa University crowned no homecoming queen in 1970, but the homecoming parade did feature the first public demonstration of the campus' GLF.

The group finally became organized just a few weeks before the homecoming parade…. At first we were kind of a loose conglomeration of people with fairly radical politics who just happened to be gay…. Whereas it may have appeared that GLF was just as much a one-issue group as some anti-war organizations, we were actually much more radical, because we were questioning not only the opprobrious laws against gay people but contesting all the ways in which society manipulates people's very being – their sexuality."[161]

Unlike at other Midwestern universities, the GLF at Iowa quickly received university recognition.[162] After a month as an official student organization, Iowa's GLF applied for and received university funding. In the words of *The Daily Iowan* reporter who wrote the five-part series,

> ...an appropriation from the University Budgeting and Auditing Committee provoked both surprise and indignation. While a few members were indignant at such a small appropriation and considered it a token gesture, most were surprised that the university was willing to give any money to Gay Lib.[163]

Also in October, the GLF held their first dance on campus at the Union.[164] Later dances were moved off campus, to the Unitarian-Universalist Church.[165] One former female GLF member, who wished to remain anonymous in 1978, recalled, "The dances were great because for once gay people could meet socially without getting a lot of shit from redneck straights."[166]

Michael Blake was a student at Iowa during the time and recalled the origins he learned of the group's formation.

> GAY LIBERATION FRONT grew out of such an informal social circle. The group of friends evolved to form a group which had been meeting on campus for more than a year. In 1971, bolstered by events occurring across the United States in reaction to Stonewall, they petitioned the Student Senate for recognition and funding. As confrontation was the mode of the times, the meeting was an intense and flamboyant event. The Senate acquiesced with funding for a regional gay conference which was attended by approximately one hundred fifty local and regional activists. By their action, the University of Iowa Student Senate became the first such entity in the nation to officially recognize and so validate by funding a gay or lesbian organization.[167]

Visibility, particularly on campus, was an important aspect to the work of the GLF at Iowa. Gary Smith summarized the radical and militant nature of the gay liberation founders there. "Visibility and confrontation were our primary aims. We had to let people know we were here."[168] Michael Blake further noted the connection between visibility and the liberation ethos of the early non-heterosexual campus organizers in Iowa City.

Visibility was important to these early activists and to be recognized as a part of the gay community became a strong political statement. Several of these local activists were also involved in the local chapter of the radical student organization, Students for a Democratic Society (SDS). For all of this group's rhetoric, its gay members were met with cool acceptance; homophobia was not exclusive to the conservative university administration. Consequently most of its gay members put the greatest share of their activist energy into the new organization.[169]

As at other Midwestern campuses, such radicalism did not survive past the early 1970s. In a retrospective article in *The Daily Iowan* in 1978, the diminishing of gay radicalism on campus was noted: "About 1972 or 1973, the general spirit of campus protest was waning and fewer gays were making the radical gay critique."[170] Ken Burch, the last chair of the GLF at the University of Iowa, reflected on the symbolism of the changing the organization's name.

Just look at the name change that took place when a new group was formed.... The new group changed its name from Gay Liberation Front to Gay People's Union. Notice the elimination of the militant overtones.[171]

One member of the former GLF, who wished to remain anonymous even in 1978, recalled the evolving nature of the membership's sense of community.

We had made ourselves visible, especially among university people, so for some the focus began to shift from assessing our activist style and to supporting other gays.[172]

By 1974, the GLF had changed, as had its membership. Michael Blake recalled the splintering of the non-heterosexual women from GLF.

LESBIAN ALLIANCE, founded in 1974, worked until 1989 within the context of the Women's center as the official lesbian voice on the many programs being formed.... Lesbian Alliance operated a coffee house for artistic and social exchange from 1978 through 1984.[173]

What Blake did not mention was that the Lesbian Alliance was formed by women who left Iowa's GLF, because of their dissatisfaction of what they felt was a lack of inclusion and a lack of focus. Across the country, women were leaving gay-focused organizations for similar reasons; those women often became increasingly involved in the women's liberation movement.[174] On university campuses in the Midwest in the mid-1970s, non-heterosexual women founded their own organizations.

By 1975, GLF's strategy of confrontation had peaked, and a new generation of activists had joined the group. To reflect a growing introspection, the group changed its name to Gay People's Union (GPU) and devoted much of its energy to developing services for gays and lesbians not being provided by the University.

Michael Blake first became involved at Iowa during this time. According to Blake, the male membership of GPU had left the revolutionary causes behind for social activities.

> I came out through the Gay People's Union in 1975. I was still a student then. Because the organization was a vehicle for me for coming out, I felt immediately involved. I wanted to pay back, in a sense.
> At that time, it was a newly revised organization. Gay People's Union, and the name change, was a very conscious attempt to make some legitimacy out of what had become party central. And I'm not meaning to say that in a derogatory way; it was just the nature of the Gay Liberation Front. Gay Liberation at that time was a very "party" atmosphere, because, "Hey, we're not hiding anymore."[175]

Still, the GPU members maintained some less than assimilationist ideas, particularly about marriage.

> The politic was, "We're going to define something new.... We're not going to recreate hetero America. It was all about creating a new culture," [... not] like a hetero construct. There was potential to actually do that, but it got interrupted, I think, because everybody had pitch in and [respond to] HIV.[176]

In 1976, the University of Iowa's GPU initiated a professionally trained crisis and information phone service. "Coming out" and validation support groups administered by gay counseling students formed. The strategy of the group during the later 1970s was to become an indispensable resource to the University population by promoting positive opportunities for gays and lesbians working and studying at the University.[177]

Southern Illinois University Carbondale, 1971–1976

A letter from John Taylor, a student at Southern Illinois University's (SIU's) main campus in Carbondale, Illinois, to gay journalist and historian Jim Kepner conveyed the founding of SIU's "Gay Liberation Organization."[178] Taylor listed the official date of the founding as April 15, 1971. He noted, "About half of the people at the first meeting were straight, including several (male-female) couples." Taylor relayed that "some of us went to the Midwest Gay Conference at Northern Illinois University" over the April 17 to 19 weekend.

> Also, this last Sat. 24th., the Gay Lib. Front of the University of Illinois has [sic] Gay Lib Dance at their Union. We gained some experience as how to organize our own activities.... Infact [sic], we are planning our first dance on May 8, in the Ball Room of our Student Union Building."[179]

Taylor's letter included a list of the officers, a copy of the GLO's constitution, along with an article from the campus newspaper, *The Daily Egyptian*, from April 9, 1971. Although the article did not survive in Kepner's correspondence files, the constitution did. Its first article stated:

> The Gay Liberation Organization of S.I.U. is an organization which seeks to accomplish the following basic goals:
>
> 1. Personal liberation – to integrate one's sexuality with the total being through a program of social interaction
> 2. Gay Community – to instill an awareness of gay brotherhood through mutual respect to recognize the diversity of life styles among ourselves and to unify them into a common culture; and to develop informal programs pertaining to homosexual problems.
> 3. Reformation – to change oppressive institutions, laws and policies through educational political activities, thereby initiating a parallel change in human attitudes.[180]

In 1976, Daniel Herzog recalled his time in graduate school at Southern Illinois University Carbondale, during the 1974–1975 and 1975–1976 academic years.[181]

Gay life in Carbondale, the hub of Southern Illinois, was a little different from gay life in Philadelphia. Carbondale is extremely rural.... When I arrived at Southern Illinois University, the campus gay organization was very loosely knit, had few members, and had very little funding from the university proper.[182]

Herzog wrote that he and his "friends" publicized the existence of the group, and it sponsored speakers and events "on borrowed money and promises. Our first big splash was to introduce Sgt. Leonard Matlovich" as a guest speaker, followed by a "gay dance" in the rented Carbondale City Hall. They capitalized on their success.

We started a gay speakers' bureau for the university classes and town clubs.... We received over 30 requests for speakers, including one from a local junior women's league. (That really made our day.)[183]

Herzog graduated and left campus, as John Taylor did, as most students do. Without a formal infrastructure within a college or university, the process of finding community and rebuilding resources was a recurring experience for successive cohorts of gay and lesbian student activists of the 1970s and 1980s.

Southern Illinois University Edwardsville, 1973–1976

Edwardsville, Illinois, is, in essence, a suburb of the St. Louis metropolitan area. In the 1970s, the campus of Southern Illinois University that had been established there was seen as a campus primarily designed for commuter students from rural Illinois. No residence halls were provided on campus, and activities for the students were scant. Nevertheless, a gay liberation group was founded over the summer of 1973: Students for Gay Liberation (SGL).

Frank Barker, Dennis Edmiston, and John Johnson, all Southern Illinois University Edwardsville (SIUE) students, decided in May of 1973 to form a gay student group. In June, they approached administrators at the campus, who informed the students there were three court rulings that indicated there was no legal reason to bar the group. By early August, SGL was recognized by both the Student Activities office and the SIUE Student Senate.[184] According to Barker, who served as SGL's first president, the group was "pushy" but not militant. Thirteen or so sympathetic heterosexuals attended the first meeting, along with 35 non-heterosexuals. The members stood outside on campus the day before meetings, handing out flyers to students.[185]

In addition to weekly "rap" meetings, SGL spent much of its time during the 1973–1974 academic year to plan for Gay and Lesbian Awareness Week. In the spring of 1974, Larry Whitsell, a student senator on the campus, served as its president; Sharon Kincaid was vice president; and John Stock was secretary-treasurer.[186] April 29 through May 3, 1974, SGL, with close to $1000 in support from SIUE, produced a Gay and Lesbian Awareness Week on campus. On the first day of the event, Whitsell and Stock provided a 90-minute panel for anyone on campus to ask questions about gay issues. They did this in the Goshen Lounge of the Campus Center (the Student Union), in what the campus magazine called "the most controversial of all programs" for the year.[187]

Reporters for the campus newspaper commented on how calm Whitsell and Stock remained many of the students called gays "fags, queers, homos and other such names,"[188] as well as on the composition of the hecklers: "Surprisingly the most vicious opponents of SGL to voice opinions on Monday were females, blacks, or persons with long hair.... After years of struggle and social movements by oppressed groups in our society we apparently still have not learned."[189] "One student told them that after he had a sexual experience, 'at least my ass don't hurt.'"[190] Whitsell responded to the negativity in a mild manner: "Gay people are people first. We are human beings, not monsters."[191]

Also during the GALA Week at SIUE in 1974, Frank Kameny and Barbara Gittings made individual as well as a joint presentation to the campus. Their joint presentation was attended by an estimated 500 people. Whitsell declared the event accomplished its purpose. "Anytime you can get 500 people in the Goshen Lounge for an activity, it's successful." Despite the detractors, he was sanguine in his observations:

> It is the sort of thing you would have seen in Chicago or New York about five years ago. Overall, this campus body is a little behind on the issues.[192]

Frank Barker, in 1976, gave an even more appreciative memory of the day.

> Of those against, the most controversial were five who were ultrahostile [sic] to the point of threatening the next gay who came within five feet of them. It was good that the violent a reaction came. It took the issue to many indifferent people – and when they saw such a violent homophobia, they empathized with the problems of being an open gay.[193]

The director of the University Center, Bob Hardy, felt the GALA Week "...gave the organization an opportunity to say what they felt, and I'm glad we did it.... I think we all benefited from it."[194]

It appears, however, that the group ceased to exist not long after their success. Larry Whitsell resigned, after repeated threats against his family.[195] Sharon Kincaid is listed as graduating in 1975. Information about the other students mentioned is difficult to find; neither does Jim Ardis provide any on Students for Gay Liberation in subsequent years. As with many of the early gay campus activists, they have disappeared into the past.

OHIO STATE UNIVERSITY, 1971–1972

The GLF at Ohio State began operations in the spring of 1971. In a letter to the editor of the *Ohio State Lantern*, the GLF wrote that:

> ...while [educating the general campus about gay and lesbian issues] is one of our goals, we as brothers and sisters exist to liberate ourselves from our own repressed attitudes as well as those of the general community.... [W]e intend to operate on all levels concerning the educational, political, economic, and religious factors of our culture.[196]

In March of 1971, GLF claimed an active membership of 25, along with 200 "non-active" members.[197] It is unclear how many of those members were actually students.

Unlike most of the other campuses covered in this study, the Ohio State University (OSU) is located in a large metropolitan area. The early founders of GLF at Ohio State did not seem to differentiate membership in their organization by status within the campus community. The distinction between students and non-students in OSU's GLF became problematic within a few years: questions from OSU's gay student organization (and student government) about the funding for the campus organization that might have been underwriting the city-based organization.

One of the first recorded actions of the Ohio State GLF was a rally in July, 1971, protesting gay discrimination. Despite lacking a permit, ten members rallied in front of the Ohio State House.[198]

In the fall of 1971, the GLF transmogrified into the Gay Activists Alliance (GAA), although it did not claim an official connection to the original, New York City-based GAA. Mark Brock, the president of the group, said that the change resulted from a new focus away from anti-war and civil rights initiatives, upon gay rights. "Although we may have personal feelings about the war and civil rights movements, GAA will not take a stand as a group." In the words of former GLF coordinator, "Many people just couldn't relate to other issues [like] liberation of the mind."[199]

Dressing for the Occasion

By winter 1971–1972, OSU's GAA had increased its membership to 48.[200] The group's focus was split between providing social outlets for non-heterosexuals to build community with other non-heterosexuals and communicating that non-heterosexuals were a minority based upon social reactions to their sexuality.

> GAA is trying to make homosexuals aware they are an oppressed minority and is encouraging accepts of gays by straight society, according to GAA member Pat Miller, a graduate student....[201]
>
> GAA was formed "so gay people could relate to each other on a more human level and know they're not alone," [said David], "who refused to give his last name fearing job reprisals."[202]

In January of 1972, the GAA held a dance in the Ohio Union. Campus police arrested three cross-dressing attendees, as Columbus ordinances prohibited wearing clothes normally worn by the other sex. GAA saw this as a symbol of the harassment non-heterosexuals faced.

> "We don't even dare walk hand in hand across the Oval between classes, while heterosexuals can make almost any display of affection they want," said Jeff Orth.[203]

Jeffrey Arnold, a graduate student at Ohio State who attended the dance, was one of those arrested. Arnold claimed the campus police were selectively targeting those who attended the dance.

The police aren't enforcing the law, just their own prejudices.... Campus police said they were investigating a rape in the area when we were busted. There's certainly no chance that anybody was raped by a homosexual.[204]

The three cross-dressers were sentenced to 80 days of incarceration, which the judge suspended on the condition that they not violate the cross-dressing ordinance in the future. The absurdity of the moment was highlighted by the fact that, appearing at their sentencing before the judge, two of the three were again in drag.[205] Eventually, the convictions were overturned, with the court deeming that the men were not trying to impersonate women.[206]

Before that case was overturned, however, the GAA filed official complaints on campus.

After seven months of testimony and review, the Faculty Council's Committee on Campus Security issued a report on OSU's police force. Of all of the charges leveled against the campus police, the Committee "found evidence" in support of only two categories of complaints: wrongful charges and partial law enforcement. Both originated from the GAA. Nonetheless, the report stated the incidents in evidence "have been the discretionary acts of individual members of the force rather than explicit policies of the director."[207]

Still, the targeted, partial, and discriminatory enforcement against cross-dressing GAA members persisted.

At 10:15 on the morning of October 12, 1972, a Columbus police officer arrested two men near the OSU Law Library, one of whom was in drag. While the officer was in the process of arresting Jack Shaw, an OSU sophomore, for "violating female impersonation laws," the other, OSU graduate student Patrick Miller, attempted to intervene.

I was trying to show the officer a Xeroxed copy of a recent over-ruling on cross dressing [sic] codes. I tried to explain that Jack couldn't be arrested because he had a beard.[208]

The officer then arrested Miller for attempting to interfere in an arrest. At the police station, Miller's claim was eventually verified.

Deputy Chief Major Francis Smith said, "Yes, the city prosecutor told me a person having a beard cannot be considered trying to impersonate a female." He added, however, "This is only hearsay. I never got anything from him in writing."[209]

So, without the veracity of the initial charges, the Columbus police formally charged both Miller and Shaw with vagrancy.

In response, GAA members "and about five 'gay friends'" picked the police station and then a sit-in in front of City Hall. Columbus Mayor Tom Moody sat with them, discussing the situation.

"I can't promise you anything.... I intended to discuss it," Moody said, "but mistakes will still be made by the police.... You won't notice the difference... when things get better, because there will still be so many mistakes."[210]

The quiet discussion was in marked contrast to the earlier picket line, which attracted a crowd of about 50 spectators.

The spectators' comments on the GAA activists reinforced the activists' point about social discrimination and fear of harassment and violence.

Chipper Fuller, also 17, and from Columbus said, "If my old man knew these people were here he'd bring down his .38 and blow their heads off."

Fifteen-year-old John Astley's solution was to "buy up some land in Gahanna and have a city for gays out there. You could call it 'Gay City.'"[211]

For his part in the events, Shaw did not complain about how the police interacted with him while he was in jail. "They treated me like a lady."[212]

Vasbinder for Vice President

As one of the coordinators for GAA in 1971–1972, Susan Vasbinder was perhaps the best-known member of OSU's GAA; she was certainly the most public lesbian on campus, despite not seeming to stand out in public. An extensive, full-page profile in the campus newspaper in April of 1972 described her.

Sue Vasbinder looks like the average college girl. Long, brown hair. Jeans. Sweater. Desert boots. Her gray-green eyes peer inquisitively through owl-eyed wire-rims. In short, when Sue walks down High Street, she probably goes unnoticed in the crowd.... Sue, a 19-year-old sophomore from Kent, had been denying her identity as a lesbian until she came out (told others she was a lesbian) about a year ago.[213]

Vasbinder's accomplishment in accepting a non-heterosexual identity so quickly was all the more remarkable given her almost immediate immersion in campus politics and gay activism. She joined the GAA (and made "first organized contact with other lesbians") in the winter quarter of 1971; by spring 1972, she was elected co-coordinator.[214]

Vasbinder was a rare non-heterosexual woman who could engage with gay men in campus organizations without feeling overly discriminated against. During autumn of 1971 some of the women in GAA at OSU felt alienated from the men and separated to form Radical Lesbians. Vasbinder's experiences in 1972 did not match those of the women who formed the Radical Lesbians at OSU. "In gay groups, though, the men seem more conscious of women's problems in society."[215]

Vasbinder commented upon what she seemed to feel were restrictive gender-based roles for non-heterosexual women.

> Lesbians realize they must act politically as a body of women if they are ever to end discrimination.... The new lesbian is the equality lesbian.... Most of us don't define each other as butch or femme.... I see myself as a woman, so why should I assume male characteristics?[216]

Vasbinder did, however, see herself as a self-conscious member of a social minority with a responsibility to change the living conditions of that minority.

> I identify with any oppressed group.... Anyone who says one person is biologically or sociologically superior to another, I'm opposed to.... With my identity, I wouldn't be happy if I wasn't fighting for homosexual acceptance.... Just because I suffer doesn't mean others should have to.[217]

The full-page feature on Vasbinder ran in the *Ohio State Lantern* just two weeks before the campus elections, just before Vasbinder announced she would vie for the position of student body vice president. Well, sort of vice president.

Jeffrey Yapalater, the then vice president of the Undergraduate Student Government (USG), and Vasbinder made a late entry into a contested election for president and vice president. Different from their competitors, the pair said they would be "co-coordinators" of the USG, sharing the responsibilities and the power. Vasbinder said, "I think gay people have been totally ignored and put down by the administration."[218] As part of her platform, Vasbinder also called for separate housing for gays on campus.

The running mates held an outdoor party on the campus Oval during the first day of voting. The *Ohio State Lantern* estimated 400 students listened to the Jeremy Clay Band; about half left when campus speakers took the stage. Vasbinder said to the crowd, "I just want to know if everybody is having a gay time."[219]

Yapalater and Vasbinder came in third, garnering 2748 votes out of a record 13,243 cast.[220] Susan Vasbinder continued her work with the gay and lesbian community. In her senior year, she was one of eight women who served as counselors for Columbus Gay Women's Peer Counseling, which was established in 1973.[221]

Changes in Gay Pride

Ohio State's GAA sponsored its first Gay Pride Week in May of 1972. Part of the events for the week harkened back to early GLF political actions, with guerrilla theater acted out on the campus Oval, depicting "situations that gay people sometimes encounter in straight society."[222] Speakers for the week included an ordained gay minister and a professor of law at OSU; Martha Shelley, one of the first GLF founders, Tina Mandel (past president of the early lesbian organization the Daughters of Bilitis), Rich Wandel (then president of GAA in New York City), and James Foriatt with the Unicorn News Service in Washington, D.C. The keynote speaker was Franklin Kameny; in 1961, Kameny had co-founded the Washington, D.C., branch of the early gay rights organization the Mattachine Society. It was an ambitious lineup of nationally known speakers who helped organize lesbian and gay activism and organizations of the past.

A dance at the Student Union was held on Saturday night, followed by a march from the campus Oval to the Ohio State House on Sunday. A free concert on the Oval Sunday night capped off the week. The Ohio Pride Committee commented,

> We do not pretend that this conference will solve all of the problems and questions, nor do we pretend to represent all the segments of gay life. We see the weekend as an opportunity for gay people to get their heads together or partially together on our stated goals.[223]

Some problems, though, were resolved through actions of the GAA. The organization made several requests during 1972 to the OSU administration. Two of the requests were eventually achieved: the end of police harassment of gays on campus, such as at the dances, and an end to the university's policy of requiring non-heterosexual students to consult psychiatrists in order to remain enrolled.[224]

By early 1975, organized non-heterosexual students on the Ohio State campus had changed. Robert J. Smith, a new officer in the group, described the difference observers would find.

> They expect long-haired radicals – that was the image GAA used to have.... But we're not into street politics or zapping people anymore. We have most of the laws on our side now. Now we're interested in helping each other on an individual basis.[225]

Even the dances on campus had become a thing of the past. Advocating for acceptance as equals within the existing structures of society, and aiding students in their coming out process, became the focus of the group.[226]

NOTES

1. Rich Cahan, "Borchers hits gay funding," *Daily Illini*, May 23, 1973, 7. In 1976, Borchers was convicted in Illinois state court for pilfering from his state-funded legislative account; he died in 1989, his legacy, such as it is, as the founder of the University of Illinois' racist mascot, Chief Illini. Illinois State University's Gay People's Alliance continued into the 2010s, as ISU Pride.
2. Wisconsin LGBT History Project, History of Gay & Lesbian Life in Milwaukee Wisconsin, Gay Liberation Organization at UWM (GLO-UWM), http://www.mkelgbthist.org/organiz/act_pol/gay-lib-org.htm
3. "Form Homosexual Freedom League," *UWM Post*, February 24, 1970, 2.
4. Wisconsin LGBT History Project, History of Gay & Lesbian Life in Milwaukee Wisconsin, Gay Liberation Organization at UWM (GLO-UWM), www.mkelgbthist.org/gayliberationfront
5. Wisconsin LGBT History Project, History of Gay & Lesbian Life in Milwaukee Wisconsin, Gay Liberation Organization at UWM (GLO-UWM), www.mkelgbthist.org/gayliberationfront
6. Background information on Phelps comes from Koreen Phelps, Interview with Scott Paulsen, November 5, 1993, Twin Cities Gay and Lesbian Community Oral History Project, Minnesota Historical Society, www.collections.mnhs.org, hereafter referred to as "Phelps Interview."

7. Phelps Interview, 2.
8. The University of Minnesota's Minneapolis campus is bisected by the Mississippi River; the west side is smaller and was slower to be developed; it is also closer to downtown Minneapolis.
9. Phelps Interview, 3.
10. Brad Theissen, "Koreen Phelps and Stephen Ihrig Discuss Early Days of Twin Cities Gay/Lesbian Community", *Twin Cities GAZE*, July 13, 1989, 10.
11. Ben Cohen, "Koreen Phelps Fought So Gays Could Live Freely," *Twin Cities Star Tribune*, July 22, 2007, B6.
12. Theissen, "Koreen Phelps and Stephen Ihrig Discuss Early Days of Twin Cities Gay/Lesbian Community."
13. "Free universities" were held in many cities, on many campuses; they offered no credit but did address topics and concerns that many students' curricula did not include, such as gay and lesbian issues.
14. Phelps Interview, 3.
15. "The Homosexual in Society" is the title of the course as Koreen Phelps remembered it in an interview in 1994; FREE member Robert Halfhill remembered it as "The Homosexual Revolution," and that is how it is referred to in a contemporary newspaper account.
16. Phelps Interview, 4.
17. S. Jane Albert, "Free U Starts 'Homosexual Revolution,'" *Minnesota Daily*, June 20, 1969, 1, 18:18.
18. Phelps Interview, 17.
19. Phelps Interview, 5.
20. Albert, "Free U Starts 'Homosexual Revolution,'" 18.
21. Albert, "Free U Starts 'Homosexual Revolution,'" 18.
22. Albert, "Free U Starts 'Homosexual Revolution,'" 18.
23. Phelps Interview, 10.
24. Dudley Clendinen and Adam Nagourney, *Out for Good: The Struggle to Build a Gay Rights Movement in America* (New York: Simon & Schuster, 1999), 57.
25. "Homosexuals Intend to Integrate 'U' Dance," *Minneapolis Star*, February 5, 1970, 27.
26. Kevin P. Murphy, "Gay Was Good," *Twin Cities GLBT Oral History Project, Queer Twin Cities* (Minneapolis, MN: University of Minnesota Press, 2010).
27. John D. Wrathall, "'What Are You After?': A History of Lesbians, Gay Men, Bisexuals, and Transgender People at the Twin Cities Campus of the University of Minnesota, 1969–1993." *Breaking the Silence: Final Report of the Select Committee on Lesbian, Gay, and Bisexual Concerns*, University of Minnesota (November 1, 1993), 48–58: 49.

28. Wrathall, "'What Are You After?,'" 49.
29. Lyn Miller, "The Dawn of Gay Liberation in Minnesota," *Stonewall 20: A Generation of Pride, Minneapolis Program,* 1989, 7–8, 10–12, 12. Jean-Nickolaus Tretter Collection in GLBT Studies, Twin Cities (TC) Pride Records, 1973–2014/1989, 1989. University of Minnesota Libraries.
30. Mike Wolff, "Gay Is Good – Should Be FREE," *Minneapolis Star,* November 19, 1969, 1B.
31. Wolff, "Gay Is Good...."
32. Wolff, "Gay Is Good...."
33. Wolff, "Gay Is Good...."
34. Wolff, "Gay Is Good...."
35. Miller, "The Dawn of Gay Liberation in Minnesota," 7.
36. Robert Halfhill, "FREE: The First Gay Liberation Group in Minnesota," *Stonewall 20: A Generation of Pride, Minneapolis Program,* 1989, 13. Jean-Nickolaus Tretter Collection in GLBT Studies, Twin Cities (TC) Pride Records, 1973–2014/1989, 1989. University of Minnesota Libraries.
37. Jack Baker's life story, even the portion of his life as president of the Associated Student Government at the University of Michigan, is beyond the scope of this book. For more information on Baker, see Michael McConnell and Jack Baker, with Gail Langer Karwoski, *The Wedding Heard 'Round the World: America's First Gay Marriage* (Minneapolis, MN: University of Minnesota Press, 2016).
38. Halfhill, "FREE: The First Gay Liberation Group in Minnesota."
39. Halfhill, "FREE: The First Gay Liberation Group in Minnesota."
40. Miller, "The Dawn of Gay Liberation in Minnesota," 8.
41. Phelps Interview, 5.
42. Miller, "The Dawn of Gay Liberation in Minnesota," 8–10.
43. Miller, "The Dawn of Gay Liberation in Minnesota," 8.
44. Halfhill, "FREE: The First Gay Liberation Group in Minnesota."
45. Halfhill, "FREE: The First Gay Liberation Group in Minnesota."
46. Phelps Interview, 13.
47. Halfhill, "FREE: The First Gay Liberation Group in Minnesota."
48. Phelps Interview, 5.
49. Phelps Interview, 5.
50. Phelps Interview, 5.
51. Phelps Interview, 13.
52. Halfhill, "FREE: The First Gay Liberation Group in Minnesota."
53. Halfhill, "FREE: The First Gay Liberation Group in Minnesota."
54. Higgins was remarkable both prior to and after the FREE march against his firing. In 1969, he was the first man granted a presidential conscien-

tious objector draft classification. In 1977, he was the activist who threw a cream pie into Anita Bryant's face when she brought her anti-gay crusade to Minneapolis. To many, he was an unsung hero of the Gay Rights Movement.

55. "Firing Protested," *Minneapolis Tribune*, February 11, 1970, 33.
56. Halfhill, "FREE: The First Gay Liberation Group in Minnesota."
57. Phelps Interview, 10.
58. Halfhill, "FREE: The First Gay Liberation Group in Minnesota."
59. Dudley Clendinen and Adam Nagourney, *Out for Good: The Struggle to Build a Gay Rights Movement in America* (New York: Simon & Schuster, 1999), 226.
60. Phelps Interview, 15; Phelps Interview, 14.
61. Michael McConnell, with Jack Baker and Gail Langer Karwoski, *The Wedding Hear 'Round the World: America's First Gay Marriage* (Minneapolis, MN: University of Minnesota Press, 2016).
62. Phelps Interview, 14.
63. Phelps Interview, 14.
64. Theissen, "Koreen Phelps and Stephen Ihrig Discuss Early Days of Twin Cities Gay/Lesbian Community."
65. McConnell et al., *The Wedding Heard 'Round the World*.
66. "ACSA removes Baker from office," *Minnesota Daily*, February 6, 1973, 1.
67. Tim Retzloff, "Outcast, Miscast, Recast: A Documentary History of Lesbians and Gay Men at the University of Michigan." *Final Report of the Study Committee on the Status of Lesbians and Gay Men, University of Michigan* (1991), 110–134, 115.
68. "PROPOSED CONSTITUTION FORM." James W. Toy Papers, Box 15, Gay Liberation Front, Folder: Membership Materials, Bentley Historical Library, The University of Michigan.
69. Tim Retzloff, "Gay Liberation: When Michigan Tore Out of the Closets and into the Streets" (June 1994), 1. Bentley Historical Library (Non-Circulating, Closed Stacks), EA 186 R441 G285.
70. James Toy, Interview with Author, September 2002.
71. Retzloff, "Gay Liberation," 3.
72. James W. Toy Papers, Box 15, Gay Liberation Front, Folder: Membership Materials. Bentley Historical Library, The University of Michigan.
73. James Toy, "Desired under the Elms": Necessary (and Obvious?) Components of a Lesbigay Agenda for American Colleges and Universities, presented at Lesbians, Gays, and Bisexuals on Campus: A Symposium on Campus Climate, University of Delaware, 4/22/1994, 1; In James W. Toy Papers, Box 19, Conference Paper, "Desired under the Elms....".

74. Jane Bartman and W. E. Schrock, "Gay Lib: Resisting Repression of the Homosexual," *The Michigan Daily*, April 12, 1970, 1, 10.
75. Bartman and Schrock, "Gay Lib: Resisting Repression of the Homosexual."
76. Hester Pulling, "'U' bans Gay Lib conference," *The Michigan Daily*, March 7, 1970, 1.
77. Pulling, "'U' bans Gay Lib conference."
78. Pulling, "'U' bans Gay Lib conference."
79. Pulling, "'U' bans Gay Lib conference."
80. Retzolf, "Gay Liberation," 4.
81. Cited in Gerald Cohen-Vrignaud, "Gay & Proud," *The Michigan Daily*, February 12, 1999; online at http://www.pub.umich.edu/daily/199/feb/02-12-99/news/news18.html
82. Dave Chudwin, "Fleming hits 'U' disruption," *The Michigan Daily*, September 29, 1970, 1.
83. Hester Pulling, "SGC Okays Gay Lib Conference," *The Michigan Daily*, June 17, 1970, 3.
84. James W. Toy Papers, Box 14, Gay Liberation Front, Meeting Minutes (Various) 1970.
85. Rich Stanford, "Goals of the Ann Arbor GLF and Organizing Toward Those Goals," Bentley Historical Library, University of Michigan, James W. Toy Papers, Box 14, Folder: Gay Liberation Front-General folder. Bentley Historical Library, The University of Michigan.
86. Stanford, "Goals of the Ann Arbor GLF and Organizing Toward Those Goals."
87. Hester Pulling, "GLF, SCG to Demand 'U' Permit 'Gay' Meeting", *The Michigan Daily*, June 3, 1970, 1.
88. Student Government Council and the Gay Liberation Front, "A Letter to Fleming," *The Michigan Daily*, June 11, 1970, 4.
89. "Fleming: A Second Chance," *The Michigan Daily*, June 10, 1970, 8.
90. Jerry De Grieck, Interview with Author, October 26, 2005.
91. Hester Pulling, "GLF Proceeds with Plans to Hold Conference at 'U'," *The Michigan Daily*, June 19, 1970, 1.
92. Pulling, "SGC Okay Gay Lib Conference," *The Michigan Daily*, June 17, 1970, 3.
93. Pulling, "GLF Proceeds with Plans to Hold Conference at 'U.'"
94. Pulling, "SGC Okay Gay Lib Conference."
95. Pulling, "GLF Proceeds with Plans to Hold Conference at 'U.'"
96. Hester Pulling, "SGC Hit Fleming, Demand Gay Conference," *The Michigan Daily*, June 11, 1970, 1.
97. Pulling, "SGC Hit Fleming, Demand Gay Conference."

98. Hester Pulling, "Fleming Cites Bad Image for 'U' in Gay Lib Case," *The Michigan Daily*, June 12, 1970, 1.
99. Pulling, "Fleming Cites Bad Image for 'U' in Gay Lib Case."
100. Lindsay Chaney, 'The People Affected Should Be Involved,' *The Michigan Daily*, July 16, 1970, 3, 6, 3.
101. Debra Thal, "Women's Liberation, GLF Hold 'Guerrilla Theatre', Blast ROTC," *The Michigan Daily*, May 28, 1970, 1.
102. Thal, "Women's Liberation, GLF Hold 'Guerrilla Theatre', Blast ROTC."
103. Bill Alterman, "General Manager Bars GLF From Using Union," *The Michigan Daily*, July 8, 1970, 1.
104. Thal, "Women's Liberation, GLF Hold 'Guerrilla Theatre', Blast ROTC."
105. Alterman, "General Manager Bars GLF From Using Union."
106. Alterman, "General Manager Bars GLF From Using Union."
107. Alterman, "General Manager Bars GLF From Using Union."
108. Alterman, "General Manager Bars GLF From Using Union."
109. Alterman, "Board to Consider Union Ban on GLF," *The Michigan Daily*, July 9, 1970, 1.
110. "Gay Lib Meets in Union, Plans Protest," *The Michigan Daily*, July 10, 1970, 1.
111. Bill Altman, "GLF Uses Union Lounge, Protest Set for Tuesday," *The Michigan Daily*, July 10, 1970, 10.
112. Altman, "GLF Uses Union Lounge, Protest Set for Tuesday."
113. James W. Toy Papers, Box 14, Folder: Gay Liberation Front. Bentley Historical Library, The University of Michigan.
114. Bill Altman, "GLF, Women's Lib, SDS Protest Union Facility Ban", *The Michigan Daily*, July 15, 1970, 3.
115. Radical Lesbians, "Letter to Editor: Radical Lesbians: Defining Deviance," *The Michigan Daily*, October 3, 1970, 4.
116. Cited in Tim Retzloff, "Gay Liberation: When Michigan Tore Out of the Closets and into the Streets," 7.
117. Cited in Tim Retzloff, "Gay Liberation: When Michigan Tore Out of the Closets and into the Streets," 7.
118. Martin Hirschman, "Fleming Backing Down on Gay Lib," *The Michigan Daily*, August 115, 1970, 1, 8: 1.
119. Hirschman, "Fleming Backing Down on Gay Lib," 8.
120. Hirschman, "Fleming Backing Down on Gay Lib," 8.
121. Jerry De Grieck, Interview with Author, October 26, 2005.
122. Bill Alterman, "Gay Lib Groups Hold State Conference in SAB," *The Michigan Daily*, August 18, 1970, 1.
123. Alterman, "Gay Lib Groups Hold State Conference in SAB."

124. Alterman, "Gay Lib Groups Hold State Conference in SAB."
125. Alterman, "Gay Lib Groups Hold State Conference in SAB."
126. "Regents Uphold 'U' Position on GLF," *The Michigan Daily*, September 19, 1970, 1, 8: 1.
127. "Regents Uphold 'U' Position on GLF," 8.
128. "Regents Uphold 'U' Position on GLF," 8.
129. Tammy Jacobs, "GLF, 'U' Continue to Dispute Over Site of Meeting on Homosexuality," *The Michigan Daily*, October 20, 1970, 1, 8: 8.
130. Jacobs, "GLF, 'U' Continue to Dispute Over Site of Meeting on Homosexuality."
131. Geri Sprung, "OSS Rebuffs 'U' on GLF Meeting," *The Michigan Daily*, October 27, 1970, 1, 7.
132. Sprung, "OSS Rebuffs 'U' on GLF Meeting."
133. "Standing firm on equal rights for homosexuals," *The Michigan Daily*, October 28, 1970, 4.
134. In 2005, Jerry De Grieck stated that he had good working relationships with some of Fleming's staff, noting particularly Knauss, with whom De Grieck said he remained in contact. Jerry De Grieck, Interview with Author, 10/26/2005.
135. Zach Schiller, "GLF Holds First Meeting of Term, Postpones Action on Conference," *The Michigan Daily*, February 8, 1971, 1.
136. Jan Benedetti, "Gay Advocates Named to New OSSP Offices," *The Michigan Daily*, December 10, 1971, 1, 8.
137. Tom Carey, Lynn Lambuth and Achy Obejas, "Gay Guide," *Indiana Daily Student*, November 28, 1978, A7.
138. Wilson E. Allen to Carol Fischer, email, April 22, 2003. Provided to author.
139. Wilson E. Allen to Carol Fischer, email, April 22, 2003. Provided to author.
140. 1974 *Arbutus*, Indiana University Yearbook, 108–109, 109.
141. Carey et al., "Gay Guide."
142. Marilyn Moore, "Lesbian Group Plans Class, Activities," *Indiana Daily Student*, February 5, 1976, 6.
143. Moore, "Lesbian Group Plans Class, Activities."
144. Carey et al., "Gay Guide."
145. Carey et al., "Gay Guide."
146. Carey et al., "Gay Guide."
147. Carey et al., "Gay Guide."
148. Dan Strang to Dear Fellow Hoosier, February 6, 1974. In Indiana University Archives, Indiana University President's Office records, 1963–1990, Box 124, Gay Awareness Conferences, 1974–1976.

149. John Struble to Dear Gay Sisters and Brothers, February 1, 1974. In Indiana University Archives, Indiana University President's Office records, 1963–1990, Box 124, Gay Awareness Conferences, 1974–1976.
150. James E. Keeler to John W. Ryan, October 30, 1975. In Indiana University Archives, Indiana University President's Office records, 1963–1990, Box 124, Gay Awareness Conferences, 1974–1976.
151. James E. Keeler to John W. Ryan, October 30, 1975.
152. John W. Ryan to James E. Keeler, November 5, 1975. In Indiana University Archives, Indiana University President's Office records, 1963–1990, Box 124, Gay Awareness Conferences, 1974–1976.
153. Bobby Knight, long-time basketball coach at Indiana University, was frequently in the press for his court-side antics, foul language, and bullying behavior.
154. John E. Scott to John W. Ryan, letter by special delivery, 2/10/76. In Indiana University Archives, Indiana University President's Office records, 1963–1990, Box 124, Gay Awareness Conferences, 1974–1976.
155. John W. Ryan to John E. Scott, 2/21/76. In Indiana University Archives, Indiana University President's Office records, 1963–1990, Box 124, Gay Awareness Conferences, 1974–1976.
156. Bill Kapp, "Gay Liberation Is Here to Stay: Finding a Consciousness," *The Daily Iowan*, October 27, 1970, 8.
157. Alan Kinsey, "Gay Lib at UI," *The Daily Iowan*, August 26, 1975, 7, 11: 7.
158. Kapp, "Gay Liberation Is Here to Stay."
159. Kapp, "Gay Liberation Is Here to Stay."
160. Brenan Lemon, "Going Public – Early Days in Gay History," *The Daily Iowan*, June 19, 1978, 1, 2: 1.
161. Lemon, "Going Public – Early Days in Gay History."
162. Lemon, "Going Public – Early Days in Gay History."
163. Bill Kapp, "Reporters Attend a GLF Meeting," *The Daily Iowan*, October 29, 1970, 4.
164. Bill Kapp, "Gay Socials: 'An Experience, A True Idea'," *The Daily Iowan*, October 18, 1970, 4.
165. Lemon, "Going Public – Early Days in Gay History."
166. Lemon, "Going Public – Early Days in Gay History."
167. Michael Blake, "Gay Lesbian Bisexual Activity at the University of Iowa," undated, Historical Papers Collection, The University of Iowa, Iowa City, Iowa, Series 1: General, Box 1.
168. Alan Kinsey, "Gay Lib at UI," *The Daily Iowan*, August 26, 1975, 7, 11: 7.
169. Blake, "Gay Lesbian Bisexual Activity at the University of Iowa."
170. Brendan Lemon, "Gay Movement Slows with Demise of Protest Era," *The Daily Iowan*, June 20, 1978, 1, 5: 1.

171. Lemon, "Gay Movement Slows with Demise of Protest Era," 5.
172. Lemon, "Gay Movement Slows with Demise of Protest Era," 1.
173. Blake, "Gay Lesbian Bisexual Activity at the University of Iowa."
174. See Margaret Cruikshank, *The Gay and Lesbian Liberation Movement* (New York: Routledge, 1992); Lillian Faderman, *The Gay Revolution: The Story of the Struggle* (New York: Simon & Schuster, 2015); and Karla Jay, *Tales of the Lavender Menace: A Memoir of Liberation* (New York: Basic Books, 1999), among others.
175. Michael Blake, Interview with Author, April 26, 2008.
176. Michael Blake, Interview with Author, April 26, 2008.
177. Blake, "Gay Lesbian Bisexual Activity at the University of Iowa."
178. John T. Taylor to Jim Kepner, April 7, 1971. Jim Kepner Papers, Coll 2011.002, Series 8: Correspondence, ONE National Gay & Lesbian Archives at the USC Libraries, University of Southern California.
179. John T. Taylor to Jim Kepner, April 7, 1971.
180. John T. Taylor to Jim Kepner, April 7, 1971.
181. Daniel Herzog, "Living Gay in Rural Illinois," *Weekly Gazette* (Philadelphia), December 10, 1976, 2, 7.
182. Herzog, "Living Gay in Rural Illinois," 7.
183. Herzog, "Living Gay in Rural Illinois," 7.
184. "SGL Builds Identity," *Focus*, February 1976, No. 12, 32.
185. "SGL Builds Identity."
186. Jim Andris, August 4, 2011, http://jandris.ipage.com/history/h74.0.html. In 1974, Andris was an assistant professor of education at SIUE, where he eventually retired as professor emeritus of Educational Foundations. His memories and transcriptions of the relevant articles from SIUE's campus newspaper, the *Arestle*, I draw upon for this section. Alas, his site does not list the page number for the articles from the newspaper.
187. "Gay Lib Controversy," *Focus*, No. 8 (October 1, 1974), 46–47.
188. Lynn Taylor, "Gay Lib Members Find Hostility During Dialogue," *Arestle*, May 1, 1974.
189. "Oppression of Rights Supported by Most Dialog Participants," *Arestle*, May 1, 1974.
190. "Oppression of Rights Supported by Most Dialog Participants."
191. "Oppression of Rights Supported by Most Dialog Participants."
192. Gary Sohl, "Gay Awareness Week Successful, According to Whitsell," *Arestle*, May 9, 1974.
193. Marc Scarpinato, "Frank Barker: 'Rapping' About Gay Lib," *Focus*, No. 6, March 1974, 50–54.
194. Sohl, "Gay Awareness Week Successful, According to Whitsell."
195. "SGL Builds Identity," *Focus*, Feb 1976, No. 12, 32.

196. The Gay Liberation Front, "Gay Lib Speaks for Selves," *Ohio State Lantern*, February 26, 1971, 4.
197. Dianne Dixon, "Gay Liberation Promoted," *Ohio State Lantern*, May 17, 1971, 8.
198. Robert Little, "Gay Rally Held Sans Permit," *Ohio State Lantern*, July 26, 1971, 2.
199. Stephan Brice, "Gay Lib: New Name and Policies," *Ohio State Lantern*, October 28, 1971, 2.
200. Mike Balduf, "Gay Activists Describe Alleged Discrimination," *Ohio State Lantern*, January 26, 1972, 4.
201. Balduf, "Gay Activists Describe Alleged Discrimination."
202. "Three GAA Members Found Guilty of Violating Ordinance," *Ohio State Lantern*, March 3, 1972, 13.
203. Balduf, "Gay Activists Describe Alleged Discrimination."
204. "Three GAA Members Found Guilty of Violating Ordinance."
205. "Three GAA Members Found Guilty of Violating Ordinance."
206. Amy Melvin, "Gays Ask For Public's Support," *Ohio State Lantern*, April 29, 1981, 2.
207. Gary Gorman, "Committee Says Police Mistakes Not Official Policy," *Ohio State Lantern*, May 5, 1976, 1.
208. A. C. DiFranco, "Gays Protest Impersonation Arrests," *Ohio State Lantern*, October 13, 1972, 1.
209. DiFranco, "Gays Protest Impersonation Arrests."
210. DiFranco, "Gays Protest Impersonation Arrests."
211. DiFranco, "Gays Protest Impersonation Arrests."
212. DiFranco, "Gays Protest Impersonation Arrests."
213. Elizabeth Vuchnich, "OSU Lesbian Works for Acceptance," *Ohio State Lantern*, April 4, 1972, 7.
214. Vuchnich, "OSU Lesbian Works for Acceptance."
215. Vuchnich, "OSU Lesbian Works for Acceptance."
216. Vuchnich, "OSU Lesbian Works for Acceptance."
217. Vuchnich, "OSU Lesbian Works for Acceptance."
218. Laura Diesing, "Two More Enter USG Race," *Ohio State Lantern*, April 6, 1972, 1.
219. Tim Bryan, "Rock Band Performs on Oval," *Ohio State Lantern*, April 12, 1972, 1.
220. "Coalition Wins in Top Turnout," *Ohio State Lantern*, April 13, 1972, 1.
221. Dale J. Gurvis, "Lesbians Extend Peer Counseling," *Ohio State Lantern*, March 29, 1975, 4.
222. Vivian Freezman, "Gay Week Promotes Pride, Unity," *Ohio State Lantern*, March 16, 1972, 3.
223. Freezman, "Gay Week Promotes Pride, Unity."

224. Amy Melvin, "Gays Ask For Public's Support," *Ohio State Lantern*, April 29, 1981, 2.
225. Joyce Tracewell, "GAA Provides Stepping Stone for Homosexuals 'Coming Out,'" *Ohio State Lantern*, January 12, 1975, 10.
226. Dale Gurvis, "Gay Activists Seek Equality," *Ohio State Lantern*, April 21, 1975, 10.

CHAPTER 3

Student Groups' Formulation of Gay Liberation Identity in the 1970s: Part II

MICHIGAN STATE UNIVERSITY, 1970–1979

Social revolution was in the thoughts of many college students during the spring of 1970, when the first non-heterosexual campus organization began at Michigan State University (MSU).[1] Prior to the actual formation, the topic of homosexuality had been highlighted, albeit briefly, by two pieces in the campus' student-produced newspaper, the *State News*. On April 6, the campus paper ran a feature in which two lesbians and two gay men were interviewed; their names were changed for their protection.[2] Different from previous mentions of homosexuality in the campus newspaper, this article stressed the positive adjustment of non-heterosexual students, despite bigotry and discrimination they felt on campus and in society in general.

This article was followed on April 13 by a letter to the editor, the writer's name again withheld upon request. The writer attempted to disabuse his readers of two notions: that gay people were mentally ill and that they should not be a part of the MSU campus culture.

> It is generally our belief that a competent psychologist or psychiatrist will understand homosexuality, seek to help his clients to adjust to themselves, and not attempt to pervert these clients to a heterosexual life which is uncomfortable, foreign, uncreative, unfulfilling, and existentially impossible for them....[3]

© The Author(s) 2019
P. Dilley, *Gay Liberation to Campus Assimilation*,
https://doi.org/10.1007/978-3-030-04645-3_3

Although it is unclear if the letters were written by one person or a collective of them, the "voice" of the letter claimed to speak for the totality of non-heterosexuals on campus.

> [A]ll of us are tired of being discriminated against, by the residence halls staff, by dormitory residents, other individuals, and "the literature" which publishes rumor and myth rather than statistic and fact.[4]

While somewhat aggressive in tone, the letter conveys a desire to be included within campus, not one to deconstruct campus.

The dissatisfaction with their experiences in the MSU residence halls seems to have prompted the first meeting of the group that would come to call itself the Gay Liberation Movement (GLM). Leonard Graff confirmed in 2018 that the genesis of Gay Liberation Front (GLF) occurred off campus, in Don Gaudard's apartment.[5] Gaudard, one of the founders of GLM, shared an apartment with his boyfriend; at what Gaudard described as the "first meeting" of the GLM, between 70 and 100 people showed up, crowding the apartment to its limits.[6] Finding more room and establishing a campus presence were first on the GLM's agenda.

A group of GLM men and women convened in Snyder-Phillips Hall, a dormitory. In addition to discussing legal issues they might face, they strategized about public relations for the fledgling collective and potential affiliation with other gay organizations.[7] They later paid for notices in the *State News*' "It's What's Happening" events column on April 27 and 29, proclaiming the group's initialization.

> The Gay Liberation Movement has been born. Live through us and with us. We offer you peace of mind, freedom from repression, and a chance to be yourself among brothers and sisters.

Not offered, however, was direct confrontation with cultural and social constructs that constrained those lives and identities.

The first publicized meeting was for Friday, May 1, 1970. On that day, an uncredited news story was published in the *State News*, proclaiming the existence of the GLM. A "co-chairman," unnamed, referenced an apparent organizing document, similar to the Port Huron Statement from the Students for a Democratic Society.[8]

"In support of the Snyder-Phillips Manifesto which states 'anyone can dance in our grill'[9] the movement culminated the meeting by doing just that," he said. "For the first time in the history of MSU, "gay" men and women danced with friends of their own sex without harassment."[10]

Given the lack of byline on the piece, along with punctuation errors uncommon in other stories published in the *State News*, I believe the May 1, 1970, article to be a publicity piece provided by the GLM, run without editing. Consequently, the statement about the GLM's purpose is probably directly from the founders:

The movement is concerned with abolishing common myths about the homosexual and creating understanding with all parts of society.[11]

According to history student Michael Carman, "This meeting represented two goals of the group: the ability to assert one's identity on campus and [the] ability to interact together in a public space."[12] These and subsequent attempts to accommodate and to integrate gays and lesbians into the larger American society, through efforts to ameliorate living conditions for non-heterosexuals on the MSU campus and to educate heterosexual students about gay and lesbian lives, defined the Michigan State groups throughout the rest of the century.

Leonard Graff was one of the founders of the GLM. He recalled the GLF having three main goals: the East Lansing anti-discrimination law, creating visibility for gay and lesbians on campus and in town, and serving as a resource for "gay people who felt alone, who were just coming out." He did note that the dancing referred to in the initial campus notice was accurate and important to the students. "How modest the goal was. [But] When you think about it, that was really radical."[13] Dancing and sponsored dances were a central activity of non-heterosexual campus organizations across the Midwest.

But dancing was not all GLM set about doing on campus. An MSU student, gender unknown, who came out by attending the second public GLM meeting wrote about the experience in a letter to the editor, published in the *State News* on June 4, 1970. The account also explains the structure and activities of the early meetings.

I first appeared at the second public meeting of the GLM with much apprehension.... [A]fter a semi-formal "throwing out" of ideas and suggestions, the members gravitated to separate committees: counseling, social, educational, etc....[14]

The letter writer continues by listing "some of the goals and ideals" [sic] that were suggested:

> draft counseling; employment counseling; a "listening" staff (We need a phone and office!) where the troubled can come to "rap" confidentially if they are afraid to appear at a public meeting; parties, swims; trips; volunteering to appear [on speakers' panels].[15]

The letter ends with a summation that represents the GLM's purpose: "Liberation is a personal perception, to a large extent," and the GLM aimed for personal change, rather than larger campus or social change.[16]

Coverage of the GLM in the *State News* continued over the summer of 1970, albeit of varying positionalities. "GLM all-day session set," which appeared on page 12 of the *State News* on August 14, does not seem to be written by someone who understood clearly the issues the group was addressing. The article, which carried no byline, indicates that the GLM "began last spring to help homosexuals decide whether they wanted the gay life." The author quoted an unnamed GLM member as saying that the group's outreach to residence hall floor advisors, to provide speaker's panels, was intended to show that the "homosexual is alive and kicking at MSU."[17] Finally, the *State News* reporter concludes, "By being organized, GLM believes it can help people decide whether they want to be gay or not."[18]

The GLM concluded the summer 1970 term on a high note. On Saturday, August 22, the GLM hosted an all-day "seminar" which they called "Gay Day" in their pre-publicity. The highlight of the day was an address by Franklin Kameny. Kameny's presentation in East Lansing was entitled "The Homosexual Dilemma: What Every Heterosexual Needs To Know." According to the *State News* reporter covering the event, approximately 200 attended Kameny's talk, which was to be followed by a question-and-answer session and an informal reception. At 8:00 that night, the GLM held its first dance in the Union ballroom, an accomplishment given the desire of the GLM founders to have a social space for non-heterosexuals to dance on campus.[19]

GLM became a registered student organization on the MSU campus by August 1970. In the fall term of 1970, when GLM decided to request office space from MSU, "extremely active" GLM member Elyse Eisenburg met with the dean of students, who told her no office space was available. She replied, "I guess if there are no offices, then we'll just have to take over the bathrooms." Conveniently, the dean found office space in 309

Student Services Building, close to the Women's Liberation office.[20] By August 6, 1970, the notice in the "It's What's Happening" column in the *State News* listed the GLM office in 309 Student Services Building.

Another response to a hostile environment in the Student Services Building showed the GLF to be as adept at adhering to the rules as some hostile administrators. To work around the MSU official who assigned student organizations meeting spaces, the GLM filed paperwork to register "numerous" organizations—including MSU Radicalesbians, MSU Radical Lesbian Sisterhood, and the Radical Gay Alliance—to allow the group weekly meeting space. According to Michael Carman, "The membership rosters of these additional groups, however, were as limited as possible, with just one or two officer positions, as police and university harassment were still a very real threat."[21]

The participation and roles of women in the early gay organizations has a contested history of lack of full acceptance of women. At Michigan State, as at many other Midwestern campuses, lesbians seem to have been more involved in the general campus gay organizations than perhaps the surviving historical record—or conventional wisdom—conveys. The 1992 MSU University-Wide Taskforce on Lesbian and Gay Issues, for instance, noted that "in the mid-1970s, GLM meetings typically hosted around 11–19 gay men, but failed to mention any female participation."[22] This is despite the involvement of members such as Elyse Eisenburg, Debbie Heinfling, and Janet Baldwin, who served as "president" of the movement.[23] Nonetheless, in Michael Carman's opinion, "the preponderance of men in the leadership and membership of the group show[s] a non-unified gay and lesbian community at MSU in the early 1970s."[24]

In an article in the *State News* on December 1, 1970, the mission and the tone of the GLF appeared to have changed. Perhaps this was due to the members of the group interviewed for the article, or perhaps it was an editorial viewpoint to emphasize something unique about this particular "liberation" organization. David Zaffer, the article's author, reported that "The movement's purposes are the education about homosexuality and the end of oppression because of sexual preference"; that, however, does not align with much of the quotes presented from (unnamed) GLF members. The first member quoted stated,

> In other places, gay groups are much more active in the outside world.... Many people [at Michigan State] are afraid that if they join, they'll have to stand outside the Administration Bldg. [sic] and beat little old ladies over the head with 'Gay is Good' signs.[25]

Zaffer continued, summarizing and directly quoting that GLF member.

> He said they [the GLM] have no desire to appear on TV and "shock the hell out of their mothers, fathers, and grandmothers.... We have to let people know that we're people interested in a number of things not even remotely related to our sexual preference."[26]

Zaffer quoted a second (unnamed) GLM member.

> One member said the name, Gay Liberation Movement, instead of Gay Liberation Front or Gay Activist Alliance, was chosen to emphasize the group's relatively conservative approach.
>
> "After all," another member said, "when you're trying to represent a fairly conservative University, you have to keep the organization pretty much conservative."[27]

Nevertheless, operating as any other student organization within the straight, rule-bound university while being homosexual could be very revolutionary. Gay student organizing challenged unspoken assumptions about issues deeper and more ingrained than organizational nomenclature. The groups brought gay and straight students into contact, often a novel experience for the straight students.

The connections felt by the MSU GLF members to other social causes, particularly the civil rights and anti-Vietnam War movements, continued during the early 1970s. In 1971, a contingent from Michigan State's GLF attended an anti-war protest rally in Washington, D.C. Notable in photographs from the time are the participation of both women and black men (Fig. 3.1).

East Lansing was the first municipality to provide protections for non-heterosexuals. Leonard Graff was a student at Michigan State and one of the driving forces behind the ordinance for those protections. Graff had transferred from Wayne State University in Detroit, where he had been involved in activist politics.

> I cut my teeth in politics in the anti-war movement.... It was a time when young people felt they could make a social change.[28]

Given the composition of the City Council, non-heterosexual students at Michigan State decided to press for inclusion of non-heterosexuals into the city's protections.

Fig. 3.1 Michigan State Gay Liberation participates in the march at Vietnam Veterans Against the War, Washington, D.C., 1971. (Copyright Steve Behrens; used with permission)

Members of Gay Liberation at Michigan State University traveled to Washington, D.C., to participate in the Vietnam Veterans Against the War march, April 24, 1971. In this photo, they are joined by members of the DC Gay Liberation Front.

East Lansing elected a very liberal city council. [We felt] the excitement of the opportunity to be first in the country to [do this.][29]

The GLF members were unaware of the mechanics of politics. "We were 18, 19, 20 years old. We didn't know there was a process."[30]

First, they had to have the proposed ordinance reviewed—and approved—by the city's Human Relations Committee. That committee was headed by an Episcopalian clergyman, Reverend Eddy.[31] Eddy was, in Graff's estimation, "somewhat conservative."

He refused to put it on the agenda for discussion, let alone a vote. So we couldn't move it to the City Council. My boyfriend at the time was Alex

McGee; Alex's father was the Episcopalian Bishop of Michigan. Coleman McGee was quite liberal, quite accepting of Alex, quite accepting of me as Alex's boyfriend; I was invited regularly to family events. I discussed with Alex, was there something his father could do, could speak to Reverend Eddy to get him to reconsider his stance, to at least put this on the agenda for discussion at the Human Rights Commission. Then I kind of forgot about it.

Then all of a sudden, a few weeks later, the ordinance was brought up before the Commission, it was approved and went sailing through over to the City Council. We had the votes there to get it passed. I later talked to Alex: "What ever happened? Did your father talk to Reverend Eddy about this?"

Alex said, "Well, let's put it this way: He let Reverend Eddy know there was an opening in the Upper Peninsula." Basically [Bishop McGee] threatened to send him to Siberia if he didn't get this moving. I'm sure he did it in a very polite, politic way. But this was our first experience of how politics works.[32]

1977: Gay-Lesbian Council

In spring, 1977, the GLM at MSU had become the Gay-Lesbian Council (GLC, sometimes referred to as the Lesbian-Gay Council).[33] As a council, the group was a part of the student government, the Associated Students of Michigan State University (ASMSU), which was composed of students elected from colleges, living groups, and minority populations. The GLC represented the issues and needs of non-heterosexual students to the governing body, akin to minority and/or residential representatives. Such a designation allowed the Council greater access to increased funds, rather than be designated a "student activity" whose funding would come from other campus fees and resources. "The Council... was a very loosely organized group."[34]

The inclusion of the GLC into ASMSU was not a smooth one. In dispute was the perception of the GLC as a political, if not partisan, group, as well as the morality or ethicality of recognizing non-heterosexuals as a part of campus life. Both of those issues came to head in 1977, with the proclamation by the National Gay Task Force of October 14 as National Gay Blue Jeans Day. "Celebrated" on many college campuses across the country, the event was intended to demonstrate both the ubiquity of non-heterosexuals in society as well as the inability to discern them from outward appearances. Dan Jones, then director of the MSU GLC, published a viewpoint in the opinion pages of the *State News*, the day prior. In it, he appealed to straight students to imagine the stigmatization non-heterosexual students felt each day, as well as for non-heterosexual students to use wearing blue jeans as a step in their own personal coming out process.

Jones ended his essay with what could be read as either sincerity or self-serving promotion.

> Finally, let me say that I would be very content to sit back and live my life. It would be much easier than dealing with all the prank calls and harassment I'll receive because of this viewpoint. I know I annoy many people (scare is a better word) by being so out in the open with my opinions. I'd love to keep them to myself, but how can I when I see so many people being hurt by gay oppression? Not the visible injustices that most people see. My sympathy is with gay people who don't feel they can live the way they want because of what other people with think.[35]

This appears to be Jones' entry into widespread public life on the MSU campus.

Dan Jones was a 20-year-old sophomore from Connecticut, majoring in horticulture. He told me that when he arrived at Michigan State, "I was desperate to find people who were like I was. Within myself, I think I had a healthy self-image, but I'd never told a soul, nobody."[36] He became involved in the GLC.

> My freshman year, I did some panel discussions, probably the most active thing the Council did at the time.... My sophomore year, I was director of that program, and then my junior year I became director of the Council.... I was the new blood coming in, energized and speaking out, and vocal.[37]

Two weeks after the contentious blue jeans event, the student body president, Kent Barry, submitted a bill to the ASMSU to strip the GLC of its standing as a council; his rationale was that the group did not represent a real minority category, as being non-heterosexual was a choice. Barry told the *State News* that he had spoken to other ASMSU members who privately agreed with him, and his entering the bill was a prompt for them to take a public stand on their views.[38]

Concurrently, the ASMSU Programming Board voted to reallocate space within the Student Services Building for all of the student organizations. GLC was to be moved from its current location to the smallest office available. Dan Jones countered, "If the Board forces us to move to 337 (the smallest office on the floor), the standing joke of the year will be ASMSU moves Gay Council into the closet."[39]

The editorial board of the *State News* took Barry to task.

> If gays "choose" their lifestyle then, by the same token, so do fraternity members or residents of co-ops. Would Barry advocate abolition of the Inter-Fraternity Council or the Inter-Cooperative Council? We think not.[40]

Jones later recalled that "there were some closeted people on the editorial board"; it would seem that those editorial board members would have concurred with Jones' estimation of Kent Barry as "a pompous ass."[41]

On Tuesday, November 9, many campus members—individuals, MSU student organizations, faculty members, and area community members—attended the ASMSU meeting to demonstrate their support of GLC. According to the *State News*, they provided "a series of emotional presentations."[42] In addition to expounding the benefits and necessity of the GLC, a technical flaw in the proposal was noted by Dan Jones: the Constitution and Code of Operations of the ASMSU did not list any criteria specifying that a council had to represent a minority group. Nonetheless, Jones continued, "Since Barry would rather not have gays identifying themselves as a minority, it has given me even more reason to believe the council must exist to report to the student representatives."[43]

Barry's bill was not passed; after the vote, he declared that in private many of the ASMSU board members had agreed with him but voiced different opinions in the public meeting. Dan Jones' letter of thanks to the board and the campus ran in the November 14, 1977, *State News*. In it, he emphasized the continued need for education about non-heterosexual issues on campus.

> Barry's move got things out in the open. The vast support shown to the board by concerned gays and non-gays was effective in increasing the sensitivity levels of the board.... We hope the move by ASMSU demonstrates to all that understanding gays requires open-mindedness and effort.... The office serves the entire MSU community.[44]

Perhaps to Kent Barry's chagrin, his effort to demote the status of non-heterosexual students in campus governance resulted in giving a public platform for the election of Michigan State's first openly gay student body president (Fig. 3.2). "That action on his part," Jones told me, "was probably one of the triggers that encouraged me to run for student government president."[45]

Fig. 3.2 Dan Jones, Michigan State University student body president campaign poster, 1978. (Courtesy of Daniel P. Jones)

Dan Jones ran for student body president at Michigan State University in 1978. His campaign poster traded on implicit male sexuality (a strategy gaining prevalence in the 1970s) as well as the notion of a gay person cleaning up the traditionally heterosexual student government.

Dan Jones as President

Jones garnered 31 percent of the vote, 3436 votes out of 11,000 votes (of the 34,000 undergrad students enrolled at Michigan State), winning a plurality of the vote. The election appears to have been important to at least some of the student body, as the number of voters exceeded the previous year by 8000 voters. In a press release about his election, Jones was quoted:

> Throughout the campaign, students got to know me as a person. I didn't deal with gayness, I dealt with issues of concern to all students. They couldn't help but realize that gayness is only one of many adjectives to describe a person. It doesn't put me way out in left field.[46]

Still, at least some viewed Jones primarily as a "gay" president. One board member, "a representative of a black fraternities group, announced that working with a homosexual would violate his Christian tenets."[47]

One of the first initiatives Jones tried to institute was intended as a way to heal the MSU Student Board of divisions that had fostered "hostility" in the organization.[48] In an editorial in the *State News*, Jones outlined his desire to improve attitudes the board member held.

> There is talk in the ASMSU wing of Student Services about labels for people. Greek, gay, Fascist, radical, etc. It's stupid. People. We are People....
>
> I hope the board can get it together. Some intense encounter group sessions are needed. Without it, board members only see each other in the sterile world of the ASMSU political arena.[49]

Jones attempted to schedule a "weekend encounter session" for the student politicians to address "negative feelings"; Jones argued that "I don't think we can deal with each other until we know each other as people." The Student Board balked at the concept and the money such a program would cost.

Jones reflected, "The majority of the Board were fraternity and sorority, and they just put up roadblocks my entire time."[50] He had campaigned as:

> a traditional liberal reformer, pointing out what he saw as the failings of the previous student government and promising to bring government "down to the level where students can get something out of it."[51]

Jones felt stymied by the traditional campus powerbrokers elected as representatives to the student government.

> It's kind of like Obama's administration during his last two years: Congress was putting up every roadblock that they could. That's what it felt like to me.[52]

After ASMSU's rebuff of his efforts to improve the Board's interpersonal attitudes toward working together, Jones focused his attention as president to initiatives he felt he could achieve.

We need to open more University offices between noon and 1 p.m. Women need more assurance of safety on campus. Pairs of women and pairs of men patrolling. Some on bicycles so more territory is covered.... We need rape education for women.[53]

During his tenure as student body president, Jones was able to convince the Michigan State administration to keep offices open during the lunch hour. He was also influential in the University's decision to install blue-light security phones.[54]

The Impeachment Vote

Jones' tenure, however, would be short. In November, Ken Stouffer, a fraternity member in his third year in ASMSU—and chair of the Board's Policy Committee—filed legislation to impeach Jones. According to the *State News*, Stouffer said that Jones had "not been a catalyst in generating input and ideas for the board... [and] failed to act as the board's leader."[55]

The editorial board of the *State News* excoriated Stouffer, all of the members of the ASMSU, and, to a much lesser extent, Jones. In an unusually lengthy editorial, the newspaper said Stouffer felt frustration, impatience and justifiable anger. But to vent those emotions on Dan Jones and his presidency is an irresponsible attempt to right a wrong.... [Stouffer's] anger is understandable, but his actions are not.

Stouffer's perception of the Student Board president's role in ASMSU is one of being a strong leader who could whip the minions into shape, create full attendance through personal charisma and sponsor rousing relevant discussion and debate among our student leaders. If that is truly what is to be expected from a board president, then Dan Jones has failed.

But that is not what is to be expected from a president. The ASMSU president is a figurehead who is, thankfully, able to accomplish things a 15-person board could never accomplish. The role of the president is not, and never has been, one of being responsible for the attitudes of individual board members. Because Dan Stouffer feels the board members have disgraced their title of representative – and, indeed, most of them have – is not reason to toss out Dan Jones as Student Board President.... [T]he Student

Board would do well to quickly get over this counterproductive, time-wasting, vindictive witch-hunt and get down to the business of what they were elected to do.[56]

On November 28, 1978, the ASMSU voted by secret ballot on the matter of removing Jones from the presidency. Jones' supporters on the Board commented on the lack of specificity in the charges and the vagueness of Stouffer's claims. Stouffer rebuffed, "Dan has not been an effective leader. He didn't know what he was getting into and hasn't fulfilled his leadership role." Jones rejected Stouffer's charges. "The point is I have taken a leadership role.... All too often you do not pass or even act on the proposals I bring before you."[57]

The majority of the Board rejected Stouffer's attempt to force Jones out of office; the vote was six in favor of the impeachment and nine against. As the board members gathered their belongings and started to don their coats, Jones tried to read a statement. Talking to one another, most of the board members ignored him, at least until he reached the point where he announced his resignation, effective January 3, 1979.[58]

Walking out of the meeting when Jones announced he was resigning, the InterFraternity Council president "indignantly muttered 'coward' under his breath and yelling SLAM! when he left because there was no door."[59] The next day, one member of the Board stated he thought Jones "should have used the board's vote a sword.... That's politics; that's what this organization is all about"; another commented, "Dan did the best thing for himself.... Having even one-third of the board against you makes the job impossible."[60]

Jones told me that he had planned the action after Stouffer introduced the impeachment legislation.

> A week before the impeachment meeting, I made the decision [to resign]. I didn't tell a single soul. But I worked on my resignation letter and vowed to myself to go through and defend myself. I was cleared of all wrong-doing. And then I stood up and read my letter.[61]

When I asked Jones why he resigned, he said, "I didn't feel I could be effective. I had been banging my head against the wall and not getting anywhere." When I asked how he felt after the announcement, he sighed and said, "I was devastated and relieved. I had struggled against this...."[62]

After leaving student government, Jones remained involved in the GLC. In addition he expanded on his work with MSU's administration, developing a gay student liaison position for the campus. During his senior year, Jones was the first to staff the position.

> I was the resource person for the campus.... Sadly, I would also get prank calls, prank letters, and then a few very sad cases of very desperately closeted gay men coming and saying, "Could I just suck your cock, 'cause I just want to see what I really am?" I would say, "No. That's not really what this position is about."[63]

Dan Jones, just the second openly gay person to be elected student body president of a college or university in the United States, graduated in 1979.

University of Illinois, 1971–1979

During 1971, the student newspaper at the University of Illinois, *Daily Illini*, published a number of articles about the GLF at the University.

According to one reporter, in the first of a two-part feature during March, social interaction was the main focus of GLF's activities.

> Ed Lisowski is president of the GLF in this area. According to him, this organization is not a structured group having definite leaders with rules and regulations behind them. Instead the group is primarily a gathering of people who are seeking emotional relationships with each other.[64]

The Illini reporter also mentioned that GLF sponsored two picnics in Allerton Park during the spring of 1970, as well as its first dance, at which approximately 150 attended. Two weeks later, in the second part, *Daily Illini* noted for readers that the "purpose of GLF is not to convince straight people of the allurements of the gay life, but to attract people who are undeniably gay but afraid to admit it."[65]

An extended comparison of the Student Organization Records of the University of Illinois' non-heterosexual campus organizations to contemporaneous newspaper accounts and organizational publications helps to convey this conflict in ideology and transition between radical and integrative ideologies while also highlighting the productive coexistence of radical and integrative activities within the campus community. At the

University of Illinois in the 1970s, student organizations had to file an application for registered organization status each year. Notably, the language used by the officers of the successive U of I gay student organizations—nominally distinct groups each year—demonstrates the apparently conflicting yet comprehensive goals of the members.

Liberation and Mobilization

On the registration forms, students had to declare the purpose of the organization, in addition to indicating what type (or types) of organization (i.e., social, service, academic, fraternal). The students' changing focus and activities for their organization were reflected in their organizations' names. Nevertheless, the groups are tied by a successive overlap of membership and leadership, as the listing of officers—as well as notations from university student affairs administrators on the forms—confirms.

Edward Lisowski, Jeffrey Graubart, and Louis Warner, students at the University of Illinois, first filed for campus registration on October 8, 1970, as "Gay Liberation." The organization's stated purpose, on its Request for University Recognition of a New Undergraduate Student Organization Not Maintaining a House, is "To advance the political and social rights of homosexuals through the education of the heterosexual community." Its membership requirements were only that one be affiliated with the University.[66]

Two flyers from September 1970 more fully outlined the group's ideology and purpose. One flyer, dated September 11, entitled "GAY LIB," stated:

> The Gay Liberation Front is an organization devoted to the advancement and defence [sic] of the rights of both male and female homosexuals through education of the general public, social organization of the homosexual community, and protest actions when necessary. It has grown out of the mass action youth movements of recent years and differs from the traditional homosexual organizations in its decentralized structure and its willingness to put the case of the homosexual aggressively before the public. The homosexual in Champaign-Urbana is subject to intense social pressure ranging from public ridicule to job discrimination or even physical attack. This forces the homosexual to lead a life of deviousness which undermines self-expression and human dignity. This is in spite of the elementary right of people to engage in sexual activity which does not harm others and in spite of considerable if not conclusive psychological evidence that homosexual

behavior is no more a physical illness than is heterosexual behavior. The GLF is open to all homosexuals and seeks the active support of sympathetic heterosexuals.[67]

Notably, the authors of the flyer seemed to conflate "Gay Lib" with the GLF: in other words, conflating the movement with one particular, contemporarily "radical" organization for homosexual representation. This language is clearly linked in ideology to the personal liberation, the need for community among non-heterosexuals, and goals for civil and legal reforms found in the civil rights movements of the times.

The connection between the general reformist GLM and the specific social deconstruction advocated by the GLF is distinct, although even contemporaneously, the members of the campus organizations seemed to use the terms interchangeably, whether that was because the members did not distinguish between the two or because another reason is not known. Still, the distinction between the two is evident when comparing the flyer quoted above with the second flyer. Dated September 24, 1970, is also entitled (in the same type font) "GAY LIB." Shorter in length and smaller in size than the September 11 flyer, the second flyer simply stated:

> The undergraduate/grad student chapter of the Gay Liberation Front is seeking University recognition. All interested people should attend an organization meeting this Thursday, September 24, in the General Lounge of the Illini Union, at 8:30 pm. The adoption of a charter will be discussed.[68]

The organizational meeting seems to have been successful. By March 12, 1971, GLF was profiled in *Daily Illini*, proclaiming its motto "step out of the closet and into the streets." According to *Daily Illini*'s reportage of an interview with GLF President Ed Lisowski, the GLF was "not a structured group... but primarily a gathering of people who are seeking emotional relationships with each other." The GLF purpose was to "preserve" basic human privileges: "We hope to change not only the attitudes of society, but also our attitudes toward ourselves."[69]

Later that spring, Gay Liberation updated its Student Organization Information Cards to reflect changes in leadership. On April 15, 1971, the group's purpose duplicated the one from its initial request for recognition. A second update, on November 28, 1971, listed the purpose as "combat oppression." The annual required update for academic year 1972–1973, filed on October 13, 1972, lists the group's purpose as "to inform public and organize social events of Gay community, also political actions."

Through 1973, despite a number of variations of the organizational nomenclature, the group was informally referred to as "Gay Lib." For the first year, the group listed an average membership of 60, which presumably included regular attendees as well as those who only occasionally attended. The officers listed Gay Liberation's purpose as "To advance the political and social rights of homosexuals through education of the homosexual community." Given the options for registration of organizations in 1970, the officers indicated Gay Liberation was both "political" and "social or recreational" in nature.

Gay liberation, and homosexuality in general, received considerable publicity in a series of articles in *Spectrum*, the weekend magazine of *Daily Illini* newspaper. *Daily Illini* staff writer Mary Ann Diehl's multiple-page article started on page 1 and focused on the group's primarily interpersonal focus.[70]

> Gay Liberation was formed with a direction dictated by members to break down the stereotypes of homosexuals and to "bring out" inhibited gay people into a world they had been deliberately hidden and excluded from in the past.
>
> It has worked to expell [sic] a guilt society has cast on the members through numerous teach-ins, dances, picnics, panel discussions in dormitories, and other activities where homosexuals could meet one another and discuss their philosophies....

Diehl extensively quoted Mark Rogers, who was listed as treasurer of Gay Liberation.

> We are trying to break down the barriers between gay people and any other kind of person.... We feel a need to combat harassment and discrimination in jobs and everyday life. Even more important, we want people to learn to accept themselves as homosexuals....[71]

Rogers indicated the group had expected a violent reaction to the forming of Gay Liberation, "But most people in the University community have reacted with little hostility."[72]

Rogers reported attendance at meetings ranged between 30 and 40, with an age range of 18–30, while "dances and other activities have drawn approximately 200 people with almost the same age variety." A second Gay Liberation member estimated group membership at 60 people, out of what he/she believed to be "a lot larger" campus gay community, "probably about 500 people here." That second member summarized the group's membership:

> Contrary to popular belief, Gay Lib are not activists... or terribly politically about radical things in general. The group is homogeneous in its conservative element.[73]
> Rogers indicated that the "majority" of Gay Lib members were male.

Additionally, he showed a particular perspective on gender relations that was not often indicated—in print—by gay men of the time.

> A general consensus shows that gay women are less social by nature due to the roles they play in society.... Fewer gay women have reached the level of consciousness or political orientation males have because homosexuality has been unacceptable in the male, but not watched or feared in the female.[74]

Perhaps it is not surprising that few women would participate in Gay Liberation at Illinois at that time, if indeed Rogers' observations were reflective of the group's beliefs. Rogers' comments confirmed that the gendered ideological division between non-heterosexual males and non-heterosexual females during the early 1970s could be found in the early Midwestern college student organizations.

On June 15, 1972, the Illinois group, formally renamed Gay Liberation Front (informally, GLF) on its registration card, organized for the purpose of "the advancement of gay people." This echoed the rhetorical positioning of the early civil rights organizations. For the 1972–1973 academic year, "political" was not an option for type of registered organizations at the University of Illinois (perhaps because of the decrease of students engaging in direct-action political protests, or perhaps because of the desire of the institution not to grant or to encourage recognition of political organizations on campus); the GLF officers indicated "social or recreational" and "service" to describe the organization.

By the spring of 1973, the GLF at the University of Illinois was no more. In a memo dated March 9, 1973, Student Organizations and Activities Associate Dean V. J. Hampton stated:

> All officers of Gay Liberation Front have resigned and indicated that the organization has dissolved. Therefore, recognition has been withdrawn

from this organization and Gay Liberation Front, account number 2837 should be closed out since it will no longer be used. There are no funds remaining in this account.[75]

A written comment on the GLF registration form, from a university administrator, also notes that the GLF disbanded in March of 1973.

The Gay Mobilizing Committee (GMC), the third iteration of non-heterosexual campus organizing at the University of Illinois, was less expansive in its goals, at least on its first application for registered organization status on July 26, 1973. The GMC formed "to promote the civil rights of homosexuals." University deposit accounts listed on GMC's registration forms, as well as the overlap in officers between the GLF and the GMC, indicates that both the students and the administration viewed this as a continuing organization rather than a new one.

On September 11, 1973, GMC updated its registration form, and in the process expanded its purview to "social" (marking through "or recreational"), "political," "service," and "other," writing in "educational." For the filers of this form, the purpose of GMC was "Gay Liberation." A second organization, Gay Women, registered as for recognition from the University of Illinois as a "support group for gay women (type: "other")" on April 11, 1974, only to disband on August 14, after only four months.

In the fall of 1974, *Daily Illini* reminded readers that Gay Liberation (now sans Front, colloquially called Gay Lib) was:

> ...an organized force of homosexuals at the University for two years, is a group of students and University employes [sic] politically and socially oriented towards civil rights.[76]

The previously mentioned on-campus dance sponsored by Gay Liberation in October of 1971 highlights the often-conflicting (relative) permissiveness on campus and constrictive interpretation (or implementation) of local and state laws. Two female impersonators attending the dance were arrested. As *Daily Illini* quoted the arresting officers' report, one was stopped "because officers suspected a female impersonator. The subject's hair was normal, but his voice sold him out and he was arrested."[77] Penalties in the city of Urbana for gender-nonconforming dress were a fine of up to $200 or six months in jail.

The Beginning of Alliance

On January 21, 1975, students registered a new organization, one which fit into three U of I classifications (political, social or recreational, and service): the Gay Students' Alliance (GSA). The GSA's purpose was "to foster a sense of pride in homosexual students, to inform the general public on the subject, and to provide an alternative to the gay bars." University administrators assigned a new funding account to the GSA, after closing the GMC's account in April 1974 (after recouping funds owed to the University by GMC). As with most of the prior iterations of gay student groups at Illinois, GSA chose "social or recreational," "political," and "service" to describe their type of organization.

A re-registration form, filed February 6, 1975, changed the purpose of the GSA: "To develope [sic] a sense of pride in the gay community and to educate the student body on homosexuality." I find it important to note that this sense of campus educational outreach first appeared on the registration forms with this iteration of the group; instead of positing their efforts to changing notions of civil rights and privileges, the GSA posed their purpose as remedial (for the non-heterosexual students) and education (to help heterosexuals understand, presumably, the non-heterosexual students); this shifted the group's outreach and actions from external change (through direct confrontation and challenge to laws and regulations) to internal support and campus accommodations.

The February 1975 GSA filers denoted the group type as "social or recreational" as well as "service"—but not "political." September 1975, however, brought another registration filing and another revision to the stated purpose of the GSA. The "political" type was again chosen (along with "social or recreational," but not "service"), highlighting a new purpose: "To provide gay people the same rights as other people." Again, this echoes the language of reform of the civil rights movement, an identity-based social movement that historians Elizabeth Armstrong or Mary Bernstein would classify as "new social movement."[78] "Such movements are conceptualized as internally directed movements aimed at self-transformation that engage in expressive action aimed at reproducing the identity on which the movement is based."[79]

An undated promotional flyer advertised GSA's "organizational meeting" on February 12, 1975. The flyer listed current and potential "functions," including outreach and involvement in non-gay-themed events:

A newsletter, for a mailing list and for the bars.
Speakers for classes.
Referrals for Hotline and Crisis Line.
Social Activities (i.e. Dances, movies, pot-luck dinners).
Group participation in community services (i.e. Dance Marathon and Walk for Mankind).
Consciousness-raising groups
A cooperative/commune.
Letter writing, petitioning, leaflet distribution on the quad, a booth in the south foyer.
Religious related events
To develope [sic] a sense of pride in the gay community!!![80]

Another undated flyer (listing the first meeting as February 12, 1975) promoted a "Gay Consciousness*Raising Group." It started with a quotation, longer than one page, attributed only to Allen Young from the early gay perspective collection *Out of the Closets: Voices of Gay Liberation*.[81] Young had been involved with Students for a Democratic Society and with student protests as an undergraduate at Columbia University, along with the Stonewall riots and the founding of the original GLF in New York City.

> Gays must organize because it is the only way a class of people that has been cut adrift by society can deal with that fact. Everywhere we find hostility, prejudice and condescension, even amongst ourselves. Most gays accept, in self-defense, the straight man's mythology that says we're sick, immature, perverse, deviant, and thus should hid our love away in tearooms, park bushes, on cruising streets and... (cruising bars). Those who reject the mythology, developing positive attitudes toward their homosexuality, are even more offensive to straights. We all risk brutalization and imprisonment and have little alternative but to use the traditional oppressive cruising institutions. These myths and institutions keep us isolated and distrustful of each other. And don't expect any help from our straight oppressors in creating alternatives. We're on our own.
>
>   In our consciousness-raising groups, we have been trying to step outside the straight man's myths and institutions, to suspend the limited ways we deal with each other, and experiment with new ways of relating. Everyone's feelings are considered in consciousness-raising, and instead of shouting each other down, consensus, a solution that is to each person's interest, can be reached. If people are silent, they are asked to contribute. This is part of the collective process. We as (people) are struggling with our eagerness to

dominate and ego-trip by being aware of the needs of others in the group, and are struggling with our tendency to intellectualize by speaking from our experience.

We are learning what has been forbidden us – to relate to one another with respect and love.[82]

On the back of that spring 1975 flyer, a different voice, reflecting Gay Illini's position, was presented.

Although the above quote is a bit strong, it does express some of the objectives of a consciousness-raising group, of being able to openly share our inner selves with other gay people and to grow (mentally) in the process, to explore and develope [sic] ourselves. Groups will meet about once a week, fairly regularly, and with about seven members to a group.[83]

The composer of the flyer then quoted a "Homosexual Encounter Group... ad in Gay Power in the late sixties, expressing a slightly different view. Groups will become what the members make them. Try it, I think you'll like it."[84]

This lengthy summary demonstrates that even creating structures parallel to those of heterosexual society, Gay Illini still postulated as an element of its core the deconstructing societal pressures. This attempted elimination of the superstructure of oppression was only somewhat congruent with the de facto goal of Gay Illini to shift the concept of homosexual in that superstructure, from a class of people based upon (illegal) activities to a class of people with a particular identity. The consciousness-raising groups were the last vestiges of "gay revolution." Once the concept of gay as an identity took root, services and functions of the campus gay groups shifted to ameliorating discord and discrimination. Rather than dismantling of the system of oppression, gay and lesbian students strove for inclusion into that system, accepting a minority social status to have standing to challenge legal and institutional statuses that were specifically anti-homosexual.

Service and Education

A "fact sheet" leaflet from January, 1976, provides insight into the specific actions of the Gay Illini; it also highlights what the membership at the time to be what its community needed: social services aimed at ameliorating dissonance between the straight campus and non-heterosexuals.

What is the Gay Illini: An organization of women and men working together to provide needed services and educational programs to the Gay and Straight Communities of Champaign-Urbana. Membership is open to all interested people in the C-U areas – students, staff and community. A membership fee of $1.00 a semester is used to defray operating costs.[85]

The fact sheet listed information on a wide range of community and campus services. Weekly meetings were held on campus on Sunday evenings, as well as a gay coffeehouse on Wednesday nights. Starting on January 12, 1976, Gay Illini operated a nightly, volunteer switchboard for referrals and peer counseling.

In addition, Gay Illini hosted the Gay Christians who, according to the 1976 fact sheet, were "a group of people who believe that being gay and Christianity are not incompatible." A Gay Resource Center, located in the Young Women's Christian Association (YWCA) Lounge of the University YW/YMCA, was also noted, as were a speakers bureau service, a gay information switchboard service, consciousness-raising groups, and a "Gay Women's Coffee House."[86]

Registration forms for 1975–1976 reflect the inconsistent focus of the "type" of organization the leadership completing the forms believed Gay Illini to be. The form dated November 23, 1975, shows the purpose of the group as "To provide gay people with the same rights as other people," as a "social or recreational" and "political" organization. The next update, dated January 26, 1976, indicated a change of name (although technically not a new organization)—Gay Illini: Gay People's Alliance at UI. The purpose was "Gay Liberation," and it typed itself as "social or recreational," "political," and "service."

In its undated application for office space for 1976–1977—its first application for such space—Gay Illini listed the number of members at 50. The general activities—which might better be understood as services—included weekly general meetings with educational programs, guest speakers, and social hours; weekly coffeehouse meetings, "an opportunity for gay people to meet and get to know each other outside the bar environment; a volunteer-staffed switchboard, [a] gay information and referral service for the Champaign-Urbana community; a resource center of materials in the University YWCA Lounge; a speakers bureau; consciousness-raising groups; and legal action through the Gay Illini Legal Action Committee, which collect[ed] testimony and investigat[ed] reported cases of discrimination on the basis of sexual preference."

The 1976–1977 office space application also listed "university-community activities" for 1974–1975, which denoted involvement in Women's Week programs, a "Professional Development symposium on homosexuality for the Office of the Vice Chancellor for Campus Affairs"; a Gay Illini Bake Sale; picnics; sponsoring a lesbian couple in the campus' Dance Marathon; a poetry reading; and three dances (Spring Glitter Ball, Beach Blanket Benefit, and the Second Annual Spring Glitter Ball). Sue Keehn, Jim DeWalt, and Kevin Cleeland, the authors of the application, indicated that "The Gay Illini will share office space with other minority group organizations."

Also in January 1976 Gay Illini started two campus initiatives. The first was the opening of a resource center. Funding for the center, which was located in the group's office in the University YMCA, was achieved through a bake sale in fall, 1975. Gay Illini collected books and ordered subscriptions to magazines.[87] In addition, a gay switchboard service, to answer questions and concerns in the Champaign area, opened on January 12.[88] The Undergraduate Student Association (Illinois' student government) matched $90 that Gay Illini had raised during a benefit at a local gay bar.[89] Volunteers from Gay Illini staffed the phone line. Sue Keehn, the switchboard coordinator, said, "About 75 per cent of our calls are from those seeking information like 'Where are the bars?' And 'Who are the Gay Illini and when do they meet?,'" as well as crisis calls that needed referral to counselors and health services.[90]

An account of the Gay Illini in campus press was quite positive, with one listing a succession of accomplishments that spanned the social and the political.

In the short span of two semesters the Gay Illini has successfully started the only Gay Switchboard in this area, opened a resource center, started a gay coffeehouse, sponsored a couple in the recent Dance Marathon, held a Glitter Ball in the Illini Union, got both mayors of Champaign and Urbana to attend their meetings as well as several City Council members, initiated a task force on discrimination against gay people, lobbied for the Human Rights Ordinance in both cities, put together a speaker's bureau and have launched a campaign to educate residents of the area with regards to the problems of gay people in a straight society. In addition, they have formed and participated in consciousness-raising groups; and panels to educate themselves as well as the rest of the community.[91]

By May, however, the members of the Gay Illini suffered from a perennial problem facing gay and lesbian student organizations: the personal might have been political, but not every person wanted to be political. A campus newsletter noted:

> According to Sue Keehn, Gay Illini member, there were different points of view within the organization regarding the direction of the group as some favored a more political perspective, while others wanted to see the organization concentrate on social activities and events.[92]

Campus and Community Service

The undated application for registered organization status from July 1, 1976, to October 1, 1977, indicated the group's office was in Room 270 of the Illini Union. The official name was listed as GAY ILLINI: The Gay People's Alliance at the U. of I. at U-C. No advisor was listed; in its place was a note to "Refer all outside calls to the Gay Illini Office... or between 7:00 pm and 1:00 am any night to the Gay Switchboard." The purpose was Gay Liberation and the type social or recreational, political, and service.

In October, *Chicago Tribune* columnist Jack Mabley wrote in a Sunday edition of "The Gay Illini: How campus has changed."[93] Mabley called the Gay Switchboard for more information about the organization and spoke to "Dave." Mabley quoted Dave's answers to his questions at length, and the responses provide insight into the specifics of the group's activities, and thus a snapshot into its members' priorities.

> We get 40 to 50 calls an evening. We get calls for information, like where the gay bars are. There are two in town.
>
> A lot of people call just wanting to talk. We offer peer counseling. We refer people to professional counseling.
>
> We operate a coffee house that's well attended by young people not old enough for bars, or by reformed alcoholics, or people who don't want to drink on a school night.
>
> Sunday night meetings are mostly business-related. We usually have about 50 per meeting. Our official members... those who have paid $1 a semester dues... is 58. A lot of people come to meetings and don't pay dues.
>
> The membership is about 20 per cent female. There's a lesbian group in town, not campus-affiliated. Most of them stick together.
>
> We're a general cross-section of everybody... faculty, librarians, lab technicians, students.

People come to us. We don't have to chase after anyone. Freshmen are
usually 17 or 18. They're too young to have thought much... they haven't
been away from parents' thinking long enough.
    Most people when they go home, go back into the closet. They haven't
told their parents.[94]

Mabley also spoke with Hugh Satterlee, Illinois' dean of students and
vice chancellor for student affairs. "We treat them as if they were another
organization. Their presence is accepted just as the rodeo club, or the
hockey team. It's not illegal. We have neither the grounds nor the social
incentive to make charges."[95]
    One activity at which the genders of non-heterosexual (and some het-
erosexuals) students mixed was the dances held by the early gay and lesbian student organizations. As with dances held on other Midwest
campuses, dances sponsored by the Gay Illini were popular social activities
for the group's members, potential sources of unrestricted revenue for the
campus group, and a space in which men and women could interact (with
either gender).
    By February 11, 1977, the group's name returned to Gay Illini; it was
back to choosing all three types ("political," "service," and "social or recreational") to describe itself. Gay Illini's goal was simply "Gay Liberation."
During the 1977–1978 academic year, Gay Illini added to its name the
tagline of "The Gay People's Alliance at the U. of I. in U-C." The purpose
on both the initial July 5, 1977, form and update on September 30 both
retained the purpose of "Gay Liberation."
    In March of 1978, the student officers listed a more delineated, if less
expansive, purpose: "Gay Illini is an organization devoted to legitimacy,
respectability, and freedom in same-sex relationships." Gay Illini kept that
self-description as its purpose through its registration forms on November
26, 1978; December 12, 1978; March 12, 1979; and May 11, 1979.

IOWA STATE UNIVERSITY, 1971–1974

Gay student organizing at Iowa State University commenced in 1971,
informally and off campus at first. The first proclamation of the group was
with a letter, complaining about perceived homosexual stereotypes in the
play *The Boys in the Band*, which was being performed on campus. The
letter was signed "Gay Liberation Front Ames."[96] A second letter, in
response to comments on the first letter, was personally signed.

Joe Franko, a 1970 graduate, had written both.[97] While the play might have been the catalyst, Franko used it as an example of "psychological stereotyping which caused Gay Liberation Groups to form."[98] Franko noted that such social conditioning was also evident in the University's only academic considerations of sexuality: "Marriage and Courtship" for heterosexuality, and homosexuality in "Abnormal Behavior."

> Only a female knows to what extent she is oppressed by "Marriage and Courtship." ... And only a homosexual... can appreciate the subtle hetero-sexual propaganda and prejudice against homosexuals in our culture.[99]

Joe Franko's life changed after he had signed his name to a letter proclaiming his homosexuality and support of other gays.

> I remember all hell breaking loose for a while after that.... The day the letter came out I got hate calls on my phone, and several friends called to offer support, while some called to say they didn't want to have anything to do with me again...[100]

On the same day that the second letter appeared, the campus newspaper printed an article about the founding of a GLF in Ames.[101] Three decades later, Franko reflected on the days following that second letter being printed.

> I think about how much courage all of us had in the beginning.... We met in the [Young Women's Christian Association] on campus, and the first meeting the campus police had come by to tell me they would be standing around outside.... I remember starting off being scared, and ending the night being elated. We had done it – we had the first openly gay meeting on campus."[102]

A campus newspaper profile of the GLF in April of 1972 reported that the goal of the GLF was "to foster a sense of community among gay people on campus."[103]

> "You have no idea how liberating it was to dance with another man on cam-pus," Franko said. "In that act of dance there was love, acceptance, joy, sexuality and pride. I will remember until the day I die those first dances, and those first real feelings of joy and pride in being who we were."[104]

Like many of its contemporaries, the gay student organization at the University of Iowa changed names frequently during the early 1970s. During the 1971–1972 academic year, its moniker was GLF. For the 1972–1973 year, the group split by gender and chose new names: Lesbian Alliance and Gay Men's Rap Group. Member Dennis Brumm believed that having a more personal, rather than political, name would draw more potential members; it worked, for at the first meeting of the Gay Men's Rap Group, "25 people showed up."[105]

For 1973–1974, the groups again changed their names to Gay People's Liberation Alliance and the Lesbian Alliance. The genders recombined for the 1974–1975 academic year, taking the name Gay People's Alliance.[106]

By 1974, the Gay People's Alliance was sponsoring dances, coffee-houses, and a quarterly newsletter. Its success in organizing events was not necessarily reflected in the group's rosters. In the spring of 1974, the group recorded 13 paying members, although more attended meetings and events.[107]

Last fall members numbered up to 30, but an ideological split apparently caused the groups [sic] membership decline, Brumm said.... "Some people just don't like to go to business meetings, so we hope the coffee houses will create a better atmosphere for people to get together."[108]

UNIVERSITY OF KANSAS, 1970–1977

The Lawrence Gay Liberation Front (LGLF) at the University of Kansas (KU) was active between 1970 and 1975 (including a time when its membership styled the group Lawrence Gay Liberation Inc.). Students who would form the organization started their collective activities in the summer of 1970, "to work for the rights of gays and to provide an atmosphere where gay members of the University of Kansas and Lawrence communities could meet freely."

The membership noted that undated press release from Lawrence Gay Liberation, Inc.

The "gay community" should not be confused with the stereotypical "homosexual" community which is as repressive and limiting as the "straight, heterosexual" community, since in both of the latter groups the limiting and harmful stereotypes that society has imposed on femininity, masculinity and sexual roles are emphasized.... the gay community offers a unique opportunity for Gays to work for a freedom and self-expression based on consideration of others as individuals, without the overtones of exploitative sexuality endemic to the straight community.[109]

In September of 1970, GLF initiated the process to become a recognized student organization at the University. KU Chancellor E. Laurence Chalmers Jr. rejected GLF's application on September 5, 1970.[110] A KU Press Bureau release, dated September 5, 1970, quoted Chalmers:

> Formal recognition of a proposed student organization confers only one significant advantage. A recognized student group may submit requests for funds to the Student Senate.
> "Since we are not persuaded that student activity funds should be allocated either to support or to oppose the sexual proclivities of students, particularly when they might lead to violation of state law, the University of Kansas declines to formally recognize the Lawrence Gay Liberation Front."[111]

The GLF attempted resolution at university level of adjudication; despite support of the Student Senate, the chancellor's decision remained. Nonetheless, the organization had an office in, and held weekly meetings, the Kansas Union. The office was reportedly staffed "daily," and the group offered confidential counseling, a periodically published newsletter, a speakers' bureau, and a legal assistance fund.

In March of 1971, GLF again applied for recognition as a KU student group, and Chalmers again denied their request. According to an unsigned, undated (but probably January 27, 1972) note from the University's University Relations and Development office, the organization filed the first form for recognition on March 3, 1971; the students listed were Joe Prados, Elaine Riseman, John Bolin, and Michael Stubbs.[112] On March 29, 1971, the LGLF charged Chalmers and Vice Chancellor of Student Affairs William M. Balfour of violating Articles 8, 10, and 20 of the Code of Students Rights, challenging the University in court.

The GLF claimed infringement of First and Fourteenth Amendments for two classes of plaintiffs, "Lawrence Gay Liberation Front and John Steven Stillwell, Steven Weaver and Joseph Prados, individually and as members...." [and] "five faculty members, a graduate student assistant, and three other listed students, all apparently non-GLF members sympathetic with the plaintiff organization's legal arguments[113] against Chalmers and Vice Chancellor for Student Affairs William M. Balfour.[114] In the suit, the GLF claimed damages of "more than $15,000" to its members.[115]

William Kunstler, who was affiliated with the Center for Constitutional Rights and had just defended the "Chicago Seven," agreed in July 1971 to represent the GLF in a legal case against Chalmers' decision. Chalmers was characterized as welcoming the challenge: "I'm frankly pleased that it is apparently going to be resolved in the courts," because he felt his decision was defendable, since it was not couched in moral reasoning. "I have, since the very outset, taken the position that this relates to the early statement by the Gay Lib people that they sought recognition in order to have access to the student activity fee, and that I did not recognize the appropriateness of expending funds – particularly student funds or state funds – in an area of private, personal choice, as it were."[116]

Meanwhile, on the KU campus, on September 16, 1971, the Student Senate reaffirmed its support of the GLF, and it called for Chalmers to address Senate on his decision, which he did on September 29. After the chancellor's remarks, the Student Senate voted to allocate $600 for GLF's legal fees. In his letter of transmission of the legislation to Chalmers, David G. Miller, the student body president, wrote, "I recommend you veto the allocation. I believe this use of funds is not appropriate for a student fund allocation and I also believe the allocation is not supported by the student body."[117]

Also at the Thursday night Student Senate meeting, the Women's Coalition announced that its reservation of the Kansas Union ballroom for a dance Friday night was really done on behalf of the GLF. The GLF, since it was not a recognized student organization, would have had to rent the ballroom, instead of reserving it for free. Despite irritation felt by both the Union staff and the administration, the dance was held on Friday, October 1. Over 300 people attended that first dance, which netted $100 for the GLF defense fund; in addition, an anonymous donor offered to pay for the rental and phone expenses for the group's office in the basement of the Union.[118]

The court case from GLF against the University was finally heard in U.S. District Court in Topeka. The judge, George Templar, barred Kunstler from courtroom.

> I cannot close my eyes to what is well known throughout the country. Your fame is notorious. You have gone all over the country deriding the judiciary.... This court finds that you are an out-of-state attorney and not eligible to practice in Kansas.[119]

Despite much conversation about representation in the case, the hearing was short.

On February 11, 1972, Templar ruled that Chalmers' decision to refuse recognition of GLF was "not discriminatory," saying,

> It is not difficult… to understand the concern of Chancellor Chalmers and his conclusion that the school funds should not be made available for the purpose of opposing or supporting the discussion of bizarre sexual activities for which plaintiffs apparently seek formal and public approval.[120]

Templar ordered the GLF to pay the University's court costs. The loss was a blow to GLF's finances and public relations.

Nonetheless, the issue of the relationship between student and campus organizations to the University continued to be refined. On February 14, 1972, the KU Student Senate Executive Council determined that "all organizations would be recognized, but that would not automatically permit them to receive allocations of the student activity fee."[121] In practice, the University eventually adopted such a strategy, although the terminology for student organizations was changed to "registered." "Registered" did not connote the approval that "recognized" would. The GLF deemed this ineffective, as the chancellor would still have the final decision.

At the end of February, GLF decided to appeal Templar's decision, and did so in May of 1972, with Kunstler representing the GLF. The U.S. Tenth Circuit Court of Appeals heard arguments on November 16, 1972, and took the case under advisement.[122] The appeal was denied in March 1973; "In the summer LGLF took the case to the SCOTUS and requested a Writ of Certiorari. The application was done in forma pauperis as the organization lacked the funds to cover the costs of such a case. The justices of the Supreme Court voted not to hear the case."[123]

A few months later, a Gay Liberation Front Emergency Position Paper was distributed on campus on April 28, 1973, detailing the discrimination experienced by attendees of an on-campus dance the Wednesday before.[124] The dance, in the Kansas Union ballroom, was to raise funds to pay for the GLF's legal defense fund; unlike "recognized" campus organizations, GLF had to pay for the ballroom: "Because of this, dances are a rare affair."

The Union ballroom has two levels: the main dance floor and a balcony above it, accessible from a different entryway. At this dance, spectators circled the balcony, "jeering… in an attempt to intimidate the gay students at the dance." In addition, a "group of four or five students grabbed the cashbox containing approximately $75 and beat-up the gay student who tried to stop them."[125]

The GLF blamed the University both for the immediate need of holding the dance to raise money and for fostering the general climate on the campus.

> By denying the Lawrence Gay Liberation Front recognition as a student organization and forcing the gay people of this campus to spend countless hours of their time, effort, and energies preparing a court case and raising hundred and hundreds of dollars for legal defense costs the university administration is to blame....
>
> We feel that non-recognition is the biggest cause of this. We are hard workers – we want to educate the students of this university to the minimum level of humanity that it takes to come to a Gay Liberation Dance without harassing, pushing around, and robbing Gay People.
>
> But why should we alone have to push the case for Gay Students? Why have you (the administration) never said anything about us. [sic] No other minority groups get official silence from your office. When you speak of minority groups why is it that the second largest minority in America – the minority of gay people – is never mentioned?[126]

To redress these issues, the GLF called for an "immediate dialogue" between the University and the "Gay Community"; for the administration "to read as many books on Gay Liberation as they read on Black Liberation a year or two ago"; for an investigation into negative experiences of gay in university housing; the initiation of a gay studies program; for the hiring of a "Gay woman and a Gay man" as full-time employees "to deal with the problems of Gay People on this campus"; for KU to investigate discrimination in employment at the University; and, finally, "that members of the administration speak out against the oppression of Gays on this campus whenever the opportunity presents itself."[127]

It would take new administrative leadership—first, Vice Chancellor for Student Affairs David B. Ambler, and then Executive Vice Chancellor (and later Chancellor) Delbert Shankel—for the GLF and its successor student organizations to have a working relationship with the KU. Ambler's staff dissolved the difference between "recognized" and "registered" organizations, eventually allowing Student Senate to allocate student fee funds to any most student organization (excepting politically partisan groups). Early in the spring, 1977 term, Shankel, then the executive vice chancellor of the Lawrence campus, wrote to Gay Services about potentially adding "sexual preference" to KU's Affirmative Action rules. "Our current thinking is to include these to some extent in the proposed guidelines. The basic premise we are working on is that our… guidelines should incorporate 'sexual preference' in all… provisions which deal with discrimination." Ambler distinguished between KU's internal policies as opposed to external requirements; for instance, the University would not add "sexual preference" to Affirmative Action guidelines, as those were governed by the federal government.[128] It was quite the change in University policy toward non-heterosexual students.

University of Missouri, 1971–1978

The Final Liberation

In 1978, the last GLF student organization remained at the University of Missouri at Columbia (nicknamed "Mizzou"). The group retained the GLF nomenclature because of its ongoing legal contest with the University. In the spring of 1971, like many other Midwestern campus gay organizations, the Mizzou GLF applied for recognition. Despite initial approval by the Missouri Student Association (the student government body of Mizzou) and the administration's Committee on Student Organizations, Government, and Activities, Dean of Students Edwin Hutchins denied that status in December of 1971.[129]

It is important to realize the campus climate on the Columbia campus in the early 1970s. Despite being the flagship campus of a multicampus system, Mizzou is located in rural central Missouri. In 1973, a student informed the newspaper in nearby Mexico, Missouri (an even more isolated locale), that a professor had worn drag to class, and another had said he was a homosexual and all cute boys should sit in the front row. The Mexico paper printed the story; a firestorm of public calumny and calamity ensued, resulting in the University instigating an investigation into determining who those faculty could be, and to rid itself of them.[130]

Over the next two years, the student group availed itself of the appeals process of the University of Missouri, first to Campus Chancellor Herbert W. Schooling and then to System President C. Brice Ratchford. Both men upheld the denial. Those actions ended with the denial of approval in early 1973. By that time, another GLF had organized at the University of Missouri–Kansas City (UMKC); administrators at the UMKC wanted to see the outcome of the challenges at the Columbia campus before they gave a final response to their campus' GLF.

The Mizzou GLF appealed the chancellor to the University's Board of Curators; an external commissioner was appointed to conduct hearing and provide a report on the issue to the Curators. In November of 1973, the Curators, in light of the findings in the report, supported the flagship chancellor in rejecting recognition to the GLF.[131]

In March of 1974, with the assistance of the American Civil Liberties Union (ACLU), the Mizzou GLF filed suit in U.S. District Court against the University of Missouri and its Board of Curators, for denying its freedoms of speech and assembly. On June 29, 1976, the District Court for Western Missouri ruled in favor of the University. The ACLU and the GLF appealed, and on June 8, 1977, the U.S. Eighth Circuit Court of Appeals overturned the District Court's ruling; in a 2 to 1 vote, the appellate court panel cited a 1972 Supreme Court case, *Healy v. James*. In *Healey*, students at Central Connecticut State College had tried to register a Students for a Democratic Society group, and the college refused recognition; the Supreme Court ruled against the college, finding that it had violated the students' First Amendment right of speech, even if the college found the speech abhorrent. On June 22, the University requested a rehearing before the entire eight-member Appeals Court judges; that request was denied on August 8, 1977.[132]

Unwilling to accept that the University of Missouri was legally bound to recognize the GLF, the Curators voted, 6 to 2, on August 11, 1977, to appeal the case to the U.S. Supreme Court. On February 21, 1978, the Supreme Court voted 6 to 3 to refuse to hear the case. Still, the University persisted its attempts to deny having a gay group on its campus. Three days after the Supreme Court refused to hear their appeal, the Curators voted 8 to 1 to file a request for rehearings to try again to convince the Supreme Court to take the case. After the Supreme Court's declining to hear the case, the Eighth Circuit Court of Appeals ordered the University of Missouri to recognize the GLF. When the University would not, the U.S. District Court approved an injunction instructing them to do so.

On April 25, 1978, the University was informed that again the Supreme Court had declined to hear the case against recognizing the GLF. After seven years, students at the University of Missouri could have a group on campus. The GLF planned for a march from their usual off-campus meeting place to the Student Union. They had notified the press and had requested from the Columbia police an escort for the six blocks they would

Fig. 3.3 University of Missouri Gay Liberation march to first on-campus meeting, April 20, 1978. (Copyright Brian Smith; courtesy of University Archives, the University of Missouri)

Glenda Dilley, strumming her guitar and singing, leads Gay Liberation at the University of Missouri to its first on-campus meeting, date. Soon after this photo was taken, the Mizzou students—along with the journalists covering their march—would be subjected to verbal harassment and physical violence.

be marching. The group realized, 30 minutes after the march's scheduled starting time, the Columbia police were not going to show (Fig. 3.3).

Glenda Dilley,[133] a graduate student, was the spokesperson for the GLF, primarily because she was not teaching and thus not afraid of the University revoking her position. She gathered her strength, and her guitar, and led the march. As she reflected in 2010,

[T]here were about twenty of us, at least to start with. We did pick up some people along the way who joined us.... I had my guitar and I think I must of played a song or two along the way.... [T]wo of the men carried a banner that said we won recognition, now let's talk. We were something....

[The march] had the potential to be treacherous, people, frat boys were out there, throwing sticks and little rocks and so on, and hooting and so forth, but the only one hit by the projectiles were press people, which, of course, put them on our side, certainly more than the people throwing the stones. So anyway, we made it over there, and then pretty much no one really bother us once we made it to the room.[134]

Reporters estimated between "75 and 100 rowdy protesters" confronted the group as they marched, "...mostly men and apparently UMC students."[135] "Traffic was forced to stop as protesters walked in the street alongside the marchers who occupied the sidewalk." Four protesters blocked the sidewalk, displaying a small banner reading "March back into your closets." The GLF went around them, chanting, "One, two, three, four, we won't shut up any more. Five, six, seven eight, we don't want your Christian hate."[136]

Protesters shot fireworks at the gay crowd; they hurled rocks; one protester took a piece of gutter pipe from a house and threw it at the marchers. Another protester ripped the GLF's banner from its poles, which caused a roar to go up from the protesters. Jane Maune, a reporter for KBIA radio, suffered a cut to her head caused by a thrown stone. The heckling and harassment continued into the Student Union, where two campus police officers were stationed outside of the meeting room.[137]

James Banning, the University's vice chancellor for student affairs, was attending a meeting down the hall. Hearing the commotion, he strode through the protesters, to stand in the doorway of the meeting room, facing the protesters. He told them, "This is an open meeting.... But it's open to all who would like to come in to participate in a less than rowdy" way. "We expect a certain level of decorum while you're in there."[138]

Ten of the protesters entered the room, as did Banning. The vice chancellor told the GLF, "I would like to apologize for the reception you received tonight outside.... I also want to indicate to you as a recognized student group that my office will do what it can to protect your rights to assemble and to be here."[139]

Later in 1978, the University of Missouri was ordered to pay the court costs for the GLF's cases, and the first Gay Pride celebration in Columbia was held. Over 20 years later, the University still refused to "recognize" non-heterosexual students. The system president, Manuel Pacheco, "contend[ed] that because of Missouri's anti-sodomy law, the university cannot grant recognition [in non-discrimination policies] to homosexuals."[140]

CONCLUSION

By the end of the 1970s, gay and lesbian student organizations at larger Midwestern state universities had become ensconced in campus life and structures. Court rulings had reaffirmed the rights of non-heterosexual students to assemble on campus, to advocate for legal and political change, and to participate in the various activities and privileges afforded by their heterosexual peers.

Some campuses' non-heterosexual students were beginning to be recognized as an economic market, particularly in bars and dance clubs. Non-heterosexual students were themselves beginning to utilize the visibility their actions could prompt in order to gain access to those marketplaces. More important, gay and lesbian student leaders persisted in seemingly endless attempts to prompt their universities to recognize them as a minority population.

NOTES

1. For more context about the origins of the Gay Liberation Movement at Michigan State University, particularly the social importance of feminism in the GLM's structure and ideology, see Michael Carman's honor's thesis, "'Not Everything Happens in San Francisco': Sociopolitical Mobilization in Identity-Politics-Era Lansing" (Michigan State University, 2011).
2. Paula Bray, "Students Affirm Gay Happiness," *State News*, April 6, 1970, 6.
3. "Gays Tired of Discrimination," *State News*, April 13, 1970, 4.
4. "Gays Tired of Discrimination."
5. Leonard Graff, Interview with Author, August 12, 2018.
6. Carman, "'Not Everything Happens in San Francisco,'" 16.
7. "End to Social Oppression Sought by 'Gay' Movement," *State News*, May 1, 1970, 5.
8. Leonard Graff did not remember such a statement. Leonard Graff, Interview with Author, August 12, 2018.
9. The "grill" referred to here was a restaurant in the Union frequented called The Grill; according to Leonard Graff, "any time, day or night," one could run into other non-heterosexual students in the area. "I don't know if it had any other name. It was a café.... Somehow, it got to be known as a gay hangout. In this section of the union, if you any kind of gaydar, you would know what's going on." Leonard Graff, Interview with Author, August 12, 2018.
10. "End to social oppression sought by 'gay' movement."
11. "End to social oppression sought by 'gay' movement."

12. Carman, "'Not Everything Happens in San Francisco,'" 17.
13. Leonard Graff, Interview with Author, August 12, 2018.
14. "Liberation: A Personal Perception," *State News*, June 4, 1970, 4.
15. "Liberation: A Personal Perception."
16. "Liberation: A Personal Perception."
17. "GLM All-day Session Set," *State News*, August 14, 1970, 12.
18. "GLM All-day Session Set."
19. "GLM All-day Session Set"; "It's What's Happening," *State News*, August 20, 1970, 11; "Speaker to Present Homosexuality Facts," *State News*, August 21, 1970, 3; Tom Spaniolo, "Homosexuality Termed Matter of Sex Preference," *State News*, August 24, 1970, 1.
20. Carman, "'Not Everything Happens in San Francisco,'" 19. Leonard Graff confirmed this to me; Leonard Graff, Interview with Author, August 12, 2018.
21. Carman, "'Not Everything Happens in San Francisco,'" 20. Carman also points out a significant issue when trying to determine this history. "The duplicate groups also confuse the historiography of early MSU queer organizing, however. The Radicalesbians, for instance, have been pointed to as a group of lesbians that did not feel the GLM met their needs, but they were in fact the GLM."
22. Carman, "'Not Everything Happens in San Francisco,'" 29.
23. Carman, "'Not Everything Happens in San Francisco,'" 29.
24. Carman, "'Not Everything Happens in San Francisco,'" 29
25. Zaffer, "Gay Lib Educates Community," *State News*, December 1, 1970, 8.
26. David Zaffer, "Gay Lib Educates Community."
27. Zaffer, "Gay Lib Educates Community."
28. Leonard Graff, Interview with Author, August 12, 2018.
29. Leonard Graff, Interview with Author, August 12, 2018.
30. Leonard Graff, Interview with Author, August 12, 2018.
31. Eddy is the name that Graff remembers; I have been unable to locate information on either the chair or the membership roster of the East Lansing Human Relations Committee for 1972.
32. Leonard Graff, Interview with Author, August 12, 2018.
33. Joe Pizzo and Kim Shanahan, 1978, "Gays Fight for Rights Amidst Stiff Oppression," *State News Welcome Week Supplement*.
34. Daniel P. Jones, Interview with Author, August 13, 2018.
35. Dan Jones, 10/13/77, "National Gay Blue Jeans Day Promoted", *State News*, October 13, 1977, 3.
36. Daniel P. Jones, Interview with Author, August 13, 2018.
37. Daniel P. Jones, Interview with Author, August 13, 2018
38. Reginald Thomas, "Gay Council May Be Eliminated," *State News*, November 3, 1977, 1.

39. Reginald Thomas, "Gay Council May Be Eliminated."
40. "Gays: The Heresy of Being Different," *State News*, November 7, 1977, 4.
41. Daniel P. Jones, Interview with Author, August 13, 2018.
42. Reginald Thomas, "Board Rejects Proposal to Eliminate Gay Council," *State News*, November 10, 1977, 1.
43. Thomas, "Board Rejects Proposal to Eliminate Gay Council."
44. Dan Jones, "Council Appreciative," *State News*, November 14, 1977, 4.
45. Daniel P. Jones, Interview with Author, August 13, 2018.
46. "For Immediate Release, Contact Dan Jones." April 4, 1978. James W. Toy Papers, Box 11, Folder: Clippings, Bentley Historical Library, The University of Michigan.
47. Steve Orr, "M.S.U. Gay Leader Applauds Tolerance," *Detroit Free Press*, May 1, 1978, 3A, 18A: 18A.
48. "Hostility Greets MSU's Gay Student President," *Ann Arbor News*, May 10, 1978.
49. Dan Jones, "Some Say Kill ASMSU – I Say It Can Still Work," *State News*, April 27, 1978, 5.
50. Daniel P. Jones, Interview with Author, August 13, 2018.
51. Orr, "M.S.U. Gay Leader Applauds Tolerance."
52. Daniel P. Jones, Interview with Author, August 13, 2018.
53. Jones, "Some Say Kill ASMSU – I Say It Can Still Work."
54. Daniel P. Jones, Interview with Author, August 13, 2018.
55. Michael Megerian, "Student Board to Consider Ousting Jones," *State News*, November 20, 1978, 1.
56. "Jones Is Not the Cause of the Board's Ineffectiveness," *State News*, November 28, 1978, 4.
57. Kim Crawford and Michael Megerian, "Dan Jones Quits Presidency," *State News*, November 29, 1978, 1.
58. "ASMSU: Victory Without Any Pride," *State News*, November 30, 1978, 4.
59. "ASMSU: Victory Without Any Pride."
60. Michael Megerian, "ASMSU Ponders Future of Board," *State News*, November 30, 1978, 1, 20: 1.
61. Daniel P. Jones, Interview with Author, August 13, 2018.
62. Daniel P. Jones, Interview with Author, August 13, 2018.
63. Daniel P. Jones, Interview with Author, August 13, 2018.
64. Pat Reynolds, "GLF Seeks Social Outlets," *Daily Illini*, March 12, 1971, 6, 10: 10.
65. Pat Reynolds, "GLF Sees Change in Nations [sic] Attitude," *Daily Illini*, March 26, 1971, 6.
66. University of Illinois Archives, Student and Faculty Organizations, Constitutions & Registration Cards, 1909–2002, Series 41/2/41, Box 10. Note: All registration information for this and its subsequent organizations comes from this file.

67. Student Affairs – Programs and Services, Office of the Dean of Students – Office for Lesbian, Gay, Bisexual, and Transgender Concerns, 1942–2014, 41/2/46, Box 1, University of Illinois Archives, University Library, University of Illinois at Urbana-Champaign.

68. Student Affairs – Programs and Services, Office of the Dean of Students – Office for Lesbian, Gay, Bisexual, and Transgender Concerns, 1942–2014, 41/2/46, Box 2, University of Illinois Archives, University Library, University of Illinois at Urbana-Champaign.

69. Reynolds, "GLF Seeks Social Outlets."

70. Mary Ann Diehl, "Gay Liberation 'Trying to Break Down Barriers,'" *Daily Illini – Spectrum*, October 16, 1971, 10, 11.

71. Diehl, "Gay Liberation 'Trying to Break Down Barriers.'"

72. Diehl, "Gay Liberation 'Trying to Break Down Barriers.'"

73. Diehl, "Gay Liberation 'Trying to Break Down Barriers.'"

74. Diehl, "Gay Liberation 'Trying to Break Down Barriers.'"

75. University of Illinois Archives, Student and Faculty Organizations, Constitutions & Registration Cards, 1909–2002, Series 41/2/41, Box 10.

76. Diehl, "GLF Sees Change in Nations [sic] Attitude," 6.

77. Margaret Bicek, "Laws Inhibit Homosexual Activity," *Daily Illini*, October 16, 1971, 10.

78. Elizabeth A. Armstrong, *Forging Gay Identities: Organizing Sexuality in San Francisco, 1950–1994* (Chicago: University of Chicago Press, 2002); Mary Bernstein, "Celebration and Suppression: The Strategic Uses of Identity by the Lesbian and Gay Movement," *American Journal of Sociology*, 103, No. 3, (November 1997), 531–565; and Mary Bernstein, "Identities and Politics: Toward a Historical Understanding of the Lesbian and Gay Movement," *Social Science History*, 26, No. 3 (Fall 2002), 531–581.

79. Bernstein, "Identities and Politics," 534.

80. Student Affairs – Programs and Services, Office of the Dean of Students – Office for Lesbian, Gay, Bisexual, and Transgender Concerns, 1942–2014, 41/2/46, University of Illinois Archives, University Library, University of Illinois at Urbana-Champaign.

81. Karla Jay and Allen Young (Eds.), *Out of the Closets: Voices of Gay Liberation* (New York: Douglas Books, 1972).

82. Student Affairs – Programs and Services, Office of the Dean of Students – Office for Lesbian, Gay, Bisexual, and Transgender Concerns, 1942–2014, 41/2/46, University of Illinois Archives, University Library, University of Illinois at Urbana-Champaign.

83. Student Affairs – Programs and Services, Office of the Dean of Students – Office for Lesbian, Gay, Bisexual, and Transgender Concerns, 1942–2014, 41/2/46, University of Illinois Archives, University Library, University of Illinois at Urbana-Champaign.

84. Student Affairs – Programs and Services, Office of the Dean of Students – Office for Lesbian, Gay, Bisexual, and Transgender Concerns, 1942–2014, 41/2/46, University of Illinois Archives, University Library, University of Illinois at Urbana-Champaign.
85. Student Affairs – Programs and Services, Office of the Dean of Students – Office for Lesbian, Gay, Bisexual, and Transgender Concerns, 1942–2014, 41/2/46, Box 1, University of Illinois Archives, University Library, University of Illinois at Urbana-Champaign.
86. Student Affairs – Programs and Services, Office of the Dean of Students – Office for Lesbian, Gay, Bisexual, and Transgender Concerns, 1942–2014, 41/2/46, University of Illinois Archives, University Library, University of Illinois at Urbana-Champaign.
87. "Gay Switchboard Service to Open," *Student Advocate*, January 14, 1976, 3.
88. "Gay Switchboard Opens," *Daily Illini*, January 27, 1976.
89. "Gay Switchboard Service to Open."
90. "Gay Switchboard opens."
91. "Gay Illini On The Move," *Student Advocate*, May 3, 1976.
92. "Gay Illini On The Move."
93. Jack Mabley, "The Gay Illini: How Campus Has Changed," *Chicago Tribune*, October 17, 1976, Section 1, 4.
94. Mabley, "The Gay Illini: How Campus Has Changed."
95. Mabley, "The Gay Illini: How Campus Has Changed."
96. Dennis Brumm, www.brumm.com/schools/gaylib/. Note: Brumm scanned clippings of many *Iowa State Daily* newspaper accounts, but not all of them are fully dated. When no date is cited, I found the article on his website.
97. Erin Randolph, "30 Years Is Just the Beginning," *Iowa State Daily*, April 1, 2002.
98. Joe Franko, "Letters to Editor: More About Boys," *Iowa State Daily*, December 14, 1971.
99. Franko, "Letters to Editor: More About Boys."
100. Randolph, "30 Years Is Just the Beginning."
101. Linda Kohl, "Gay Liberation Front Organizes Here," *Iowa State Daily*, December 141,1971, A18.
102. Randolph, "30 Years Is Just the Beginning."
103. "Gay Liberation Frowns on Stereotyping," *Iowa State News*.
104. Erin Randolph, "30 Years is Just the Beginning."
105. Brumm, www.brumm.com/schools/gaylib/
106. Brumm, www.brumm.com/schools/gaylib/
107. "'Gays' Plan Activities for Fall," *Iowa Student Daily*, August 8, 1974.
108. "'Gays' Plan Activities for Fall."

109. Lawrence Gay Liberation Inc., undated press release (probably 1972). University of Kansas Student Organization Records, University Archives, RG-67, Kenneth Spencer Research Library, University of Kansas, 67/66, Queers & Allies, Box 1.

110. *Up Front: The Official Newslettre* [sic] *of Lawrence Gay Liberation Inc.*, 1, no. 1. University of Kansas Student Organization Records, University Archives, RG-67, Kenneth Spencer Research Library, University of Kansas, 67/66, Queers & Allies, Box 1.

111. KU Press Bureau, press release, 9/5/1970, University of Kansas Student Organization Records, University Archives, RG-67, Kenneth Spencer Research Library, University of Kansas, 67/66, Queers & Allies, Box 1.

112. University of Kansas Student Organization Records, University Archives, RG-67, Kenneth Spencer Research Library, University of Kansas, 67/66, Queers & Allies, Box 1.

113. "KU's Gay Libbers File Federal Suit," *Topeka Capital*, December 14, 1971.

114. "Gay Liberation Front Take Case to Court," *Wichita Eagle*, December 16, 1971, 14.

115. "Gay Liberation's Request Denied," *Topeka Capital*, February 12, 1972.

116. "Chalmers Welcomes Test of His Gay Liberation Decision," *Lawrence Journal-World*, July 22, 1971, 3.

117. David G. Miller to E. Lawrence Chalmers, Jr., October 1, 1971. University of Kansas Student Organization Records, University Archives, RG-67, Kenneth Spencer Research Library, University of Kansas, 67/66, Queers & Allies, Box 1.

118. Mimeographed *Lawrence GLF News*, no 2, April 7, 1972. University of Kansas Student Organization Records, University Archives, RG-67, Kenneth Spencer Research Library, University of Kansas, 67/66, Queers & Allies, Box 1.

119. "Topeka Judge Bar Kunstler," *Lawrence Journal-World*, January 27, 1972, 1.

120. "KU Gay Lib Recognition Loses in Court Attempt," *Lawrence Journal-World*, February 12, 1972, 1.

121. "New KU Effort May Recognize Gay Liberation," *Lawrence Journal-World*, February 14, 1972, 16.

122. "Kunstler Requests Court Order KU Gay Lib Okay," *Lawrence Journal-World*, November 17, 1972, 20.

123. *Up Front*, 1, No. 1, 2. University of Kansas Student Organization Records, University Archives, RG-67, Kenneth Spencer Research Library, University of Kansas, 67/66, Queers & Allies, Box 1.

124. Gay Liberation Front Emergency Position Paper. University of Kansas Student Organization Records, University Archives, RG-67, Kenneth Spencer Research Library, University of Kansas, 67/66, Queers & Allies, Box 1.

125. Gay Liberation Front Emergency Position Paper. University of Kansas Student Organization Records, University Archives, RG-67, Kenneth Spencer Research Library, University of Kansas, 67/66, Queers & Allies, Box 1.

126. Gay Liberation Front Emergency Position Paper.

127. Gay Liberation Front Emergency Position Paper.

128. *The Yellow Brick Road*, January and February, 1977. University of Kansas Student Organization Records, University Archives, RG-67, Kenneth Spencer Research Library, University of Kansas, 67/66, Queers & Allies, Box 1.

129. Erin Niederberger, "The Gay Lib Controversy: Social Change Versus Social Norms at the University of Missouri," *Artifacts*, April 2016, artifactsjournal.missouri.edu

130. "Ratchford Says Homosexuals Already Under Investigation," *Columbia Daily Tribune*, March 29, 1973; "University Investigates Homosexuals," *Columbia Missourian*, March 30, 1973, 1, 15.

131. Niederberger, "The Gay Lib Controversy."

132. Niederberger, "The Gay Lib Controversy."

133. No relation to the author.

134. Glenda Dilley, Interview with Jim Andis, August 10, 2010. jandris.ipage.com

135. Ron Lee, "Protestors Heckle Gays During March to First Campus Meeting," *Columbia Daily Tribune*, April 21, 1978, 1.

136. Tom Evans and David Bushman, "Gay Lib Takes March of Victory," *Columbia Missourian*, April 21, 1978, 1A, 14A; Ron Lee, "Protestors Heckle Gays During March to First Campus Meeting," *Columbia Daily Tribune*, April 21, 1978, 1.

137. Evans and Bushman, "Gay Lib Takes March of Victory."

138. Evans and Bushman, "Gay Lib Takes March of Victory."

139. Evans and Bushman, "Gay Lib Takes March of Victory."

140. Josh Flory, "MSA Rights Proposal Gains Ally," *Columbia Daily Tribune*, February 12, 1999; clipping in University of Missouri Archives, vertical file "Gay Lib."

CHAPTER 4

Gay and Lesbian Student Groups Struggle to Serve Campus in the 1980s

Although seen at the time and remembered as a period of conservatism in the United States, the 1980s for some college students was a time of activism.[1] The apartheid government in South Africa was a notable civil rights issue that drove much campus activism: universities had invested in enterprises owned or controlled by the racist South African government. For gay and lesbian students, in particular, university investment (or lack thereof) into the campus rights of non-heterosexual students prompted many forms of action, from "zap"-like protests of the early 1970s to private (or at least as private as anything ever is on a college campus) negotiations between students and administrators.

The core of that activism remained equity of access to and participation in campus recognition, protection, and funding. The efforts in the 1970s to force campuses to allow access to campus had largely succeeded; in the 1980s, would the university—both its administration and its ever-changing student population—recognize non-heterosexuals as a minority akin to ethnic minorities? If so, would non-heterosexual students receive subsequent services and funding from the university?

University of Illinois, 1980–1984

A large advertisement for the Gay Illini appeared on page 17 of the January 18, 1980, edition of the *Daily Illini*. It listed activities through March; "forum" topics included "Women's Music," "Gays in University Housing,"

© The Author(s) 2019
P. Dilley, *Gay Liberation to Campus Assimilation*,
https://doi.org/10.1007/978-3-030-04645-3_4

"Local Gay History," "Constitutional Amendments," "Equal Rights Amendment," and "Game Night." Clearly, despite earlier members' comments to the press, Gay Illini's focus remained political as well as educational and social.[2]

A flyer indicating Gay Illini's schedule for March 1980 conveys a shift in programming. The month's activities began with a game night followed by a BYO (Bring Your Own refreshment) social at a member's home (which typically was planned after each general meeting). Two nights later met "with several other campus groups (including Inter-fraternity/Panhellenic Councils!)" as part of Arts for Change Consortium, planning a festival in April. The general meeting on March 16 focused on the experiences of "Gay Businesspersons."

While political programs did comprise part of the schedule, they did not consist of direct action by the campus organization. Gay Illini did indicate it was "sending people to this hearing" on "state gay rights bills" in Chicago. The general meeting on March 9 focused on "Libertarianism," with speakers from Students for Libertarianism. A statewide meeting of the Illinois Gay Rights Task Force was scheduled on campus for March 29, but "If you can't make the meeting, join us for cocktails at The Bar afterwards."

A slightly modified statement continued was used on the student organization registration form for 1982–1983.[3] A change of type of registered organization then included "Rights/Freedoms," which Gay Illini chose through 1986–1987. Accompanying this change, though, was a shift in purpose. In 1982–1983 forms, the purpose was stated as "To assure legitimacy, respectability, and freedom in same-sex relationships. Education and promotion of gay rights." The March 23, 1983, form, to cover the summer of 1983, however, changed the purpose drastically: "We are devoted to the legitimacy and respectability in same-sex relationships." This is a far cry from the initial Gay Liberation focus on deconstructing the heteronormative confines of gender, sexuality, and relationships.

A flyer dated August 1983 stated:

> The purpose of Gay Illini is to promote respectability, legitimacy, and freedom in same-sex relationships. We attempt to help educate the general public, and Gays themselves, as to the difficulties Gays encounter in our society, and ways in which these can be overcome.... Gay Illini is presently made up mostly of students, but staff and faculty of the U. Of I. Are warmly invited to join. People who are not associated with the University are just as welcome, as are any people who support Gay Rights.[4]

The (undated) 1983–1984 form stated, "Legitimazation [sic] of same-sex relationships," while the one dated May 1, 1984, stated, "Promote respectability in same-sex relationships," as did the one dated November 27, 1984.

Gay Illini produced a fact sheet, dated July 22, 1984, that listed two bars: Chester Street, "gay owned and operated bar and disco... [at which] Many non-gay customers may be present on Tuesday and Thursday night"; and the Silver Dollar Saloon, at which "There are no cover charges and few non-gay customers." It also listed gay coffeehouses and lesbian coffeehouses.[5]

The applications for registration for academic year 1985, November 16, 1984, listed the purpose of the organization as "Gay Illini is dedicated to the legitamacy [sic], respectability, and freedom of same-sex relationships," as did successive forms for summer 1985 and academic year 1986–1987. Notable, however, was the moniker the organization registered under in the November 16, 1984, registration form: the group included its distaff members, becoming Gay and Lesbian Illini.

Clearly, though, the changes were not simply inclusivity of gender nor leaders responsible to the University for the group. Gone were the (express) goals of social and political change, or connection to other identity-based groups that originated from the civil rights movements of the 1960s; gone was the notion of liberation—of gay liberation—from the social constructs of a normative heterosexual culture. Gay Illini desired to become respectable, to fitting in to a place within the normative culture. The ideology of revolution was replaced by one of assimilation.

UNIVERSITY OF MICHIGAN, 1981–1983

By 1981, gay and lesbian students were able to avail themselves of a plethora of activities, across a spectrum that was intended to serve their political, religious, athletic, social, and medical needs. The "GAY MALE/ CO-ED CALENDAR" for January and February of 1981 noted weekly and special events. Worship groups for Presbyterian/Episcopal and Metropolitan Christian Churches were listed for Sundays, as was the Lutheran Campus Ministry, which also had a support group, Lutherans Concerned, which met monthly. Further, Integrity, a support group for non-heterosexual Episcopalians, had a contact name and support number listed.[6]

Other support groups were noted, with mailing addresses and phone numbers: one for bisexual males (meeting in Ann Arbor) and a second for bisexual married men (meeting in Pontiac). Other phone numbers included "Womanspace," Women's Crisis Center, Assault Crisis and Crisis Counseling hotlines, Express Teen Clinic, and Ozone youth services. Free gay and lesbian venereal disease clinics were open Monday evenings; in addition, a group for "med. students, nurses, physicians, & others interested in gay health concerns" convened every other Tuesday.

Thursday evenings were reserved for the Lesbian/Gay Political Caucus, which met in the Michigan Union. "Gay Volleyball" was held on Friday nights in the Central Campus Recreation Building. An office-campus, co-ed dance was listed for Saturday, January 24. Other special events listed included a breakfast meeting of the Ann Arbor Consortium of Business Professionals, an Inauguration Day workshop on "Gay Concerns in Political Activism," and a showing of *Diversions & Delights*, featuring Vincent Price as Oscar Wilde.

Gay Pride

But perhaps no campus or community activities of non-heterosexual students were as obvious to their heterosexual peers as were those of Gay Pride Week. Ann Arbor's Lesbian-Gay Pride Week in 1981 occurred June 20 through June 28, sponsored by the Gay Liberation Front (GLF) of Ann Arbor, UM's Human Sexuality Offices, and the Gay Community Services of Ann Arbor; it was, as most campus Pride Week celebrations on Midwestern campuses were, a melange of social, educational, and activist activities.

Akin to Pride Weeks on other campuses, this one lasted longer than seven days. Prior to the initial Saturday march and rally was a "Pre-Pride Week Sign-Making Session and Wine and Cheese Party" on Monday, June 15. The march and rally "focus[ed]... on the link between the lesbian-gay rights struggle and those of other oppressed groups."[7] In this regard, Michigan students were a bit ahead of the curve, as most Midwestern campuses did not strive to make this connection at Gay Pride events for another decade; instead, most early Gay Pride events focused on the empowerment of coming out, along with social acceptance of non-heterosexual students on campus.[8]

Also on Saturday was a "Lesbian-Gay Talent Night," held at the Michigan Union. Sunday offered a Pot-Luck Pride Week Kick-Off Party, followed by a concert featuring "nationally known gay male singer-song writer from Seattle" Charlie Murphy and "local lesbian singing duo" "Trees."

Brown-bag luncheons in Liberty Plaza, a large city park in Ann Arbor, were scheduled Monday through Friday, for non-heterosexuals "to socialize and remind the community that lesbians and gay men are out to stay." Sunday through Thursday, the student organization sponsored educational workshops on such tentative topics as:

Sexism and the Origins of Lesbian-Gay Male Oppression
Minorities and Minority Oppression in the Lesbian and Gay Male Community
Lesbian-Gay Life in Mexico
Job-related Concerns for Lesbians and Gay Men in the Business and Working Worlds
Legal Concerns for Lesbian and Gay Male Couples
The Process of Coming Out
Separatism and Non-separatism in the Lesbian-Gay Liberation Movement "(for wimin)"
Overcoming Sexism within the Gay Male Community (for men)
Fighting the Repressive Right

Friday night, June 26, was reserved for a film night. Two films were given two showings each. *Outrageous* was a 1977 Canadian comedy concerning a hairdresser for drag queens who longed to be on the stage himself. *A Comedy in Six Unnatural Acts* was a send-up of cliché images of lesbians.

On Saturday, June 27, 1981, Gay Community Services of Ann Arbor held a general meeting in the afternoon. Saturday night, however, was the entertainment highlight of Pride Week: the Lesbian-Gay Pride Week Dance at the Unitarian Church. A last-minute addition, to be held prior to the dance, was Theater Lambda's "triumphant return of The Anita Bryant Follies with the indescribable Velma La Velma" (an alter ego of local thespian Rob Reiniche). The week concluded with a picnic, volleyball and canoe trip on the Huron River on Sunday afternoon, and a discussion of gay and lesbian history, "Herstory, Hisstory, Ourstory," Sunday evening.[9]

As with most volunteer-driven events, the schedule was subject to change; potential last-minute Pride events listed on the Tentative Schedule of Events included roller skating, a bowling night, a showing of the documentary *Word Is Out: Stories of Our Lives*, an afternoon coffeehouse gathering, and an ecumenical religious service. Nonetheless, the 1981 Pride Week schedule set the template for subsequent events at the University of Michigan and Ann Arbor for years to come.

In 1982, students at the University of Michigan reorganized the Ann Arbor GLF as the Michigan Gay Undergraduates (MGU). According to a membership form from the time, "MGU is a non-profit, gay, 50 member, student organization which is recognized by both the Michigan Student Assembly, and The University of Michigan. Our purpose is to provide an alternative social setting to the bars.... We also sponsor special events... [and] have regular bar runs, throw parties, and even have bake sales in the Fishbowl."[10]

According to notations in the James W. Toy Papers, MGU was active between 1982 and 1987. Its undated Operating Paper (a seven-page document detailing in minutia everything from obtaining voting rights to disciplinary procedures and actions) listed the group's purpose as "to provide a positive, social environment at the University of Michigan, as well as all other interested people."[11]

Although visibility for non-heterosexuals in U.S. society increased during the 1980s, the images were not always positive in their portrayal of gay men and women. In the early 1980s, as AIDS began to be recognized in the United States, the representations in the media of non-heterosexuals were often shaped by a narrative of disease and death; in response to AIDS, and the U.S. culture's lack of response to the epidemic, gay men and lesbians coalesced to provide services and education on campus, as well as to confront the country's disregard politically. As noted by a campus reporter, "Gays on the Ann Arbor campus, however, have slowly become more political and more open in the last several years."[12] Within this context, the first configuration of the Lesbian and Gay Rights Organizing Committee (LaGROC) emerged at the University of Michigan.

"The Year of the Queer"

The Year "1983 will be seen as the year of the queer": so a speaker in front of the Ann Arbor federal building at an August 6, 1983, rally was predicted.[13] The rally was in response to a man "threatening a group of gays with a shotgun" during a Lesbian/Gay Pride Week rally on June 25.

Donovan Mack, one of the student leaders of the campus group LaGROC, presented what became a symbol of gay activism at Michigan during this time. As he approached the microphone to speak, he donned a paper bag over his head, "representing the 'straight' masks gays are forced to hide behind."[14] As this typical, invisible gay man, Mack chided straight society, presenting the perceived social consequences of not a few gays and lesbians about coming out. "What's a self-respecting queer to do?... You have sex, you get AIDS. You put on an apron and go to work, you get fired. If you come out to the world, some cuckoo points a gun at you."[15]

"It is plain to see that Ann Arbor is not used to (gays) asking for equal rights," Mack continued. Noting the press at the rally, he said, "It is great to get media coverage, but we are looked at like we are troubled kids."[16] Instead, Mack called for a new approach and a new organization to utilize it. "Since the beginning of the year, a group calling itself the Lesbian and Gay Rights on Campus (LaGROC) has been campaigning to require the University to state that it will not discriminate on the basis of sexual orientation."[17]

Mack, along with the other members of LaGROC, was among the firsts of a new wave of student activists to "play" the media. Harkening back to the initial guerrilla theater that inspired the GLF at Michigan, LaGROC staged very public satires to admonish straight society's discrimination against non-heterosexuals. LaGROC (and its sibling, QuAC, the Queers Action Committee) orchestrated these demonstrations while simultane-ously—and publicly—engaging in the University's process and procedures for creating policy change on their campus.

LaGROC: Disruptive and Droll

Founded during the 1982–1983 academic year, LaGROC was organized to attempt "to seek redress, through political action, for the past injustices gay men and lesbians had suffered at the University of Michigan."[18] Chief target of their actions was the University's anti-discrimination statement, which prior gay and lesbian student groups at Michigan had argued needed to include "sexual orientation" as a protected category. According to an existing draft of a history of LaGROC, in February of 1983, LaGROC published "position paper that addressed the need and effect of amended anti-discrimination by-laws that they demanded the regents enact."[19] The paper, produced with financial support from the student government, the Michigan Student Assembly, outlined the goals of the organization and the need for a "formal policy" to protect the rights of homosexuals on campus. The paper said that the University's bylaws should include a clause protecting homosexuals from discrimination.[20]

Those positions, sometimes referred to by LaGROC as "demands," were delivered to the University administration in December of 1982; one of the points included in the position paper was for the Michigan President Harold Shapiro to recommend to the Board of Trustees for such an amendment to the bylaws. In the ensuing semester, "The members of LaGROC found that administration action on their proposal was not forthcoming and were forced to stage political actions."[21]

Such a bylaw change would potentially put the University in conflict: how would it—how could it—reconcile a policy of condemning gay discrimination while still allowing the practice of discrimination to continue by organizations, such as Reserve Officer Training Corps (ROTC) and the U.S. military, as they operated on campus? The Pentagon was threatening colleges and universities that attempted to disallow them to operate ROTC and/or recruit on their campuses would result in a withdrawal of Department of Defense funding. At the University of Michigan, the amount of such funding exceeded five million dollars. Aaron Bruce, however, did not disagree with the potential loss; nonetheless, "LaGROC's position on the military issue, however, is that it is a civil rights issue and is therefore 'beyond cost-benefit analysis.'"[22] Although Michigan's president met with LaGROC in April of 1983, LaGROC member Jonathan Ellis "said the group received no response from Shapiro since their April meeting."[23]

The typical administrative response to gay initiatives on campus, whether they involved equality statements or direct support, was to stall: delay giving answers, refer the matter to an underling or a committee for "study," promise decisions at a later time. Often this was done with a hope that student agitators might graduate, become disinterested in pursuing such an elusive goal, or simply come to the realization that one "can't change the system."

Chief campus administrators continued these tactics into the 1980s, often leaving it to other, often more sympathetic, staff members (who were ultimately powerless to make institutional change) to interact with the complainers. This letter, from LaGROC's Jonathan Ellis to Jim Toy, dated July 5, 1983, conveys the frustrating runaround experienced by students in such situations.

I left a note in Shapiro's office this morning (Monday, July 5th) asking if there would be a five minutes sometime in the next day or so when he could give me a brief status report on the telephone about our proposal.

I got a call back this afternoon from Susan Lipschutz who is an assistant to the president. She said that Shapiro had been out of the office for two weeks and just got back today. She did not think he would be able to get back to us by phone, so she said she was giving us a message from him.

That message was (1) although he had hoped to make a decision in early July, for his schedule would now have him focusing on a decision for us in two weeks or even longer. (2) He remained committed to consulting with us on the wording of any statement after he made his basic decision.

I asked if the decision he hoped to make, in two weeks or whenever, was a question of what avenue to take, e.g. by-law change through the Regents or presidential policy statement. Susan Lipschutz said, yes, that was the decision he was still considering, and he would then contact us....

She said she could continue to be a contact for us if we wanted to call his office again, but that we should not expect anything for "several weeks or longer."[24]

In essence, Shapiro sent an implicit message that he was still deciding what and when to decide what manner in which to decide to express equal rights for non-heterosexuals on campus. For LaGROC, the message was clear; any response would need to transcend routes of official communication.

By the beginning of the fall 1983 term, LaGROC had planned a series of incrementally more disruptive actions on the Michigan campus. They began with attending one of the University's most conventional traditions: the annual tea hosted by the president. According to news accounts, "a group of about 50 gays rights activists" worked the event, distributing stickers and buttons that stated "Oct. 14," the deadline they were about to give the University to address their concerns listed in the December 1982 position paper.[25]

One of the spokespersons for LaGROC was Bruce Aaron, who used the informal event to deliver to Shapiro a letter from LaGROC, protesting the University's delay in including sexual orientation in the non-discrimination statement. Aaron said that Shapiro "expressed concern for their cause" but was undecided on whether he should take the issue to the University Regents for a bylaw change or simply make a presidential policy statement himself.[26] The group demanded a response to their continued requests by October 14, "or else," which Aaron indicated had not yet been determined, but "[t]he longer Shapiro waits, the more likely disruptive tactics would become necessary."[27] According to press reporting of the event, "Shapiro refused to say what he plans to do, although he said he understood their position."[28]

On March 10, 1984, over 50 people, described in the campus paper as "activists... pushing for a campus non-discrimination policy for gays," occupied President Shapiro's office. After a march that began on the Diag at 12:30, the group arrived at Shapiro's office, where they were told he was out to lunch. They stayed in the outer office, chanting, "Two-four-six-eight, Tell Shapiro we can't wait!"[29] When Shapiro finally arrived, he smiled and allowed the students into his office. Photographs in the local press show Shapiro literally surrounded by members of LaGROC, expressing their frustration waiting 15 months for the policy change they had asked for from the president.

Shapiro did himself no favors in his responses to the students. "I think it's unfortunate that it's taken so long.... But I'm not ready to issue a policy statement now." In response to the activists' not unexpected disappointment, Shapiro said, "I've probably worked a good deal more than anybody in this room on this."[30] That, probably as much as his refusal to offer a policy statement (or even a timeframe for doing so), infuriated the protesters. Was it another example of an oppressor trying to claim to the oppressed that his actions were really benefiting them?

LaGROC responded by stepping up their public demonstrations. At 2:00 on Friday, March 9, a baker's dozen of female members of QuAC gathered in the Diag and placed paper shopping bags upon their heads, upon which were written statements such as "Another U-M employee in the closet," "My friends tell faggot jokes and I can't come out," and "Let me out of the closet."[31] For an hour they marched across campus, their destination: the Fleming Administration Building. "The only sound during the protest was the beat of a coffee can... used as a drum" (Fig. 4.1).[32]

The first stop was in the Office of Affirmative Action. Next, the protesters marched to the president's office, where they were informed by a secretary that Shapiro was out of town. The women then "sat in a circle holding hands."[33] After ten minutes, Molly Adams, the spokesperson for the action, demanded that Shapiro issue a statement to protect non-heterosexuals on campus; she said, "We won't be silent anymore and we will be back."[34] QuAC member Cathy Godre complained, "We're tired of waiting for Shapiro.... A lot of things are holding up (the passage of the policy), but he is the man who is holding us up."[35]

Fig. 4.1 Masked protesters occupy president's office, University of Michigan, 1984. (*Ann Arbor News*, courtesy of Ann Arbor District Library, copyright Barcroft Media; used with permission)

The "Unknown Comic" was a short-lived celebrity in the mid-1970s; he wore a paper bag over his head when he performed, to save him from public ridicule. These protesters at the University of Michigan in 1984 used that concept to demonstrate both the ubiquitous ubiquity of non-heterosexuals on campus along with the fear of coming out on campus that many felt. These protesters had just marched across the campus, ending at the office of the university president, to bring attention to the University's lack of attention to their calls for codifications of campus rights and protections.

The QuAC demonstration seems to have prompted Shapiro to take action. On March 13, the president announced that his administration had completed drafting a policy statement to protect non-heterosexuals from discrimination at Michigan; despite not needing to, Shapiro decided to present it to the Board of Regents for their consent. He did so, nonetheless, despite feeling gays and lesbians were already "well protected" by existing non-discrimination statements. Further, he told the press, "No one has presented any solid evidence to me that there's a particular problem with discrimination of gays."[36]

QuAC's members demonstrated mixed assessments of the policy. Marcy Sherman said, "I question whose interest the University is trying to protect by excluding the government, the military, and the ROTC from this policy."[37] But Shapiro's statement would only be a presidential policy, which could be changed by a new president or overruled by a future Regents' bylaw. Cathy Godre noted that Shapiro's statement was only a step: "I'm really pleased that a policy statement is going to come out. I think that this is indeed a victory... (but) there are bigger and better things to pursue."[38]

Bruce Aaron, LaGROC's spokesperson, was less enthusiastic. In a "Campus Meet the Press" event on March 14, Aaron decried Shapiro's dismissal of the lived campus experiences of the University's non-heterosexual population; what, precisely, would constitute "solid evidence" for Shapiro? In Aaron's view, "[i]t's discrimination to prevent people from being who they are," which was at least in part the intention behind anti-gay and anti-lesbian slurs and graffiti on campus. "It's not cool to refer to blacks as niggers," Aaron argued, "but it's still cool to refer to homosexuals as fags and dykes."[39]

LaGROC had also requested for Shapiro to make a public announcement of the non-discrimination statement, an inclusion of the statement in the official logos that included equal opportunity and non-discrimination statements, clearly outlined grievance procedures, and an effort to educate students and faculty about homosexuals.[40]

The Presidential Policy Statement

On March 21, 1984, Michigan President Shapiro finally issued a policy statement concerning discrimination based upon sexual orientation.

> Among the traditional factors which are generally "irrelevant" are race, sex, religion, and national origin. It is the policy of The University of Michigan that an individual's sexual orientation be treated in the same manner. Such a policy ensures that only relevant factors are considered and that equitable and consistent standards of conduct and performance are applied.

In part, Shapiro provided what LaGROC was demanding. Shapiro's statement solidified gay and lesbians as a minority with (some) protections at the University; it did not, however, extend beyond the scope of its programs.

It should be noted that this policy does not apply to the University's relationships with outside organizations, including the federal government, the military, and ROTC.

While not carrying the weight of an official bylaw, this statement was viewed as "the beginning of the end of discrimination against lesbians and gay men on the campuses of the University of Michigan."[41] After a dozen years of protest and petition, non-heterosexual students at Michigan had some measure of protection and redress. But as LaGROC reminded the University of Michigan campus the next day,

> ...we are under no illusion that today's statement, or any other University document, alone will secure our rights. We intend to see lesbian/gay discrimination ended once and for all at the University. The presidential policy statement now in effect gives us one more means to struggle for such justice.[42]

The presidential policy statement was a major accomplishment. No doubt, Shapiro hoped the issue resolved. LaGROC's student leadership would graduate and move on, as no doubt Shapiro expected. Perhaps to his surprise, a few years later Shapiro would be brought to task over gay and lesbian issues on campus. While the group confronting the University of Michigan administration in later years was also called LaGROC, its origins and members were quite different.

The University of Kansas, 1984–1985

Year 1984 began with the Gay and Lesbian Services of Kansas (GLSOK) striving for minority recognition from the University's Student Senate. The senate's Minority Affairs Committee had taken up the issue when the spring term commenced, entering into a "month-long dispute over whether homosexuals should be included" in the committee's definition of "minority."[43] Two years earlier, GLSOK member Ruth Lichtwardt had been chosen director (sometimes called "president") of the group (Fig. 4.2).[44] Lichtwardt (who was also working as the secretary in the University of Kansas [KU] Student Senate office) and GLSOK member Kevin Elliott, aided by Shirley Gilley, a member of both GLSOK and the Minority Affairs Committee, argued for inclusion of gays and lesbians within the definition.[45] They must have been convincing; by March, the committee decided

Fig. 4.2   Ruth Lichtwardt of Gay and Lesbian Services of Kansas, circa 1985.
(Kenneth Spencer Research Library, University of Kansas Libraries, The University
of Kansas)
Ruth Lichtwardt being interviewed by KJHK radio, mid-1980s. Lichtwardt
was the longest-serving leader of the non-heterosexual student group at the
University of Kansas. She was at the center of one of the most controversial eras of
discrimination and harassment of gays and lesbians at KU, one much more insidious than was generally known to the public.

upon a definition expansive enough to include many groupings of students: "any part of the University's population differing from others in
some characteristics and often subjected to differential treatment."[46]

The arguments in the committee meetings and in the campus press
reflect a clear change in the rhetoric of such debates. In the 1970s, gay and
lesbian campus groups routinely stated that "coming out" was, at least in
part, an acceptance of a lifestyle, one that rejected (at least some) of the
values of the dominant, heterosexual culture; in the 1980s, argument that
non-heterosexuals were an inherent minority replaced the language of a
chosen gay "lifestyle," which social opponents of homosexuals conflated
with immoral, illicit, and inhumane practices. Lichtwardt responded, "Who
would choose a lifestyle that is discriminated against in every aspect?"[47]

The attention of senate committees upon GLSOK was far from over,
though. For 1983–1984, the previous Student Senate had approved $493
for GLSOK. In late March of 1984, like other student organizations at the
University, GLSOK petitioned for $2882 in student-fee funding for the

next academic year. At a hearing of their application in the Student Senate Finance Committee, GLSOK officers were asked for a list of their members. By university rules, only organization officers had to be listed on official forms, and for groups like GLSOK, "official" membership lists were problematic: many students attended meetings less frequently than those who attended social or service events. Still, members of the Finance Committee wanted a list of names, because GLSOK was "one of our most controversial fundings." Lichtwardt had prepared, with the aid of the American Civil Liberties Union, a response, and GLSOK refused to provide a list. That did not satisfy the Finance Committee.[48]

In April, the Student Senate voted not to fund GLSOK, claiming that GLSOK could fund its activities through income generated through the dances it sponsored.[49] The dances had been quite popular for a decade, but were not generating the attendance numbers as in the early 1970s.[50] KU Student Body President Carla Vogel said she would veto any funding bill from the Senate that did not include GLSOK.[51]

In the ensuring week, an undergraduate KU student, Steve Imber, started circulating a petition in opposition to university or student funding of GLSOK. Imber told the press that the "purpose of the petition is to inform the students on the issue and to inform the student body president and Student Senate as to how some students feel in regards to the issue."[52] Within three days, Imber claimed 1000 students had signed his petition. Nonetheless, he claimed that someone was stealing petition forms he distributed. GLSOK had a counterpetition, to support restoring funding, which over 200 had signed.[53]

In the meantime, Ruth Lichtwardt and GLSOK were still fighting to obtain funding for the 1984–1985 academic year. The Student Senate, perhaps in response to Carla Vogel's veto threat, finally approved $505 for GLSOK. That amount was not enough to pay for anticipated phone and rent fees for the GLSOK office in the Kansas Union.[54] Some student senators stated that since the dances had made GLSOK so much profit, Student Senate did not need to fund their activities. Doug Stallings, the GLSOK treasurer, tried to disabuse them of that fallacy: "In the past, we borrowed money from rich gays and paid it back."[55] It seems those days, and those gays, were over.

By April 24, Imber reported he had 1600; 2300 were required to force a referendum. Given the timing of the semester, and the required time outlined by the Student Senate Code for such procedures, it appeared that the referendum, including checking the validity of the signatures on the petition, would have to be postponed until the fall, 1984, semester.[56]

In September, the start of the 1984–1985 academic year, the face of GLSOK's future funding was still undecided. Ruth Lichtwardt returned as president of the group, facing pressure from both Steve Imber and the members of KU's student government, who wanted to dismantle the precariously funded activities of GLSOK. Lichtwardt told the campus newspaper, "What it boils down to is that our members is largely gay.... That is what people object to."[57]

Fagbusters

On September 25, the *University Daily Kansan* (*UDK*) published a two-article expose about the appearance on campus of "Fagbusters" T-shirts, which had begun to appear on campus a few weeks earlier.[58] Appropriating the logo of the then popular film *Ghostbusters*, the front of the shirts displayed a red circle and slash emblem over a ghost; however, "The ghost has a limp wrist, an earring, and long eyelashes." Above the image, in bright red, was the word "Fagbusters." Lichtwardt made clear the seriousness of the analogy.

> If people make racist statements about blacks or Jews or handicapped people, they wouldn't get away with it for very long.... But to do the same toward homosexuals is still acceptable, at least to large groups of people.[59]

Student Body President Carla Vogel responded to the T-shirts' appearance with a challenge to the campus and its leaders.

> This shows fear of things we don't understand. We can't ignore that there is discrimination on this campus. These shirts opened it up for people to think about it; it's there and it's blatant, and we need to do something about it.[60]

Also revealed in the September 25 *UDK* articles was the provenance of the T-shirts. A reporter, neither denying nor declaring he was such, went to the Arcadia fraternity house; at the door, he asked if he could buy a Fagbusters T-shirt. The brother who sold him the shirt said that about 400 of the shirts had been printed. That Arcadia brother was Steve Imber.[61]

The *UDK* noted that just 12 days earlier, Imber had denied having any involvement with the T-shirts. Multiple sources within the KU Greek system confirmed, however, that Imber, along with other Acadia members, had attended meetings at many fraternity houses, selling the shirts over the previous weeks.

The Student Senate Elections Committee, responsible for validating the petition and organizing any resultant referendum that the Student Senate might choose to call, was in a quandary: as they checked and counted signatures on Imber's petition, should they include signatures of students who were enrolled in spring 1984 but not fall 1984? How would they even have access to that information (which, in the times before online enrollment, were not readily available, even to the KU's administration)? Should a petition from a previous academic year even be valid the next year? Those were the questions its members faced as they examined the petition in order to make a recommendation on it to the full Student Senate.[62]

More pressingly, however, was the feeling among many on campus that the petition was but an example of the harassment being experienced by GLSOK members, as well as other non-heterosexual students, on campus. The fact that Imber originated both the petition and the T-shirts made student leaders question the impetus of the former. Dennis Highberger, the KU student body vice president, declared, "It takes any credence out of Steve's contention that he was just interested in seeing the group was self-sufficient.... It's obvious that the petition was directed at gay people just because they are gay." Thom Davidson, a student senator and chair of the Elections Committee, concurred: "In my opinion now, it's pretty obviously a cut and dried case of discrimination."[63] After an hour of discussion, the Elections Committee determined that Imber's petition was "discriminatory," and thus they voted unanimously to invalidate it.[64]

Indeed, the KU gay and lesbian community was experiencing even more blatant—and physical—harassment than in the previous semester. The day after the expose was printed, Lichtwardt and another GLSOK member, Howard Rogers, set out to a GLSOK meeting. As Rogers started to drive his car, he realized something was amiss. Three of his car's wheels had been tampered with; "preliminary police reports showed that someone apparently loosened the car's lug nuts, which hold the wheel to the car's axle."[65] That same day, at a beer bar in town, the DJ repeatedly played the theme song from *Ghostbusters*, turning down the volume each time the title was to be said, so that patrons could yell, "Fagbusters." One patron yelled, "We're at war with the GLS – and I love it!" Across the street, in front of the town's only gay bar, people threw stones at people going into and out of the bar. In addition, GLSOK office staffers and members in general had received multiple anonymous phone calls, threatening death or castration "almost regularly this fall."[66]

Despite—or perhaps because of—the public scrutiny, the next week the Student Executive Committee (StudEx), which was composed of the leadership of the Student Senate, rejected the Elections Committee's recommendation about Imber's petition, and sent the petition back to the Elections Committee for reconsideration, rather than forward it, with the committee's recommendation, to the full Senate. In the words of student senator and chair of StudEx, Michael Foubert, "the charge of the committee was to 'look only at the wording of the petition and at the validity of the signatures, and that it not judge whether the petition was discriminatory.'"[67]

Other factors might have been in play, however: the vote on the petition by the full Student Senate could possibly approve the petition. Foubert, who was also a member of the gay community at KU, might have been implementing a procedural action to delay the Senate from being in a position to make such a final decision. The chair of the Student Senate Finance Committee (a student senator who had consistently voted against funding GLSOK) stated, "Student Senate should not have the right to question the right of the student body to question the Senate." For his part, "Imber said... that he thought GLSOK could be self-supporting and that the issue was financial, not moral."[68]

At the second Elections Committee meeting, Foubert addressed the notion that members of the Senate sent the petition back for review was because of a threat of veto. "The reason that we decided to bounce it back to you is because this is the proper form in the rules and regulations," Foubert stated. The chair of the committee, Student Senator Thom Davidson, opined, "I think that allocations of monies based on a popular vote is a dangerous precedent." The Elections Committee student representatives again debated the petition, for 90 minutes, parsing the meaning of specific words. The petition called for student groups with "potential" to be self-supportive would include most of the student organizations at KU. Committee members found this wording too broad; again, the Committee voted to reject the petition. Student Body President Vogler indicated that she thought Student Senate would follow the Elections Committee's recommendation.[69]

Steve Imber decided to appeal the Elections Committee's second decision. Imber's appeal would go to the University Judicial Board, headed by faculty but including staff and students. Imber reiterated his contention that the petition "wasn't done with any prejudice." Lichtwardt, speaking for GLSOK, responded that the group would challenge the legitimacy of

the petition. "We'll go through University channels as far as we can go....
And we'll take it to outside courts if necessary."[70]

During the second week of November, KU's executive vice chancellor,
Robert Cobb, sent letters to all faculty and staff of the University, declaring that the University would not tolerate discrimination; Vice Chancellor
for Student Affairs David A. Ambler sent similar letters to some 300 student leaders. Both sets of letters included a copy of an excerpt from
Chancellor Gene A. Budig's 1983 convocation address. "Clearly, there
can be no place in this university for bigotry, intolerance, racial or sexual
discrimination, anti-Semitism, and the like. These are the products of a
closed mind."[71]

This effort to address the campus climate beings experienced by non-
heterosexuals on campus inadvertently backfired. In the moment, the
University's intent was welcomed; Lichtwardt told the campus newspaper,
"I think it is a step that will definitely help stop the harassment. I think
that people knowing the administration backs our civil rights is a big
step."[72] Non-heterosexual students noticed, however, that the chancellor
did not specifically address the violence and harassment they were experiencing; worse, the statement provided did not even include the words
"gay" or "lesbian." Although the GLSOK students were busy attending
to other issues in November of 1984, this response—or lack of it—would
haunt KU administration's relationship with its campus non-heterosexual
population for a decade.

In December, a second petition, specifically denouncing GLSOK and
demanding its removal from campus was circulated, backed in part by a
new organization on campus, Young Americans for Freedom. Students
staffing the GLSOK office reported harassing students coming to the
office to confront them.[73] Meanwhile, members of GLSOK had been joining Student Senate committees, to participate directly the decision-making
processes.

An Ethical Dilemma

The spring semester of 1985 opened with the University's Judicial Board
upholding Imber's appeal of the invalidating of his petition, stating, "This
is a highly charged political matter. It is our belief that the [elections]
committee did not proceed in as careful a manner as the circumstances
dictate."[74] Facing the probability of the petition making it to the floor of
the full Student Senate, GLSOK leaders were feared the real possibility
that the Senate would approve the petition, placing a referendum to the

student population that had been so violently vocal and demeaning of gays and lesbians. It was time, they decided, to use a tactic they had hoped not to have to use.

Steve Imber was gay.

Members of Gay and Lesbian Services had known this for some time. While Imber was not identifying publicly, or even privately, with a non-heterosexual identity, he had been having sex with men. Some of those men told gay and lesbian leaders, in both GLSOK and Student Senate, of their sexual experiences with Imber. None wanted to state so publicly, as they were not "out," either.[75]

Lichtwardt, accompanied by other gay leaders, arranged to meet privately with Imber. They informed him of their knowledge and their willingness to go public with the information and, if necessary, provide proof. Of course, such an action would not only tarnish Imber's reputation and position but also force his sexual partners' identities to be made public, which would help none of the involved parties. It was blackmail, to be sure, but GLSOK suggested a compromise: declare a public truce. Imber could save face for himself while still ending the referendum, and GLSOK would hold onto the truth.[76]

On Friday, January 17, Imber and Lichtwardt issued a jointly signed statement, declaring that both GLSOK members and Imber had allowed issues to grow out of hand; the statement included multiple sentences indicating that both parties were equally at fault for the climate on campus. While this was not true, it allowed Imber a path not to admit to his guilt at fomenting an anti-gay crusade on campus at least in part to disguise his homosexuality.

Lichtwardt appeared very accommodating: "Both Steve and I feel that things have gotten out of line.... We hope to show people who have jumped on the bandwagon and harassed others that there is no longer a bandwagon to jump on." Imber told the *UDK*, "I feel good about this. I just hope others follow the example we're setting."[77]

Imber's agreement to the truce, however, was short-lived: one weekend. On Monday, he indicated that he was continuing to pursue his petition. "I feel obligated to pursue this; people have even asked me to continue the petition." When asked about his change of heart, Imber told the campus press,

In the joint statement we were agreeing to disagree.... Now attention should return to the original issue – should the organization be funded?... It's one thing to accept homosexuals.... And it's another to fund them."[78]

Imber called GLSOK's bluff, banking that they would not reveal their blackmail information.

Publicly, Lichtwardt responded to Imber's breaking of the peace in a way that still left GLSOK's threat in play. "It's too bad that Steve is continuing this petition. I was hoping this was all over. This issue has made people afraid of being harassed and now we don't have money."[79] Privately, however, Lichtwardt and the GLSOK were at a crossroads: do they stick to their principles of right of privacy for those who were non-heterosexual, or would they expose the hypocrisy that was fueling the wave of discrimination and campus and threatening the organization's existence? The leadership decided they could not, in good conscience, expose men who were not "out" to public scrutiny; they would take their chances with convincing the Student Senate.[80]

GLSOK ended the month January holding a dance. It was the first to make a profit ($100) since the Fagbusters incidents began. They had hired extra security for their Halloween dance, which ended up losing $300 for the group; the expenses for the December dance also exceeded income, by $200. This drained the funds that GLSOK had saved from the previous years' dances, each of which could make the group up to $600.[81]

Steve Imber claimed GLSOK was losing income because the group was falsely claiming to be a victim.

> I think their financial loss is due more to their own attempts to get sympathy.... They tried to get so much sympathy for acts of harassment that didn't happen, they scared away a lot of people. They are just as responsible as I am for creating a negative attitude.[82]

Whatever his reasoning, he was steadfast in the need for his petition. Lichtwardt, however, pointed out the flaw of Imber's analysis.

> The petition's whole argument was that we are self-sufficient.... But because of his actions against us, we're going broke. If they keep it up, they will ruin their argument that we are self-sufficient.[83]

Without cash on hand, the group would have to petition the Student Senate for funds to fulfill their obligations for the upcoming Gay and Lesbian Awareness Week.

April continued to be the cruelest month for GLSOK. The group requested funding for the next year, but the group also, for the first time, attempted to request $165 for Gay and Lesbian Awareness Week, which was scheduled for later in April. KU's student funding regulations allowed student organizations to apply for unanticipated funding needs, to be distributed from funds that were not yet allocated for the current fiscal year.

On Monday, April 1, 1985, the Student Senate Finance Committee recommended approving $256 for the 1985–1986 academic year. GLSOK had requested $728, to cover rental and phone costs for the office in the Kansas Union. Still, there was time to petition student senators to raise the amount when the full Senate considered the funding bill. The Finance Committee did approve the funding for Gay and Lesbian Awareness (GALA) Week; after the vote, however, Tim Henderson, the chair, overturned the vote, declaring the bill requesting the funds "null and void."

While Lichtwardt had submitted the funding request bill through the Finance Committee, David Hardy, GLSOK member and student senator, presented a copy to the StudEx committee, in order to attempt to have the Senate vote on the funding directly, circumventing the Finance Committee. The chair of StudEx, Student Body Vice President Jeff Polack, indicated in their meeting he was not forwarding the request without review by the Finance Committee; Henderson then determined that the Finance Committee agenda was only to complete "old business," and thus the funding request could not validly be considered. Consequently, Lichtwardt told reporters that GALA Week would have to be canceled. "We can't have it, we can't postpone it."[84]

Enough members of the Finance Committee were convinced to call for an emergency meeting on Tuesday. They debated the bill late into the night, with disagreements often shaped by religious feelings. In the words of one member, "If we take the morals and ethics out of the decision then we could have a computer do this job." Eventually, the Finance Committee opted not to forward the GALA Week funding bill. Further, they rescinded their approval from the night before for GLSOK's 1985–1986 budget; as the campus newspaper reported, the committee "early this morning voted to let the fall Senate decide on the group's funding."[85]

Prior to the senate meeting that week, StudEx, chaired by Michael Foubert, suspended the rules to allow the full Student Senate to vote on whether to consider the GALA Week funding bill. On a vote of four to three, Foubert was able to bring the option to bypass the normal legislative process. He was not, however, able to garner the threshold of two-thirds of the senate required for the full Senate to hear the bill, eliminating all chances of GLSOK to receive funding for the event.[86]

After reading of the Student Senate's action, KU faculty and students came to the GLSOK office, to donate money. Through those contributions, Gay and Lesbian Awareness Week 1984 could still go on. Moreover, it demonstrated that members of the campus believed in the worth of GLSOK's efforts on campus. Ruth Lichtwardt reflected the emotions of most in the group: "I've gone through most of the year thinking no one cared and suddenly people are showing support. I think it was anger that had some people feeling that they wanted to contribute. GALA Week is very important."[87]

Meanwhile, the specter of the current and future student referenda about student organization funding loomed. The Student Senate considered two bills aimed to prohibit popular student votes to eliminate funding for particular student organizations. The first failed, by only two votes. Michael Foubert and Thom Davidson brought forward the second bill, which was referred to the Elections Committee. Foubert argued that the majority should not be able to decide, by popular vote, to deny funding for minority-based student organizations. "I think that's discrimination. I think that avenue should be blocked."[88]

A member of the Elections Committee suggested that such referenda could be an opportunity for minority groups to educate the majority about the issues and discrimination they experienced. A new member of the Elections Committee questioned such a strategy: "Who's going to pay for the education?" she asked. That member, Ruth Lichtwardt, answered her own question. "It's the group that's going to be allocated. Just by bringing up the issue, whether GLSOK won the vote or not, would have killed the group."[89]

Still, the Imber petition was still hanging over GLSOK. The Elections Committee, of which Michael Foubert was a member, indicated it would review the petition—for the third time—before the end of the semester.[90] The issue was brought before the 1985–1986 Student Senate in the fall. David Hardy, a student senator and a member of GLSOK, said, "I think they've beaten it to death. I think it's a dead issue." Imber had graduated in August and was no longer a student; consequently, who was advocating for the referendum was not known. The *UDK* reported that "Imber said last week that although he hoped the petition would eventually pass, he had no further ties with KU and wanted nothing to do with the petition."[91] Imber stated, "I'm not going to pursue it because it's not in anybody's best interest.... It would not be good for the school, not good for GLSOK and not good for me."[92]

Seventeen months after it was sprung upon the campus, Steve Imber's attempts to eliminate support for gay and lesbian students at the KU finally died. The GLSOK members who confronted Imber on his sexual activities hid that portion of the story for decades.

Ruth Lichtwardt was elected as an off-campus senator to KU's Student Senate in 1984 and re-elected twice; she also served as the chair of the Minority Affairs Committee. She was not a very vocal senator, but nonetheless her presence bred enmity: in the words of one of her political detractors, "I haven't seen a direct obvious impact from her... but she could be working behind the scenes."[93]

University of Iowa, 1986–1987

While perhaps the Gay People's Union at the University of Iowa was not "social" enough (as Michael Blake recalled of the late 1970s), the group's reach extended into campus education activities outside of the classroom.

In June of 1986, it brought openly lesbian actress Pat Bond to campus, and in November of that year, it hosted Jonathan Net Katz, an early historian of sexuality and gay and lesbian history. The public extension of GPU started earlier, though. In November of 1982, the organization flew in English ex-patriot bon vivant Quentin Crisp, whose memoir *The Naked Civil Servant* had brought attention—and a memorable face—to non-heterosexual issues in Europe and the United States. As Michael Blake recalled,

> We all said, "Oh, Quentin Crisp would never come to Iowa, for God's sake; he's a New Yorker." So Steve (Freedman, a GPU leader and faculty member at the Iowa Writer's Workshop) just picked up the phone, dialed New York Information, got Quentin on the phone, and said, "Will you come to Pride?" He said, "Of course." Two or three months later, I have Quentin sitting in my kitchen, like with the Twelve Apostles around him. He was mesmerizing.[94]

Gay People's Union (GPU) was also successful in securing funding from the University of Iowa's student government during the 1980s.

> There [were] very liberal [student] senates in the earlier days, so we took advantage of that and liaisoned with a lot of the liberal/other organizations at the time. At the time, the dynamic, the political dynamic was such that a couple of the real liberal organizations took over the senate.... It was this broad spectrum of these very liberal people, and a lot of them were out gay and lesbian.[95]

For the 1987–1988 academic year, the GPU, on behalf of its "100 members," requested $10,330.54 from the Student Senate. Over 60 percent of that amount was requested for the GPU Health Committee, "the single largest source of information, support services and education on AIDS in Johnson County." According to the Supplemental Form for 87 Funding attached to the request, "The health committee has sponsored more than 65 programs on AIDS within the past year, reaching out to dorm residents, medical and nursing students, and the general public."[96]

According to a press release from the GPU dated May 6, 1987, the organization "was allocated an unprecedented sum" from the student government: $6980.01 for 1987–1988. Of that amount, $4947.50 was given for health education, particularly safer sex and HIV and AIDS educational programming.[97] The press release quoted the Student Senate president, Joe Hansen, about the health education funding.

> We don't normally give $4947.50 to student organizations, much less for single priorities, but I think this falls into the category of extraordinary circumstances.[98]

It also falls into the category of non-heterosexual students again providing services and education that rightly should have been the responsibility of the higher education institution.

> Gay People's Union requested almost six thousand dollars for health education because, as one officer of the organization said, "The University isn't doing anything about it. (U of I) Student Health Services hasn't allocated a penny this year for A.I.D.S. education, and we have a top administrator here who has been quoted in the press twice this past year as saying "We're more concerned about measles right now."[99]

Also included in the 1987–1988 budget was $331.80 to produce a newsletter, $680.71 for office expenses, and $1020.00 for outreach and support groups.

UNIVERSITY OF ILLINOIS, 1986–1987

Becoming a Minority: Tasks and Forces

The Gay and Lesbian Illini spent the 1986–1987 academic year continuing their ongoing efforts to have sexual orientation added to the University of Illinois' non-discrimination policy. The amendment to include such a clause had been submitted by the Conference on Conduct Governance (CCG) on April 10, 1985. The proposal, submitted by Professor Charles H. Smith, chair of the CCG, to Chancellor Thomas E. Everhart was six pages in length; it outlined the history of the development of the proposal as well as comparing the University to peer and aspirational peer institutions, along with ethical considerations involved in making the addition. Smith noted that the CCG approved the recommended change by a vote of ten to one.[100]

Everhart forwarded Smith's recommendation to his senior staff, requesting their opinions, and over the next few months, a number did respond. Everhart's files include responses from the Vice Chancellor for Academic Affairs, the Associate Chancellor for Public Affairs, and the Vice Chancellor for Student Affairs. On January 22, 1986, Everhart formally rejected the proposed change. "After eight months of deliberation, the chancellor indicated his refusal…: 'There appears to be no strong evidence of an immediate pressing problem.'"[101]

On January 27, the Monday after Everhart made his decision, the Gay and Lesbian Illini picketed in front of Swanlund, the campus building where Everhart's office was located. They chanted a familiar campus protest refrain for non-heterosexuals in the 1980s: "What do we want? Gay rights. When do we want them? Now." Approximately 35 demonstrators picketed during the noon hour. The chancellor was having lunch with the president, but he agreed to meet with the protesters at 1:45.

According to student affairs administrator Clarence Shelley, the meeting appeared to have placated the students for the moment, but they wanted more time to press their case. From Shelley's email (rife with typos) to Stanley Levy:

> Riegle wanted someone fro [sic] Student Affairs to be there, and I agreed to since I know their leadership and was familiar with the Chancellor's statement…. The chancellor agreed to meet with the group for only 15 minutes.
>
> The campus police were on the third floor, but out of sight…. Everhart, Rowand and me; along with Dollins and Moore standing near the doors. The students were all in the room about 20 of them. Some I recognized-including Terry Cosgrove. Chancellor explained his response to CCG. Students were given copies of the statement hich [sic] none of them had read. The meeting went well- no acrimony only Cosgrove made any vaguely hostile comments. The students appreciated the statement but felt that the phrase sexual orientation was crucial as a sign that the campus recognized their existence.

> TEE [Everhart] agreed to another meeting for no more than an hour.
> Students told of instances of harassment, violence, loss of jobs, loss of hous-
> ing etc. the usual litany. I now suspect than [sic] some of the group weren't
> our students Mar Lee Sargent fro [SIC] Parkland was with them....
> The strategy seems to be to try to change TEE's mind. Failing that they
> want to escalate the issue to the Trustee level.[102]

Everhart did not believe the matter of gay rights important enough to
risk public approbation nor his salary. As he stated in a letter to a faculty
member, in response to the faculty member's request to include sexual
orientation,

> Like my predecessor, I do believe that the lack of consensus by our society
> does have some relevance. The question is how much. We depend on society
> to provide tax dollars to pay your salary and mine. One of my responsibilities
> is to administer the affairs of this University so that those tax dollars are not
> jeopardized. How I feel about issues as an individual may need to be tem-
> pered as I make decisions for all members of the campus community, and try
> to consider all aspects of the consequences of such decisions....
> Let me conclude by thanking you for your concern in your letter, and
> also by assuring you that I intend to try to build greater understanding in
> this campus community to promote tolerance toward people whose beliefs
> we may not share, and respect for each other's right to disagree, as well as
> each other's right to privacy.[103]

Finally, in what was perhaps equal measure of an attempt to stall action
and to appear active, Everhart announced on February 10, 1986, the formation of the Task Force on Sexual Orientation.

> I have asked the task force to address the problem of ensuring the rights of
> all individuals on this campus, regardless of sexual orientation.... We should
> all be strongly committed to the idea that all human beings have certain
> basic rights, and that these rights should be protected by society.[104]

Buried on page two of the press release was Everhart's clear indication of
both his lack of belief in the anecdotal evidence of harassment and discrimination supplied to him and his openness to unbiased evidence.

> I ask the Task Force on Sexual Orientation to investigate and document for
> me instances of discrimination against individuals in our university commu-
> nity whose sexual orientation places them in the minority. Further, I ask the
> Task Force to suggest how the university might implement a process of

social education to improve conditions on this campus for members of the gay and lesbian community.[105]

Everhart charged the Task Force to provide him with a preliminary report by May 23 and a final report by December 19, 1986.

A February 26 membership list of the Task Force included student representatives from the InterFraternity Council and the Pan Hellenic Council, along with one undergraduate student (Kristina Boerger) and three students whose affiliation was non-declared. Mary Ellen Shanesey, a health educator, was chair. She asked for 22 members.

> "The current task force is composed of 21 people: six students, four faculty members, three administrators, four academic professionals [a classification at the University at Illinois that denotes a form of continuing, non-tenured administrator who works with students], three non-academic members, and one religious worker, according to Shanesey.[106]

Shanesey attempted to have enough members to achieve a comprehensive report.

> I have chosen to set the ultimate size of the total committee around twenty allowing the three subcommittees on Education, Policy and Campus Climate to consist of five to seven dedicated, working members.[107]

Kristina Boerger, a leader in Gay and Lesbian Illini (GLI) who had been vocal about her feelings over Everhart's and the University's inaction, declined the invitation "because of the time commitment and her 'mixed feelings' about the force."[108]

Kristina Boerger

Kristina Boerger came to the University of Illinois in 1983. In 1985, between her sophomore and junior year, she had a summer job in Minnesota.

> I was 20 years old working a summer job for a college and being fired for being a lesbian. I was still politically naïve. I thought this was the land of liberty and justice for all, and that everyone would get a fair shake.[109]

She soon realized, however, that such actions by employers were entirely legal, even at the University of Illinois.

I thought, Well, I cannot permit that what I just experienced should befall anyone else. So I took a vow that I would not leave that town until I had seen to it that the University passed protections for the equal right of queer people to work and be publicly accommodated at the school, participate in all the aspects of university life....[110]

Boerger's friend, Mike Friedman, had recently been kicked out of his fraternity when it discovered he was gay. Together, they decided to join the Gay Illini and to become politically active.

He was furious, I was furious, so we started attending meetings of the organization. We set our sights on changing the rules governing student organizations.... We felt that since it was a state institution, and that all students were paying into it, that it was not right that any organization should have a barrier based on any real or perceived sexual orientation.

My buddy Mike Friedman and I got busy pretty quickly. We were elected co-presidents.... We changed the name to the Lesbian and Gay Illini....[111] We started by agitating against the chancellor and this particular policy governing registered student organizations, but what we quickly saw was that we needed a university-wide policy governing all employees and all students. So we doubled down, set our sights on that, and really opened a two and a half year campaign of constant agitation, with some really good mentorship from studied and experienced student organizers.[112]

Some of that mentorship came from historian Mary Lee Sargent, who was at the time teaching history and women's studies at nearby Parkland Community College.[113] Boerger credits Sargent for providing the activists' understanding of how to create change.

As an historian, she was able to explain to student activists, any time change is successful it's because there is constant pressure and action, both using the middle of the road, polite liberal tactics but also on a radical wing. Unless there is a radical wing, really pushing the envelope so that detractors can point to them and say those people are completely crazy, we're not going to give them what they want, then they default back to the more "reasonable" position taken by the liberal letter writers. But it's the radical fringe pushing that determines where the center can be.

Those were very convincing historical lessons for me, and that's why I made sure we were always working on both of those front, the respectable, liberal, proper channels.... I collected hundred and hundred and hundreds of names on petitions; I wrote editorials all over the place. I wrote letters. I did all the polite stuff you were supposed to do.

But at the same time, we were just outrageous, outrageously truthful and bold on the other end. And of course, that is way more fun, to have a kiss-in or to deface an administration building with a bunch of chalk in the middle of the night. When the cops come up and take your name down, and you say your name is "Mary Wollstonecraft," they ask you how to spell it. That is way more fun than sending a petition to your boring trustee member. But we did it all....

You have to have actors pushing within the system, and you have to have actors pushing [from] without. Neither faction can get anywhere without the other, and instead of blaming each other taking the wrong tactics, they need to be grateful to each other. That was a tremendous lesson, and I've never forgotten it.[114]

Prior to 1995, the trustees of the University of Illinois were elected directly by voters of the state. Albert N. Logan was a Democratic trustee from the South Side of Chicago, one of only two African-American trustees. Boerger developed a professional relationship with Logan; she, and the Gay and Lesbian Illini, actively and vocally supported his efforts to press the University to divest of its holdings in apartheid South Africa.[115]

These two black trustees who certainly had some kind of a consciousness about how money does or doesn't support systemic racism were grateful to those of us students who were activists for this cause. They came to understand that a lot of us were also queer or supportive of the queer movement on campus that Mike and I were spearheading.[116]

To Boerger, the University's appointment of a task force to study, in essence, what non-heterosexual students had been telling them for years was "ridiculous."

I saw it as a diversionary tactic and a huge postponement. I thought, the right thing to do is so obvious. Just do it. It was not even dignified to debate this. I was not going to get involved in [a] study [of] whether this is the right thing to do....

[University of Illinois President Stanley Ikenberry] did appoint a couple of people who I do consider allies, and they went ahead and did their work as best they could, because they may have seen that this is the way a university does something like this....

I think that despite any intentions [Ikenberry] might have had, some of the individuals on the task force gather important data and made some important recommendations. Nobody [in the administration] intended to follow those, and if we hadn't kept the heat on, they would have molded in the grave for another generation.

He never had any intention to provide leadership on this, and he never did. Eventually, we recognized the real fight was over his head, with the board of trustees. He was basically dodging it. I didn't have time for that shit; I was busy doing kiss-ins.[117]

Marching On

Spring of 1987 on the Illinois campus brought organized activism in support of "civil rights for homosexuals" on campus.[118] The deadline for the final report, December 19, 1986, had passed; Mary Ellen Shanesey, a health center counselor and chair of the task force, indicated the delay was because "Members of the task force asked for a delay to do a student survey in January."[119] Alan Ellis, a graduate student and task force member, stated the survey "was set up as a delay tactic."[120] The survey, reportedly, was distributed to 73 individuals, of whom 50 responded, although anonymous survey collection was ongoing; interested responders could contact Ellis for a survey.[121]

On January 30, 1987, an estimated 75 to 100 people marched from the Illini Union to the Swanlund Administration Building, at which campus police officers lined the hallways (Fig. 4.3). The protesters did not enter Swanlund, instead rallying in front of it. Boerger spoke to the crowd through a megaphone: "We want the university to know that we're disgusted with the way they've been handling the issue.... They've been giving us the runaround." Boerger stated at the time that the remedy for addressing the protest, and discrimination on campus, would be a short amendment to include sexual orientation in the University's non-discrimination statement. "Something of that order is all it would take."[122]

Dan Savage, the future sex opinion columnist, was a junior at Illinois and co-president of the GLI. The night before the march, he and Boerger received death threats.

(The caller) asked me if I was going to participate and then he asked me what kind of bullet I wanted. He said I was going to be shot if I marched.... If they think they can intimidate me and get me to stop demanding my rights, then they're wrong.... I'm tired of them. I just wish they'd grow up, get a life.[123]

No administrators met with the protesters. Chancellor Everhart was reportedly at lunch and did not see the protests. After the protest, the chancellor spoke with a reporter for the campus newspaper. "He said he wanted to get the view of all students before making a decision." Everhart

Fig. 4.3   Protesters at the University of Illinois, 1986. (Jean Lachat, copyright *Daily Illini*, courtesy of University of Illinois Archives, the University of Illinois) Student supporters of gay rights march in protest of the University's continued refusal to codify gay and lesbian protections on campus, January 30, 1987.

was quoted as saying "he would present the report to the board [of trustees] 'if appropriate,' and 'if it's a balanced report and if it's documented.'" Everhart also said, of those threatening GLI members with death, "That sort of harassment is unconscionable in a University such as ours." The harassers, whom he regarded as a few crazies, were "acting outside the bounds of accepted behavior. I'm very ashamed of them."[124] Of the protesters, Everhart said, "I think I understand their desire to have such a clause.... I'm waiting for the report of the task force and the survey."[125]

Daily Illini reporter Orrin Schwarz spoke with three passersby during the protest. One, Deborah Kupner, who was a junior in education, stated, "I'm a Christian and I don't think it's right.... It's biblically wrong. I feel for them. It's pretty sad." Arthur Greene was a town resident who was watching the march. "That's disgusting, isn't it?... This world is going down and that's part of the reason why. I think they're a bunch of insecure people."[126]

Another person who was perhaps insecure about gay and lesbian issues was University of Illinois President Stan Ikenberry. Kristina Boerger recalled the first time she met him, when he asked to meet with her at the president's house.

> He was getting really fatigued of my agitation, the group's agitation under my leadership.... He asked me basically to call off the dogs, to cut it out. That day I met him, he had sweat circles under his armpits that went all the way to his bottom rib. He was so nervous just to talk to me.
>
> I just laughed in his face and said, "No, I'm not gonna stop. Look, you know I'm a senior in college, but don't get excited, because if I graduate and this hasn't been accomplished, I'm just staying here, I am not leaving until this gets done.
>
> He was so pathetic as to actually, personally request me to stop. Like I was gonna stop? What do these stupid white boys think? That was really dumb.[127]

The Board of Trustees met on March 14, and its first order of business was to receive, formally, Ikenberry's letter of May 6. In that missive, Ikenberry outlined the policies concerning non-discrimination at the University of Illinois up to that point. In order to prevent further ongoing confusion, Ikenberry proposed formal policy from the Board to prohibit discrimination based on sexual orientation. The Board then heard from the GLI's Kristina Boerger, who formally presented the organization's "basic request" for the Board to explicitly make a statement ordering all university non-discrimination policies and statements reflect the University's prohibition of discrimination based on sexual orientation. In support of GLI's legal interpretation and need for this change, Jane Whicker, an attorney from the ACLU, spoke to the Board. After, according to the official minutes, a brief discussion, the Board voted unanimously to accept Ikenberry's letter and to grant GLI's request.[128]

By the end of March, however, the report was still not released and the Code of Campus Affairs remained unchanged. Indeed, the issue had still not been brought before the Board of Trustees. On March 26, Krista Boerger led a baker's dozen of protesters to one of Everhart's breakfasts with the chancellor meetings. The usual format for the meetings was for a student to speak to the chancellor about issues and questions, primarily a one-way form of communication from the students to the chancellor. "For the first half of the breakfast, members of the organization refused to talk to Everhart, mimicking the attention they believed they had been denied," according to GLI's spokesman Warren Taylor.

According to Taylor, "Everhart admitted the tactic was effective and asked for questions." George Danos, co-president of GLI, told a *Daily Illini* reporter that "he wanted to remind Everhart of the importance of civil rights to homosexuals and lesbians. He said once civil rights are gained, people will not be fearful to admit they support gay and lesbian rights." The student intern for the chancellor, who organized the series of breakfasts, complained that the GLI "monopolized the breakfast, which he said was unfair to other students" in the meeting.[129]

Eventually, 92 (self-)selected student and staff members "who admitted being homosexual" completed the survey,"[130] a random distribution collected results from another 1031 students and staff. The results confirmed what GLI members had stated: non-heterosexual students experienced overwhelming discrimination. Ninety-one percent feared being labeled non-heterosexual by others, two-thirds feared for their safety, and 88 percent feared being open about their sexual orientation would harm their chances for advancement at the University. Almost all had concealed their sexual orientation to avoid harassment, although over a third had experienced public ridicule in class.[131]

The data from the randomized survey was just as revealing. Eight percent knew of job discrimination on campus due to sexual orientation; ten percent witnessed personal harassment or verbal threats made to non-heterosexual campus members. Eighteen percent of the random sample respondents did not want to be a member of a group that had a non-heterosexual member, 29 percent were afraid to be alone with a homosexual, and 18 percent agreed that "All homosexuals should be locked up."[132]

Chancellor Everhart expressed that he was unaware of the extent of such problems. And, despite the homophobia reflected in the surveys, 74 percent of the randomized sample supported the University create a policy to counter discrimination based on sexual orientation, along with grievance procedures for such a policy.

The task force report was released on April 27, 1987. At the same time, Chancellor Everhart proposed changing the Code of Campus Affairs, the Academic Staff Handbook, the Campus Administrative Manual, and "other appropriate campus codes and guidelines."[133] Everhart recommended these changes only to the Urbana-Champaign campus, requiring only approval from campus constituent bodies, such as the Faculty Senate. The chancellor did not intend to propose the change to the Board of Trustees; consequently, the changes would not apply to the Chicago campus or the College of Medicine. Terry Cosgrove, GLI's political action director, deemed the proposal "very limited in scope"; Dan Savage, who had been a member of the chancellor's task force, called Everhart's action "a very half-assed thing."[134]

Nonetheless, Everhart's proposal added sexual orientation to the list of prohibited factors of discrimination, including "race, color, sex, religious or political beliefs, age and handicap."[135] In addition, Everhart wanted a chancellor's council to combat discrimination to be formed, to advise his office on responding to all aspects of discrimination on campus.

Everhart told a reporter for the *Daily Illini*,

> I'm sorry it took as long as it did.... I think the campus community owes (the task force) a vote of gratitude.... I think it takes a long time to change people's attitudes in an area like this. But this is a step, I hope an important step in the right direction.[136]

The University of Illinois became the seventh Big Ten university to add protections for non-heterosexuals. But the controversy was not over.

April 28, 1987—the day after the task force report and the chancellor's statement—University President Stanley Ikenberry stated that the University Board of Trustees would not be presented with a policy to prohibit sexual orientation discrimination. Calling Everhart's statements "basically an elaboration of the existing University policy," Ikenberry declared that a 1978 board resolution already protected non-heterosexuals on campus. Written in response to the U.S. Supreme Court decision in *Regents of the Univ. of Cal. V. Bakke* (438 U.S. 265), the resolution proclaimed that the University was committed to "eradicate prohibited... discrimination in all its forms, foster programs within the law which will eliminate, and comply fully... with applicable federal and state laws relating to nondiscrimination."[137]

Unsurprisingly, the GLI were not confident, given the data at hand, that the University would do so. George Danos, a GLI co-president, stated that "the chancellor's proposal [was] good interim... coverage must come from the trustees." The chancellor's policy could be overturned by another administration, as well as "lack[ing] breadth and depth" over the entirety of the University. Further, "Why if (the 1978 policy) is sufficient, did Everhart come up with his proposal?"[138]

In May of 1987, GLI, buoyed by their progress, petitioned the Board to adopt "a policy prohibiting discrimination based on sexual orientation that would affect all University campuses."[139] GLI's position was that such a policy would make permanent the Board's March vote, rather than simply a ratification of a presidential order.

Terry Cosgrove, an Illinois graduate student and GLI's political action coordinator, stated to the *Daily Illini* that the presidential order was a step of a five-year goal, as outlined in the task force report, for the creation of a university policy specifically prohibiting discrimination based on sexual orientation. The first step was completed by Chancellor Everhart adding to the Code of Campus Affairs a clause that prohibited discrimination of homosexuals; Chancellor Ikenberry's "clarification" of university codes and guidelines was another.[140] Ikenberry and the GLI made presentations for such a change at the Board meeting in May.

The GLI met with both success and stymie at the Board's June, 1987, meeting, where the Board voted to add the following, rather specific statement, to the University's Code of Campus Affairs, Academic Staff Handbook, and Campus Administrative Manual:

> All individuals enrolled at or employed by this campus shall be entitled to freedom from invidious discrimination and harassment, whether or not prohibited by law, regardless of their race, color, sex, sexual orientation, religious or political beliefs, age or handicap, except as specifically exempted by law. It is university policy to comply fully with federal laws. Existing campus complaint and grievance procedures may be used when discrimination or harassment in any of these categories is perceived to have occurred.[141]

In addition, the trustees voted unanimously to change the language of its policy of non-discrimination to extend "to foster programs within the law which will ameliorate or eliminate, where possible, the effects of historic societal discrimination" while complying fully "in all university activities and programs with applicable federal and state laws relating to non-discrimination and equal opportunity."[142]

The trustees stopped short, however, of enacting a university policy specifically enumerating protections for non-heterosexual students. Threading a political needle, Ikenberry and the trustees seemed to be attempting to foster change incrementally, without having the University seem to endorse homosexuality. Neither the president nor the Board was willing to specify any of those groups that might have been prey to "historical societal discrimination," apparently finding a difference between a campus statement and a university policy, a difference which could give them personal and political "cover" should public blowback occur. Trustee Albert Logan made a motion to specify who was covered by the policy, but his motion failed; President Ikenberry stated being "concerned that any modification, no matter how well intentioned, if it is made explicit for one group, has the effect of weakening it [the policy] for all others."[143] Dissatisfied and stymied in their efforts again, the GLI members attending walked out prior to the meeting's conclusion, "chanting 'We will be back.'"[144]

By the fall of 1989, media coverage of GLI reflected the group's change in ideation: no longer was "gay," as an identity, seen to be one in opposition to a normative heterosexual society, but rather as one of many social identities that comprised American society. On November 3, 1989, the *Daily Illini* reported on a panel discussion the night before, sponsored by Interracial, "the minority student organization," and led by members of GLI, that stressed their identification as a distinct minority of the population deserving of recognition as such. In the words of reporter Jessica Goldbogen, "The discussion was intended to show that homosexuals are another minority."[145]

In the words of Chris Martin, a senior majoring in engineering, "It's a hidden minority, because you can't always tell...." Martin also outlined four forms of discrimination experienced by gay students: physical abuse, verbal abuse, verbal discrimination, and non-verbal discrimination. Additionally, Martin and his co-presenter Ben Madamba, a senior in liberal arts, noted social stigmas that inhibit gay students from showing expression in public.[146]

None of these pieces of information were novel or unique, but the contextualization of them was. By positing the forms of discrimination as actions done upon non-heterosexuals by heterosexuals, rather than as responses of non-heterosexuals because of society in general, ideological and structural connections between the non-heterosexuals and racial minority groups became apparent. Once the connection was made clear, the equivalency of their status as minority became a political and social tactic.

UNIVERSITY OF MICHIGAN, 1984–1989

During the mid-1980s, the University of Michigan Board of Regents still refused to amend Bylaw 14.06. Democratic regent Paul Brown conveyed perhaps the most liberal of the Regents' attitudes: "I don't think we can start including in our non-discrimination policy every group that feels they are being discriminated against."[147] The matter was not simply a moral or ethical dilemma for the Regents; if they granted protective status to "every group," what would it cost the University—and what would it cost the Regents, in terms of political capital?

Carol Wayman matriculated to the University of Michigan in 1984. While she did not self-identify as lesbian when she arrived, she soon came to realize that identity (Fig. 4.4). In an interview in 1987, she remembered students in the dorm yelling at her,

> "Hey Lesbian!" "I walked up to them and said, 'Oh, hi, are you gay, too? Have you heard of the lesbian/gay support group...?'" They didn't know what to do... they don't expect that, they want you to be really hostile." Despite the jeer, she indicated that the slur "didn't really offend me... it was like yelling, "Hey, straight person.'"[148]

Fig. 4.4 Carol Wayman of the University of Michigan's LaGROC, circa 1985. (Courtesy of Carol Wayman)

Carol Wayman was the founder of the second iteration of LaGROC at the University of Michigan. Wayman's political style utilized brazen public confrontations to draw awareness to issues non-heterosexual students faced, which often served to shame the administration.

Seeking personal connections, she first gathered a group of friends in her dormitory, Bursley Hall, on the far north side of campus. "I created a lesbian group; it was more of a social group."[149] As a consequence, "...she started finding messages such as 'fucking lesbians' written on her [dorm] room door."[150]

Soon, however, she expanded beyond her dorm.

> There was a fair amount of anti-gay violence and harassment, professor saying inappropriate things.... I realized we needed more political approaches [to] things on campus. There was no LGBT visibility.... It felt like we didn't have a way to communicate or share our opinions or speak out about things.[151]

Wayman, along with her girlfriend at the time, Alicia Lucksted, and other students, created a new iteration of LaGROC. This time, the organization's acronym came to stand for Lesbian and Gay Rights Organizing Committee.

In that 1987 interview, she stated one of the goals for LaGROC: "We want people to realize that you don't have to be heterosexual" to live a normal life. Wayman said, "We want them to say, 'It's OK to be gay, and we'll protect you.'"[152] Wendy Sharp, Michigan Student Assembly (MSA) vice president, was a member of LaGROC. "She's great at making people feel comfortable in a very uncomfortable situation.[153]"

Wayman's memory of the time confirms reporting in *The Michigan Daily* of the time: approximately 30 people were "regular" members of the organization. Chief among their goals was changing the campus climate, which was hostile to gays and lesbians, from the administration to on-campus housing, from the campus police to the social spots of Ann Arbor.

One of the most personally transformative experiences for the students in LaGROC and their allied student organizations was the initial "Integration Night" in November of 1987. According to *The Michigan Daily*, 77 members and spectators participated in the event, and "Wayman said that the purpose of the Integration Night was to demonstrate how homosexuals are discouraged from displaying affection publicly."[154]

Wayman recalled in 2018 the impetus for the event was in part to demonstrate the solidarity between LaGROC and other student anti-discrimination groups and in part to include very visible non-heterosexuals in heterosexual social environments.

> Almost everybody in LaGROC was white.... We were trying to ally with a pretty strong anti-racism group, UCAR [United Coalition Against Racism], that had been building around the time we were building [LaGROC]. When they would have protests against join them....
>
> We wanted to show that gay people could be anywhere, we should be allowed to go to a [straight] club. UCAR went along with it; "We want to help you." [So] we did what we called an "integration...."[155]

For the first event, she chose Dooley's, a basement sports bar in Ann Arbor popular with campus jocks, as well as fraternity and sorority members.

> We went on a frat night. We all had lambda t-shirts that I ordered. We synchronized our watches. At a certain time, everybody started dancing [as] same-sex couples. We said we'd do this for 20 minutes, half an hour, and then we'd go back to the Union and talk about it.[156]

At the appointed time, the UCAR and LaGROC members switched from mixed-gender dancing couples to same-gender couples. At first, the disc jockey refused to play any slow songs; almost immediately, the straight crowd threatened violence.[157]

> It was really scary. When we did it, some of the women I knew were kissing on the floor; some of the women were UCAR women, dancing with UCAR women; the guys dancing together were straight, UCAR guys.
>
> The vitriol – I still remember this woman's face, just screaming at me, these vicious anti-gay slurs. I thought, It's probably what a lynching audience looks like. These are people here, who are at college with me.[158]

The event prompted greater empathy and solidarity from their straight allies than Wayman anticipated.

> We went back to the cafeteria, and [this one] UCAR guy, who had not really been pro-gay – he was trying, he was doing this – he was straight, and a big guy. He was really shaken. He was, like, "Wow, I did not expect that to happen."
>
> I don't think we ever did something like that at a straight bar again, although we did go to restaurants. I remember going up the stairs. There were bats and things on the wall, hockey sticks. I remember thinking I should have done better reconnaissance, because if someone pulls one of the things off the walls and beats us, somebody's going to get really hurt. I should have picked a bar without sports equipment on the walls.[159]

Virginia Nordby

Virginia Nordby was the director of the Office of Affirmative Action at the University of Michigan. One of the highest-ranking women in the University of Michigan's administration, Nordby was tasked with representing the University in dealing with LaGROC in their efforts to change the University's bylaws and non-discrimination statements. Carol Wayman recalled Nordby "just seemed incredibly uncomfortable with gay people and incredibly uncomfortable with the issue."[160]

In November of 1987, Nordby and LaGROC entered into a public disagreement about the outcome of a meeting they had had regarding potential changes to university policies. Alicia Lucksted, representing LaGROC, quoted Nordby to the campus newspaper as saying she would "strongly support" adding sexual orientation to the University's Affirmative Action "logo" (really a statement included on all official materials).[161] Lucksted further claimed that Nordby "promised... to ask President Harold Shapiro to take steps against discrimination based on sexual orientation."

Nordby, however, stated that amending the logo was a "dead issue," since only the Board of Regents had the authority to amend it. Nordby had a point: the Regents had not even been receptive to a non-discrimination statement. Further,

> Nordby... said she refused to endorse an anti-gay and lesbian bigotry poster campaign specifically, leaving the method of promotion open. "The word 'advocate' is not appropriate, but I am going to be making recommendations (to Shapiro) along these lines."[162]

Shapiro, for his part, refused to comment to the newspaper until he had spoken to Nordby.

Carol Wayman recalled feeling during this time that "...they [the University of Michigan administration] felt they didn't need to do anything to support gay or lesbian students."[163] She had reason to feel that way, along with reason to doubt the sincerity of what Nordby told the press. During the interview about the discrepancy between what LaGROC and Nordby were reporting from their meeting, Nordby told a *Michigan Daily* reporter that the Affirmative Action Office's campaign against sexual harassment had included protections for gay and lesbians, but as the reporter pointed out "... posters already in existence say nothing about sexual preference."[164]

On November 17, 1987, the University of Michigan student government unanimously passed a resolution for the University to change its bylaws and non-discrimination "logo" to include gays and lesbians as a protected category. One MSA member stated, "It is clearly a homophobic attitude being expressed by the administration"; in addition, the resolution called the administration's attitude "heterosexist." Another MSA representative declared, "This is one group that has made demands last spring and has not received the kind of attention and concern they deserve."[165]

As a consequence of what LaGROC's members must have felt was Nordby's shifting position, if not outright two-faced behavior, LaGROC decided to occupy her office. They brought along journalists, in an attempt to record precisely what Nordby's intentions were toward supporting non-heterosexual rights on campus, as well as the actions Nordby intended to take to ensure those rights (Fig. 4.5).

Given the difference of memory over the outcomes of their prior meeting with Nordby, LaGROC requested a written response to their concerns from Nordby. They waited as she wrote the memo. In her responses, Nordby indicated clearly that she supported changing the non-discrimination "logo," developing posters for campus that would indicate methods of redress for those experiencing discrimination, and including the topic in orientation meetings. She tried to assure the students: "I will carry this concern to President Fleming."[166]

Robben Fleming was to return to serve as interim president in January. LaGROC feared that he might choose to rescind Shapiro's presidential policy, which was the only protection they felt they had on campus. When the protesters in her office asked why she would not support changing the university bylaws, which they viewed would give them stronger protection, Nordby simply said, "I am not at liberty to discuss changes in the bylaws."[167]

In their naïvety about how power worked in institutions of higher education, the students believed she had agency to match her titular authority. In photos from the sit-in, Nordby looks on at the protesters in her office, her face in her hand, listening again to their repeated needs and demands. To me, she seems skeptical and put out.[168]

Carol Wayman reflected on the occupation 30 years later.

> I think the sit-in was good, because we weren't getting anywhere.... It was pretty clear if you want something changed, you have to target the people who have the power to change it. She and the Administration had the power to change it, so that's what we did.[169]

Fig. 4.5 LaGROC occupies Virginia Nordby's office at the University of Michigan, 1984. (*The Michigan Daily*, The Michigan Daily Digital Archives, Bentley Historical Library, The University of Michigan)

LaGROC occupies the office of the University of Michigan's director of Affirmative Action, Virginia Nordby, whose back is to the viewer in this photo. Nordby and LaGROC had publicly contradicted each other over the understood outcomes of a meeting about enacting protections for non-heterosexuals on campus. To ensure a greater understanding, LaGROC decided to visit Nordby, bringing along the press, to ensure a record of the conversation. Carol Wayman is on the left side of the photo, second from the top.

Nordby in reality probably did not have the power to make the changes the students thought she did. In the hierarchy of the University, she was doubtless only empowered to follow legal instructions and/or to implement policy decisions made by the president or the regents. I believe her comments when she stated that the changes sought by LaGROC were out of her purview. I am uncertain, though, how strongly—or how well—she attempted to persuade those above her, who perhaps thought she was doing too much to encourage or to accommodate non-heterosexual student agitators.

As Nordby appeared unable or unwilling to advocate for a bylaw change, LaGROC took their argument to the offices of the administrators LaGROC deemed more able. LaGROC went over Nordby's head, literally—the Office of Affirmative Action was in the basement of the administration building, while the president's offices were on the second floor.

Increasing Pressure

As 1988 dawned, Michigan Regent Deane Baker again was complaining of gays on campus; specifically, he was requesting the University investigate "homosexual activity" in the men's room in the basement of Mason Hall, a classroom building. At their January meeting, the Michigan Regents again voted seven to zero not to change Bylaw 14.06. Regent Thomas Roach stated his reasoning: such a change would force the University to cut ties with any organizations that banned gays and lesbians. "We don't want to get bogged down in that quagmire of 'Let's cancel all government action."[170] Instead, the Regents voted to endorse, finally, the presidential policy statement made by Harold Shapiro in 1984.[171] No action was taken on the other initiatives LaGROC discussed with Nordby. Instead, it was Regent Baker's ongoing attempts to ferret out non-heterosexuals.

In response, over 30 LaGROC members—and one parent—assembled on the second floor of the Fleming Administration Building on January 22, from 9:30 a.m. until 5:00 p.m. The assemblers took turns "guarding" the men's restrooms outside of President Shapiro's office suite; those not in the johns were in the halls, in a sit-in protest.[172]

Members of the group met with Robert Holmes, Assistant Vice President for Academic Affairs, and Henry Johnson, Vice President for Student Services.[173] Johnson expressed his belief that student protests to prompt institutional change for treatment of non-heterosexuals on campus were inappropriate as well as ineffective. He recommended students file individual grievances through the University and the civil courts.[174] *The Michigan Daily* summarized his advice to the protesters: "Demonstrations such as the sit-in 'dramatize the felt urgency of the problems, but those problems are resolved in the courts,' he said."[175]

Robert Holmes answered questions from the protesters. He said he would relay LaGROC's concerns to other administrators (including Fleming, who was out of town), but he declined to say if he would recommend a bylaw change.[176]

Alicia Lucksted, a LaGROC leader, stated the objective of the bath-room occupation. "The protest is basically to point out how ludicrous Regent Deane Baker's request was.... We object to him equating our struggle for equal rights with sex in public bathrooms." As Wayman recalled,

> It was just outrageous. We're bringing real issues of discrimination, vio-lence, and harassment. Around that time, I was getting threats on the phone. We had a LaGROC office at the Student Union; people would write "Die Fag." Every time I reported something, I got harassed more by the police.[177]

Baker was nonplused by the protest: "It seems to me they should support such an investigation calling attention to the need to enforce the laws of the state of Michigan."[178]

Wayland recalled that particular protest as effective.

> My mom came in, drove in from Cleveland. She wore a really nice pants suit, and brought her needlepoint. She was just sitting by the men's urinals, doing needlepoint.... The administration was surprised there was a parent there. That seemed to make them pay more attention.... I think we stayed for a few hours.[179]

LaGROC used the restroom occupation to call, again, for the regents to amend its bylaws to include gays and lesbians as a protected minority on campus. At the same regents meeting that Baker had called for investigat-ing tearoom sex on campus, the Board of Regents had finally, four years after then President Shapiro proffered it, voted to endorse the presidential policy of 1984. This act was seen by some as "a sign of its commitment to protecting gay rights on campus."[180] Interim President Robben Fleming had drafted an anti-discrimination policy to protect non-heterosexual stu-dents from harassment, but LaGROC viewed both "too weak." LaGROC believed that a change in the bylaws would provide a stronger statement of support and better protection of their rights on campus.[181]

Like many of the protests and events of both iterations of LaGROC, irony placed a prime role in pointing out the discrepancy between the lived experiences of straight and non-heterosexual students. Wayman reflected that there was no particular analytic strategy to their style of pro-tests. "We were just young and being outlandish. It was a really good group of people I worked with."[182] Perhaps the irony was unintentional, but it brought attention to the issue and called into question why the actions seemed so audacious.

The continued lack of response from the administration, coupled with a curtailment of student rights, prompted more direct action from LaGROC. The story is complex, involving internecine struggles between students and administrators at the University of Michigan. Interim President Robben Fleming, in a purported attempt to curb campus discrimination, had proposed a revised student code of conduct. Fleming had asked for the Regents' approval of such changes at their January meeting, citing his right to do so through Regental Bylaw 2.01, which granted Michigan's president "power to promote the 'maintenance of health, diligence, and order among the students.'"[183]

Invoking Bylaw 2.01 allowed Fleming to bypass formal channels of approval for student non-academic conduct.[184] Student leaders from across the Michigan campus saw the revision to code as an attempt to curb dissenting speech without student input; the purpose, to them, was clearly to stifle student voices, particularly as administrators and faculty were not covered by similar codes.[185] In addition, Fleming threatened to cut funding and appoint professional staff to be in charge of *The Michigan Daily* and the Campus Broadcasting Network, in order to have more control over what was presented to the public.[186]

Michigan's student government association, the MSA, blasted what they viewed as strong-armed attempts to squelch student rights. The president of the student body (as well as the MSA), Mike Phillips, stated, "The administration doesn't care about students anymore. They did in the first place."[187]

On April 14 and 15, 1988, LaGROC joined an effort, organized by Michigan's student government association, to protest the new code and to demand its repeal. Students disrupted the Regents' meeting on Thursday, entering the room with picket signs and chanting, "Hey hey, ho ho, Fleming has got to go"; the meeting was forced to be relocated to a more secure location on the second floor.[188] A group protested on the Diag on campus during the first day of the Regents' monthly meeting, a group occupied the administration building overnight,[189] and 60 gathered at 9:30 Thursday night to protest in front of Fleming's house on campus.[190] About 40 protesters disrupted the Regents' meeting and occupied the bottom floor of the administration building.

Fleming and Regent Deane Baker exited the closed-session Regents' meeting together. Baker told the protesters, "Don't blame the president (for the policy). The regents vote; the regents run the University."[191]

Perhaps coincidentally, Virginia Nordby was appointed at the April 1988 Board of Regents meeting to become the University's vice president for governmental relations.[192]

Physical Attacks

The summer of 1988 was hotter than normal in Ann Arbor; the gay and lesbian campus community's temper was almost as hot over what they viewed as a continuing disregard for their rights—and their physical safety. On July 26, a woman leaving one of the "gay nights" held at the Nectarine Ballroom was assaulted by a man who called her "lesbian." He tore off her sweater and hit her in the head. After similar assaults—and lack of what was felt appropriate police responses—the members of LaGROC, along with the gay and lesbian community in Ann Arbor, had had enough.

On August 9, somewhere between 150 and 300 "vociferous," self-described "concerned and angry citizens" rallied in response to the July 26 assault.[193] Shouting chants such as "Two, four, six, eight, Ann Arbor cops discriminate," the protesters marched from the Nectarine Ballroom down Maynard Street, through the Nickels Arcade shopping center, past Tower Plaza (site of the July 26 assault), ending in front of the Ann Arbor City Hall, where they were met by the chief of police. At the rally in front of the police station, witnesses to the July assault also complained that police were insensitive.[194] Michigan graduate student Patti Myers declared, "We will not tolerate having our rights violated because we are lesbian, because we are gay."[195]

As an outcome of that rally, members of LaGROC and the community formed an "Anti-Violence and Discrimination Task Force" to address the issue of anti-gay violence in Ann Arbor. The task force met with Ann Arbor Police Chief William Corbett, who indicated he understood their concerns and "agreed then to try to relieve them."[196]

The hot weather continued into the fall, and so did the harassment of gays and lesbians around Ann Arbor. In November, LaGROC established a "Community Defense Watch" (CDW) for gay nights at the Nectarine Ballroom. LaGROC released a statement to the public, announcing their CDW.

> The CDW will provide protection and an escort to people concerned for their safety, a visible presence which will deter attacks from happening in the first place, and rescue victims of assaults. There will also be a group of people outside the Nectarine to witness and photograph any violence which does

occur. It is hoped that photographic evidence and witnesses will be enough to force the police to arrest gay bashers.[197]

LaGROC's Linda Kurtz, who had been one of the organizers of the August demonstration, served as spokesperson for the CDW. She criticized the Ann Arbor police force in the campus newspaper.

> The fact is, the police are, in general, only interested in stopping assaults against white, presumably heterosexual men and women. In at least three instances in which lesbians and gay men have been verbally or physically attacked, the police have refused to go in pursuit of their attackers.[198]

The deputy police chief for Ann Arbor conceded that police offers had perhaps not acted in as "caring and empathetic" a manner as they should have over the summer, but denied not pursuing attackers.

It would seem that in 1988 being identified (rightly or wrongly) in a public space presumed to be for non-heterosexuals was as physically dangerous as being in places that had not. LaGROC conducted a number of public activities that simultaneously brought non-heterosexuals to the public's attention while potentially putting themselves at risk.

Queering Michigan

One visibility strategy popular in the late 1980s and early 1990s involved "being" gay or lesbian in traditionally heterosexual spaces, such as restaurants or shopping centers. Inspired in part by the tradition of civil rights sit-ins as much as ACT UP and Queer Nation strategies, non-heterosexual students would be conspicuous in their personal interactions in public spaces.

LaGROC sponsored such events. The meeting minutes from May 17, 1988, note the group's reflections on "Shopping Day" the previous weekend. "About 12" members went to Briarwood Mall on May 14.

> ...we got stared at by dumb-founded straight weekend shoppers who never expected gay people to patronize *their* shopping mall. According to Blane, the women were a lot more affectionate.

Brainstorming ideas for future public events,

Blane suggested that we all break down our own **homophobia** and try to do more PDA.[199]

Students like Blane were soon to have their wish, as campus gay and lesbian organizations (such as the KU, Iowa State University, and the University of Minnesota) began sponsoring "kiss-ins," a throwback to a Gay Liberation Movement strategy, where same-gendered couples kissed each other in highly trafficked areas of campus. Kiss-ins were in use at Michigan through the early 1990s.[200]

Earlier campus gay and lesbian organizations had utilized public displays to demonstrate that non-heterosexuals were on campus, including marches on the University of Michigan campus in which members wore paper bags over their heads. These newer forms of public display, however, were intended not just to show non-heterosexual students on campus but also to challenge social norms that delimited what was deemed acceptable for gays to do on campus. Gone were the strategies of hiding and concealment while protesting; in their place were those protest actions that matched (unquestioned) straight behaviors on campus.

In October of 1989, as part of National Coming Out Day events on campus, LaGROC presented nine demands to the administration.[201] The group had intended to give the list to new Michigan President James Duderstadt; he was out of town, so LaGROC settled for Charles Moody, the Vice Provost for Minority Affairs. LaGROC believed their demands would fit into the spirit, as well as the actual goal, of Duderstadt's "Michigan Mandate," a plan for advancing minority representation at the University. Not including non-heterosexuals in the plan "shows that the University does not take us seriously...," said Patricia Bach, a LaGROC spokesperson.[202]

LaGROC's full list of demands was printed in full in *The Michigan Daily*.

1. Change Bylaw 14.02 to include "sexual orientation."
2. Offer regular courses in lesbian and gay studies, leading toward the development of an academic department.
3. Creating mandatory courses on racism and sexism, including heterosexism.
4. Improve the library's holdings of non-heterosexual works and topics.

5. Establishing a lounge or community space for non-heterosexuals, which could eventually become a resource center.
6. Reform the University's housing policies.
7. Include "sexual orientation" in the Michigan Mandate.
8. Appoint an openly gay member to the university's AIDS Task Force.
9. Declare October 11 to be an annual Coming Out Day at the university.[203]

Other National Coming Out Day events included a rally during the noon hour, which drew 150 people.[204] According to Bach, it was intended "to make the University aware that gay people exist, to empower gay people and allow them to see that more exist and to make the demands to the university."[205] In addition to making speeches and displaying hand-painted signs encouraging coming out, members of LaGROC staged a skit on the steps of the Graduate Library to allow students to come out of the closet—a small structure with a door, in which a student would stand and then exit. LaGROC member Linda Kurtz declared the activity a success: "It was good, powerful, empowering for the people there to come out on the steps of the Grad."[206]

Ohio State University, 1982–1989

The experiences at the non-heterosexual student group at Ohio State University (OSU) were similar to those of other large, Midwest state universities. The group changed its name frequently during the decade—from the Gay Alliance (GA), later to be renamed Gay and Lesbian Association (GALA) and Bisexual, Gay and Lesbian Association (B-GALA)—representing how college non-heterosexual groups across the country became more aware of and more inclusive to multiple forms of non-heterosexual identity.

Throughout the decade, the group offered a variety of services, programs, and special events. In 1982, for instance, the student volunteers of the GA staffed their campus office an average of 35.5 hours per week in 1982 and 38 hours per week in 1983. During those hours, they answered 6078 questions (in person or via phone) in 1982 and 6010 in 1983.[207]

Still, the campus conservatism of the later 1970s held sway at OSU. Gay Awareness Week, for instance, focused on showing films on campus, as well as presentations about gay rights from the dean of students and a law professor. The GA advertisements for the "week" also invited persons to join the group at a "Disco and Party" at an off-campus bar, on the first and second Fridays of May 1981.[208]

In 1981, the GA was headed by a three-person "council," elected by its member: Brian Knedler, Larry Sims, and Jerry Mallicoat. By the fall quarter of 1990, the organization had adopted a more traditional leadership structure. Thomas Fletcher was president, Amy Price and Michael Scarce co-vice presidents, Marc Conte treasurer, and Skip Myers secretary.[209]

Tom Fletcher was a sophomore at Ohio State University in 1989 and newly elected as the president of GALA. Still balancing between the Columbus community and the university campus, GALA had selected new officers, including Fletcher, who, he indicated, had "a more positive approach to homosexuality," focusing "on issues gays should think about, like AIDS, relationships and a positive attitude."[210]

In a profile of him in the campus newspaper in November of 1989, Fletcher credited his parents for the courage of his convictions.

> "I got the strong conviction through my parents that I'm always as good as anyone else and I should stand up for what I believe in.... If you stand by your principles, eventually, even if you don't get what you want, at least there is the satisfaction of knowing you're doing what is right." Still, he noted the harassment he experienced: "In other organizations, there is no association [in people's minds] linking you to it."[211]

The 19-year-old echoed standard sentiments of building self-worth within the student membership—and assimilation of gays and lesbians into the existing collegiate and national cultures. "Gays are people you hear about. They need to be shown as ordinary people, and then the stereotypes would go."[212] Among his plans for GALA included more outreach for lesbian involvement and an increase in the membership's understanding of the politics of the time. Fletcher stated that "[b]eing politically minded in my mind means you stand up for your rights, and you fight for what you deserve. I don't think it necessarily means marching in the streets."[213]

By May of 1990, Fetcher's convictions led him—and he led others—to march the sidewalks and streets.

NOTES

1. See Robert A. Rhoads, *Freedom's Web: Student Activism in an Age of Cultural Diversity* (Baltimore, MD: Johns Hopkins University Press, 1998), and Helen Lefkowitz Horowitz, *Campus Life: Undergraduate Cultures from the End of the Eighteenth Century to the Present* (New York: Alfred A. Knopf, 1987).

2. Student Affairs – Programs and Services, Office of the Dean of Students – Office for Lesbian, Gay, Bisexual, and Transgender Concerns, 1942–2014, 41/2/46, Box 1, University of Illinois Archives, University Library, University of Illinois at Urbana-Champaign.

3. University of Illinois Archives, Student and Faculty Organizations, Constitutions & Registration Cards, 1909–2002, Series 41/2/41, Box 10. Note: all registration information for this organization comes from this file. Also, I was unable to locate in that file the forms between 1979 and 1982.

4. University of Illinois Archives, Student Affairs, Programs and Services, Offices of Lesbian, Gay, Bisexual and Transgender Concerns, 1942–2014, 41/2/46, Box 1, Gay Illini.

5. University of Illinois Archives, Student and Faculty Organizations, Constitutions & Registration Cards, 1909–2002, Series 41/2/41, Box 10.

6. James W. Toy Papers, James W. Toy Papers, Box 17, Folder: Michigan Gay Undergrads, Bentley Historical Library, University of Michigan.

7. "Ann Arbor Lesbian-Gay Pride Week '81 Tentative Schedule of Events 20–28 June," undated. James W. Toy Papers, James W. Toy Papers, Box 17, Folder: Michigan Gay Undergrads, Bentley Historical Library, University of Michigan.

8. "Ann Arbor Lesbian-Gay Pride Week '81 Tentative Schedule of Events 20–28 June," undated; James W. Toy Papers, James W. Toy Papers, Box 17, Folder: Michigan Gay Undergrads, Bentley Historical Library, University of Michigan.

9. "Ann Arbor Lesbian-Gay Pride Week '81 Tentative Schedule of Events 20–28 June," undated; James W. Toy Papers, James W. Toy Papers, Box 17, Folder: Michigan Gay Undergrads, Bentley Historical Library, University of Michigan.

10. Michigan Gay Undergraduate Membership Form, James W. Toy Papers, Box 17, Folder: Michigan Gay Undergrads, Bentley Historical Library, University of Michigan.

11. Michigan Gay Undergraduate Membership Form, James W. Toy Papers, Box 17, Folder: Michigan Gay Undergrads, Bentley Historical Library, University of Michigan.

12. Jackie Young, "Campus Gays Come Out Politically," *The Michigan Daily*, September 3, 1983, 1, 2: 1.
13. Jackie Young, "Gay Rights Backers Rally Against Anti-gay Bias," *The Michigan Daily*, August 9, 1983, 1, 3–4, 3.
14. Young, "Gay Rights Backers Rally Against Anti-gay Bias," 3.
15. Young, "Gay Rights Backers Rally Against Anti-gay Bias," 3.
16. Young, "Gay Rights Backers Rally Against Anti-gay Bias," 3.
17. Young, "Gay Rights Backers Rally Against Anti-gay Bias," 4.
18. "A History of LaGROC," draft, undated but after 1987. Bentley Historical Library, University of Michigan. James Toy Papers, Box 16, Lesbian and Gay Rights on Campus (LaGROC).
19. "A History of LaGROC."
20. Young, "Gay Rights Backers Rally Against Anti-gay Bias," 1.
21. Young, "Gay Rights Backers Rally Against Anti-gay Bias," 1.
22. Rachel Gottlieb, "Shapiro Aggravates Gays," *The Michigan Daily*, March 15, 1984, 1, 2: 2.
23. Gottlieb, "Shapiro Aggravates Gays."
24. Jonathan [Ellis?], letter to Jim [Toy], July 5, 1983. Bentley Historical Library, University of Michigan, James W. Toy Papers, Box 16, Folder: LaGROC, Correspondence, 1983–1988.
25. Barbara Misle, "Hundreds Come to Share Hal's Donuts and Cider," *The Michigan Daily*, September 30, 1983, 1, 9.
26. Misle, "Hundreds Come to Share Hal's Donuts and Cider," 9.
27. Misle, "Hundreds Come to Share Hal's Donuts and Cider," 9.
28. Misle, "Hundreds Come to Share Hal's Donuts and Cider," 9.
29. Georgea Kovanis, "Gays Call for Action," *The Michigan Daily*, March 2, 1984, 1, 3: 3.
30. Kovanis, "Gays Call for Action."
31. "Gay Rights Protest (photo)," *Ann Arbor News*, March 10, 1984, A4; Sharon Silbar, "Gay Activists Protest Silently Before Visiting Shapiro's Office," *The Michigan Daily*, March 10, 1984, 1.
32. Silbar, "Gay Activists Protest Silently Before Visiting Shapiro's Office."
33. Silbar, "Gay Activists Protest Silently Before Visiting Shapiro's Office."
34. "Gay Rights Protest (photo)."
35. Silbar, "Gay Activists Protest Silently Before Visiting Shapiro's Office."
36. Georgia Kovanis, "Shapiro Issues Policy Shielding Gays," *The Michigan Daily*, March 13, 1984, 1, 5: 1.
37. Kovanis, "Shapiro Issues Policy Shielding Gays."
38. Kovanis, "Shapiro Issues Policy Shielding Gays."
39. Rachel Gottlieb, "Shapiro Aggravates Gays," *The Michigan Daily*, March 15, 1984, 1, 2: 2.
40. Gottlieb, "Shapiro Aggravates Gays."

41. "President Shapiro Issues 'U' Policy Statement" handout, undated. Bentley Historical Library, University of Michigan, James W. Toy Papers, Box 16, Folder: LaGROC, Correspondence, 1983–1988.

42. LaGROC, "Op-ed: Non-discrimination Policy Takes Effect," *The Michigan Daily*, March 22, 1984, 4.

43. Mary Saxton, "GLSOK Fighting for Classification as Minority," *University Daily Kansan*, February 20, 1984, 3.

44. Tad Clarke, "Lichtwardt Has Dream of Equal Rights for Homosexuals," *University Daily Kansan*, April 10, 1985, 1, 5.

45. Saxton, "GLSOK Fighting for Classification as Minority," 3.

46. Mary Sexton, "Committee Defines 'Minority,'" *University Daily Kansan*, March 1, 1984, 6.

47. Cindy Holm, "GLSOK Says Senate Panel Shows Bias," *University Daily Kansan*, February 14, 1984, 1.

48. Mary Sexton and Cindy Holm, "Senate Committee May Ask Groups to List Members," *University Daily Kansan*, March 23, 1984, 1, 5: 1.

49. Cindy Holm, "Senators Vote Not to Finance Gay Services," *University Daily Kansan*, April 11, 1984, 1; Mary Sexton, "GLSOK Did Not Expect Budget Cutoff," April 12, 1984, 1.

50. Partly this was due to non-heterosexuals having more social outlets in the 1980s, such as bars, in Lawrence. For more, see Patrick Dilley, *Queer Man on Campus: A History of Non-Heterosexual Men in College, 1945–2000.* (New York: Routledge Falmer, 175–177).

51. Holm, "Senators Vote not to Finance Gay Services"; Sexton, "GLSOK Did Not Expect Budget cutoff."

52. Mary Sexton, "Student's Petition Opposes GLSOK Financing," *University Daily Kansan*, April 17, 1984, 3.

53. Mary Sexton, "Student 1000 Back End to GLSOK Funds," *University Daily Kansan*, April 18, 1984, 8.

54. Cindy Holm, "Senate Tentatively Extends GLSOK Funds," *University Daily Kansan*, April 19, 1984, 5.

55. Holm, "Senate Tentatively Extends GLSOK Funds."

56. Mary Sexton, "Student Wants to Force Referendum on GLSOK," *University Daily Kansan*, April 24, 1984, 5.

57. John Hanna, "Funding to GLSOK in Doubt," *University Daily Kansan*, September 6, 1984, 1, 5: 5.

58. John Hanna, "Petition's T-shirt Sales Stir GLSOK," *University Daily Kansan*, September 25, 1984, p. 1, 5; John Hanna, "Doubt Cast on Referendum Drive," *University Daily Kansan*, September 25, 1984, p. 1, 5.

59. Doug Hitchcock, "Anti-homosexual T-shirt Stirs Protest at KU," *Lawrence Journal-World*, September 26, 1984, 6.

60. Hitchcock, "Anti-homosexual T-shirt Stirs Protest at KU."

61. Hanna, "Petitioner's T-shirt Sales Stir GLSOK."
62. John Hanna, "Senate Panel Must Check List of Names," *University Daily Kansan*, September 18, 1984, 1.
63. Hitchcock, "Anti-homosexual T-shirt Stirs Protest at KU."
64. John Hanna, "Committee Calls GLSOK Petition Discriminatory," *University Daily Kansan*, September 28, 1984, 1.
65. John Hanna, "Gay Group Angry After Car Tampering," *University Daily Kansan*, September 28, 1984, 7.
66. C. S. Manegold and Shelly Phillips, "'Fagbusters'" Turning Violent on U.S. College Campuses," *Elyria* (Ohio) *Chronicle-Telegram*, December 23, 1984, C-8. This was a syndicated story on the Knight-Ridder news service, so it appears in multiple papers, under different headlines, on various days in this time period.
67. John Hanna, "Petition on GLSOK Money to Get Second Chance," *University Daily Kansan*, October 4, 1984, 1.
68. Hanna, "Petition on GLSOK Money to Get Second Chance."
69. John Hanna, "Committee Kills Imber's Petition on GLSOK Funds," *University Daily Kansan*, October 5, 1984, 1, 7: 7.
70. John Egan and John Hanna, "Imber Will Appeal Decision Disallowing Campus Vote," *University Daily Kansan*, October 11, 1984, 5.
71. Doug Hitchcock, "KU Administrators Hope Steps Will Stop Intolerance," *Lawrence-Journal World*, November 12, 1984, 1, 18: 18.
72. Mary Carter, "KU Officials Issue Harassment Policy," *University Daily Kansan*, November 9, 1984, 1.
73. Nancy Stoetzer, "Appeal's Fate in Limbo After Board's Meeting," *University Daily Kansan*, December 5, 1984, 5.
74. Nancy Stoetzer, "Judicial Board Says Petition Wrongly Invalidated," *University Daily Kansan*, January 16, 1985, 1.
75. Ruth Lichtwardt, Interview with Author, January 2002.
76. Ruth Lichtwardt, Interview with Author, January 2002.
77. Nancy Stoetzer, "GLSOK Leader, Foe Promote Truce," *University Daily Kansan*, January 18, 1987, 1.
78. Nancy Stoetzer, "Imber Still Seeking GLSOK Referendum," *University Daily Kansan*, January 21, 1985, 1, 5: 1.
79. Stoetzer, "Imber Still Seeking GLSOK Referendum."
80. Ruth Lichtwardt, Interview with Author, January 2002.
81. Sharon Rosse, "GLSOK Dance Shows Profit After 3-Month Lag," *University Daily Kansan*, January 28, 1985, 3.
82. Rosse, "GLSOK Dance Shows Profit After 3-Month Lag."
83. Rosse, "GLSOK Dance Shows Profit After 3-Month Lag."
84. Nancy Stoetzer, "GLSOK Awareness Week Cancelled, *University Daily Kansan*, April 2, 1985, 1, 5.

85. Nancy Stoetzer, Panel passes GLSOK back to Senate, University Daily Kansan, 4/3/85, 1, 5: 1.
86. Julie Mangen, "Senate Rejects Request for GALA Week Funds," *University Daily Kansan*, April 4, 1985, 1, 5.
87. Nancy Stoetzer, "GALA Week Resurrected with Private Funds," *University Daily Kansan*, April 5, 1985, 3.
88. Michael Totty, "Senate Could Limit Effect of Petitions," *University Daily Kansan*, April 17, 1985, 3.
89. Totty, "Senate Could Limit Effect of Petitions."
90. "Petition to Get Review in Two Weeks," *University Daily Kansan*, April 16, 1985, 16.
91. Nicolette Kondratieff, "Student Senate to Consider GLSOK Petition Once Again," *University Daily Kansan*, August 26, 1985, 9.
92. Bonnie Snyder, "GLSOK Petition Dies Again," *University Daily Kansan*, October 15, 1985, 1, 2.
93. Clarke, "Lichtwardt Has Dream of Equal Rights for Homosexuals," 5.
94. Michael Blake, Interview with Author, April 26, 2008.
95. Michael Blake, Interview with Author, April 26, 2008.
96. Supplemental Form for 87 Funding. Records of the GLBTAU, RG 02.03.18, University of Iowa Archives.
97. Gay People's Union, Press Release, March 6, 1987. University of Iowa Archives, RG 02.03.18, Records of the GLBTAU.
98. Gay People's Union, Press Release.
99. Gay People's Union, Press Release.
100. Charles H. Smith to Thomas E. Everhart. University of Illinois Archives, Student Affairs – Dean of Students, Office of the, Stanley A. Levy Papers, 1948–1998, 41/1/21, Box 11, Folder: Gay Rights.
101. Dawn Bushaus, "Amid Scorn, Task Force Rolls," *Daily Illini*, March 17, 1986, 15.
102. Email from Clarence Shelley to Stanley Levy re: GLI meeting with Chancellor Everhart, January 27, 1986. University of Illinois Archives, Student Affairs – Dean of Students, Office of the, Stanley A. Levy Papers, 1943–1998, 41/1/21, Box 11, Folder: Gay Rights.
103. Thomas E. Everhart to H. George Friedman, Jr. Associate Prof of Computer Science, January 27, 1986. University of Illinois Archives, Student Affairs – Dean of Students, Office of the, Stanley A. Levy Papers, 1943–1998, 41/1/21, Box 11, Folder: Gay Rights.
104. University of Illinois News Bureau, January 27, 1986. Student Affairs – Dean of Students, Office of the, Stanley A. Levy Papers, 1943–1998, 41/1/21, Box 11, Folder: Gay Rights.
105. University of Illinois News Bureau, January 27, 1986. University of Illinois Archives, Student Affairs – Dean of Students, Office of the, Stanley A. Levy Papers, 1943–1998, 41/1/21, Box 11, Folder: Gay Rights.

106. Bushaus, "Amid Scorn, Task Force Rolls."
107. Mary Ellen Shanesey to Thomas E. Everhart, March 18, 1986. University of Illinois Archives, Student Affairs – Dean of Students, Office of the, Stanley A. Levy Papers, 1943–1998, 41/1/21, Box 11, Folder: Gay Rights.
108. Bushaus, "Amid Scorn, Task force Rolls."
109. Kristina Boerger, Interview with Author, September 27, 2018.
110. Kristina Boerger, Interview with Author, September 27, 2018.
111. At least in the press, the title of the organization was the Gay and Lesbian Illini. Boerger notes the "kind of unfortunate appropriation of Native American imagery" of the still contested University of Illinois' mascot, Chief Illini. In an odd connection, the Illinois Republican who talked to the press about the abnormality of sucking cock, Webber Borchers, hitch-hiked to North Dakota to obtain the costume for the original mascot, back when Borchers was an undergraduate student at Illinois.
112. Kristina Boerger, Interview with Author, September 27, 2018.
113. Mary Lee Sargent was women's rights—and gay and lesbian rights—activist and organizer in her own right, helping shape efforts in the Champaign-Urbana area on gay and lesbian issues for 40 years. She was a faculty member at Parkland Community College, from 1968 until 2001. She continued serving as the director of the Office of Women's Programs and Services until 2003.
114. Kristina Boerger, Interview with Author, September 27, 2018.
115. The anti-apartheid movement was a global protest against investments in segregated apartheid government-held businesses and projects. For more information, see Philip G. Altbach and Robert Cohen, "American Student Activism: The Post-Sixties Transformation," *Journal of Higher Education*, 61, No. 1 (January–February, 1990), 32–49.
116. Kristina Boerger, Interview with Author, September 27, 2018.
117. Kristina Boerger, Interview with Author, September 27, 2018.
118. Cheryl Thompson, "Protesters Criticize UI Anti-discrimination Delays," *Champaign-Urbana News Gazette* January 31, 1987.
119. Thompson, "Protesters Criticize UI Anti-discrimination Delays."
120. Orrin Schwarz, "Threats Fail to Hal Gay Activists," *Daily Illini*, Feb 2, 1987, p. 3, 7: 7.
121. Schwarz, "Threats Fail to Hal Gay Activists," 7.
122. Schwarz, "Threats Fail to Hal Gay Activists."
123. Schwarz, "Threats Fail to Hal Gay Activists," 7.
124. Schwarz, "Threats Fail to Hal Gay Activists," 7.
125. Schwarz, "Threats Fail to Hal Gay Activists," 7.
126. Schwarz, "Threats Fail to Hal Gay Activists," 7.
127. Kristina Boerger, Interview with Author, September 27, 2018. My conversation with Boerger occurred the night of the U.S. Senate's Committee

on the Judiciary's hearing of Dr. Christine Blasey Ford's testimony and Brett Kavanaugh's response. The national mood affected both of us. Boerger told me, "My comments are off the chain after today."

128. Meeting of the Board of Trustees of the University of Illinois, March 14, 1987, 259–261.
129. Rebecca Dohleman, "GLI Urges Everhart to Back Anti-discrimination Policy," *Daily Illini*, March 27, 1987, 3.
130. Robert Loerzel, "Report: Homophobia Prevalent," *Daily Illini*, April 27, 1987, 1, 5.
131. Loerzel, "Report: Homophobia Prevalent"; Laurie Goering, "Report Says Bias Haunts U. of I. Gays," *Chicago Tribune*, April 28, 1987.
132. Loerzel, "Report: Homophobia Prevalent," 5.
133. Robert Loerzel, "Policy Proposed for Protection of UI Homosexuals," *Daily Illini*, April 28, 1987, 1–5: 1.
134. Loerzel, "Policy Proposed for Protection of UI Homosexuals," 1.
135. Loerzel, "Policy Proposed for Protection of UI Homosexuals," 1.
136. Loerzel, "Policy Proposed for Protection of UI Homosexuals," 5.
137. Nancy Slepicka, "Board Will Not Hear Gay Rights Proposal," *Daily Illini*, April 29, 1987, 1.
138. Slepicka, "Board Will Not Hear Gay Rights Proposal."
139. Catherine Spellman, "GLI to Ask for Action by Board of Trustees," *Daily Illini*, May 13, 1987, 1, 9.
140. Spellman, "GLI to Ask for Action by Board of Trustees," 9.
141. "Ikenberry, Board Affirm UI Policy Protects Gays," *Illini Week*, June 11, 1987.
142. "Ikenberry, Board Affirm UI Policy Protects Gays."
143. "Ikenberry, Board Affirm UI Policy Protects Gays."
144. "Ikenberry, Board Affirm UI Policy Protects Gays."
145. Jessica Goldbogen, "Discussion Centers on Gays as Minority Group," *Daily Illini*, November 3, 1989, 3.
146. Goldbogen, "Discussion Centers on Gays as Minority Group."
147. Georgea Kovanis, "Campus Gays Still Waiting for Policy," *The Michigan Daily*, March 9, 1984, 1, 5: 5.
148. Jim Poniewozik, "Gay Activist Fights for Recognition Through LaGROC," *The Michigan Daily*, December 9, 1987, 1, 5: 5.
149. Carol Wayman, Interview with Author, August 14, 2018.
150. Poniewozik, "Gay Activist Fights for Recognition Through LaGROC," 5.
151. Carol Wayman, Interview with Author, August 14, 2018.
152. Poniewozik, "Gay Activist Fights for Recognition Through LaGROC," 5.
153. Poniewozik, "Gay Activist Fights for Recognition Through LaGROC," 1.
154. Poniewozik, "Gay Activist Fights for Recognition Through LaGROC," 5.
155. Carol Wayman, Interview with Author, August 14, 2018.

156. Carol Wayman, Interview with Author, August 14, 2018.
157. Poniewozik, "Gay Activist Fights for Recognition Through LaGROC," 5.
158. Carol Wayman, Interview with Author, August 14, 2018.
159. Carol Wayman, Interview with Author, August 14, 2018.
160. Carol Wayman, Interview with Author, August 14, 2018.
161. Stephen Gregory, "Nordby Says She Supports Gay Demands," *The Michigan Daily*, November 13, 1987, 1.
162. Gregory, "Nordby Says She Supports Gay Demands."
163. Carol Wayman, Interview with Author, August 14, 2018.
164. Gregory, "Nordby Says She Supports Gay Demands."
165. Barbara Misle, "U-M Student Government Fights 'Homophobic' Policy," *Ann Arbor News*, November 18, 1987, A9.
166. Elizabeth Atins, "Group Occupies Nordby's Office," *The Michigan Daily*, November 19, 1987, 1, 3, 5.
167. Atins, "Group Occupies Nordby's Office," 5.
168. Atins, "Group Occupies Nordby's Office."
169. Carol Wayman, Interview with Author, August 14, 2018.
170. Jim Poniewozik, "Regents Refuse Demand to Include Gays in Logo," *The Michigan Daily*, January 18, 1988, 1, 5: 1.
171. Poniewozik, "Regents Refuse Demand to Include Gays in Logo," 5.
172. Barbara Misle, "Activists for Gays Occupy Bathroom to Protest Statement," *Ann Arbor News*, January 22, 1988, A5; Jim Poniewozik, "LaGROC Sits in at Fleming Building," *The Michigan Daily*, January 25, 1988, 1, 5.
173. Henry T. Johnson was the first African-American hired at Michigan at such a level, having been appointed in 1972. Johnson was an active leader in the field of higher education, serving as a voting delegate for the National Association of Student Personnel Administrators (NASPA) and as commissioner-at-large for the North Central Association of Colleges and Schools. He was trained as a psychiatric social worker. Given his background in student affairs and civil rights, Johnson's responses to LaGROC are all the more indicative of an administration that really had little interest in doing anything for non-heterosexual students than it was forced to do. It is difficult to fathom an officer of a university encouraging students to file grievances and lawsuits against that university.
174. Misle, "Activists for Gays Occupy Bathroom to Protest Statement"; Poniewozik, "LaGROC Sits in at Fleming Building."
175. Poniewozik, "LaGROC Sits in at Fleming Building," 5.
176. Poniewozik, "LaGROC Sits in at Fleming Building," 5.
177. Carol Wayman, Interview with Author, August 14, 2018.
178. Misle, "Activists for Gays Occupy Bathroom to Protest Statement."
179. Carol Wayland, Interview with Author, August 14, 2018.

180. Misle, "Activists for Gays Occupy Bathroom to Protest Statement."
181. Misle, "Activists for Gays Occupy Bathroom to Protest Statement."
182. Carol Wayman, Interview with Author, August 14, 2018.
183. Steve Knopper, "Officials Discuss Code Draft," *The Michigan Daily*, January 18, 1988, 1, 3.
184. Knopper, "Officials Discuss Code Draft."
185. Jim Poniewozik, "Civil Rights Board Hears 'U' Testimony," *The Michigan Daily*, April 18, 1988, 1, 5.
186. Steve Knopper, "CBN Fears Fleming's Funding Cut Threat," *The Michigan Daily*, April 15, 1988, 3.
187. Jim Poniewozik and Ryan Tutak, "Chaos Disrupts Regents' Meeting," *The Michigan Daily*, April 15, 1988, 1, 5: 1.
188. Poniewozik and Tutak, "Chaos Disrupts Regent's Meeting," 1.
189. David Schwartz, "Code Approval Prompts Protest," *The Michigan Daily*, April 18, 1988, 1, 2.
190. Poniewozik and Tutak, "Chaos Disrupts Regent's Meeting."
191. Schwartz, "Code Approval Prompts Protest," 2.
192. Steve Knopper, "Nordby Appointed to Gov't Relations Position," *The Michigan Daily*, April 18, 1988, 3.
193. Amy Smith, "150 Rally, March to Protest Assaults on Gays, Lesbians," *Ann Arbor News*, August 10, 1988, 3. Smith counted 150 protesters, while *The Michigan Daily* report counted "Nearly 300." Anna Senkevitch, "300 Rally Against Police," *The Michigan Daily*, August 12, 1988, 1, 4: 1.
194. Smith, "150 Rally, March to Protest Assaults on Gays, Lesbians."
195. Senkevitch, "300 Rally Against Police," 1.
196. Lisa Winer, "LaGROC Organizes Defense Watch," *The Michigan Daily*, November 11, 1988, 3.
197. Winer, "LaGROC Organizes Defense Watch."
198. Winer, "LaGROC Organizes Defense Watch."
199. LaGROC meeting minutes, March 17, 1988. James W. Toy Papers, Box 16, Folder: Meeting Minutes, 1987–1988. Bentley Historical Library, University of Michigan.
200. Henry Goldblatt, "Students Rally on Diag in Support of Gay, Lesbian Rights," *The Michigan Daily*, February 15, 1991, 1.
201. Heather Fee, "LaGROC Holds Rally on the Diag," *The Michigan Daily*, October 12, 1989, 1, 2.
202. Fee, "LaGROC Holds Rally on the Diag," 1.
203. "LaGROC Demands," *The Michigan Daily*, October 12, 1989, 2.
204. Fee, "LaGROC Holds Rally on the Diag."
205. Fee, "LaGROC Holds Rally on the Diag," 1.
206. Fee, "LaGROC Holds Rally on the Diag," 1.

207. *OFF The Wall, OSU Gay Alliance Newsletter,* Winter 1984. The Ohio State University Archives, Vice-President for Student Services (RG: 9/a/58), "Gay Alliance: A Student Organization: October 3, 1979-May 6, 1982," Accession 103/96.

208. Amy Melvin, "Gays Ask For Public's Support," *Ohio State Lantern,* April 29, 1981, 1; Gay Alliance Gay Awareness Week advertisement, not dated. The Ohio State University Archives, Vice President for Student Services (RG: 9/a/58), "Gay Alliance: A Student Organization: October 3, 1979–May 6, 1982," Accession 103/96.

209. Gay and Lesbian Alliance at OSU, Calendar of Events, Fall Quarter, 1990. The Ohio State University Archives, Vice President for Student Services, (RG 9/a), Box 2, "Gay/Lesbian/Bi-Sexual Student Services: 1993–1994," Accession 103/96.

210. Lynn Echelberger, "Gay Program is Changing," *Ohio State Lantern,* November 7, 1989, 3.

211. Echelberger, "Gay Program is Changing."

212. Echelberger, "Gay Program is Changing."

213. Echelberger, "Gay Program is Changing."

CHAPTER 5

Student Groups Assimilate Despite Campus Resistance in the Early 1990s

The early 1990s for non-heterosexual student organizations on campus focused upon assimilation of non-heterosexuals into campus and beyond. The question of non-heterosexuals serving in the military came to the fore of political policy discussions in the United States. Gay and lesbian (and increasingly included bisexuals), having achieved significant gains in procuring non-discrimination statements on their campuses, saw the Department of Defense (DOD) policy prohibiting non-heterosexuals from serving in the armed forces as an issue that could be leveraged for political advantage. At many postsecondary institutions across the country in the early 1990s, the issue polarized students and administrators; not unlike the issues that surrounded apartheid in the 1980s, Reserve Officer Training Corps' (ROTC's) involvement on campus was often viewed as a monetary and political necessity by administrators and viewed by students as hypocritical.

The campus activists in this time period hoped that by highlighting the irreconcilable discrepancy they saw between the DOD policy and the institutions' claiming that non-heterosexuals could not be excluded or discriminated against on campus, they could advance gay rights in one of two ways. Either the policy would be changed, or the institutions would have to expel the military and its ROTC programs. None seriously thought their institution would give up the funding that came from ROTC programs on campus—nor, moreover, the lucrative military contracts that the DOD warned would be severed if a campus dropped ROTC. Still, the

© The Author(s) 2019
P. Dilley, *Gay Liberation to Campus Assimilation*,
https://doi.org/10.1007/978-3-030-04645-3_5

activists hoped, publicity of their actions might be enough to prompt the universities to lobby the Pentagon (and/or Congress) to change the military policies they deemed discriminatory. This is a far cry from the draft counseling provided by, and the anti-war sentiment embedded in, many of the original Gay Liberation Front (GLF) movements on the Midwestern campuses.

Another area of activism for non-heterosexual college students during the early 1990s had to do with campus housing policies. Older students, particularly graduate students, attempted to avail themselves of "married student housing" or "family housing" on campus. Besides being close to campus, it was often less expensive than apartments in town; given the limited stipends of most graduate students, those with a partner would benefit from such a housing option.

Institutions, however, did not wish to be seen equating "marriage" with such a partnership. Despite gains in change on campus inclusion in other areas, most administrators were hesitant to be seen as responsible for what at the time was still a radical concept. As the head of University Housing at the University of Kansas (KU) said in a meeting I attended in 1993 concerning recommendations from the University's Gay and Lesbian Concerns Study Committee, "Show me an official piece of paper that says they're married, and I'll draw up a contract for family student housing." Such licenses, however, were decades away.

MICHIGAN STATE UNIVERSITY

Gay and lesbian students (and their allies) protested similar administrative resistance at the Michigan State University (MSU), for sexual orientation was still absent from the MSU Board of Trustees bylaws. For some non-heterosexual students, their exclusion from "family" or "married student" housing caused an inequity of experience and financing, when compared to their straight peers. Charley Sullivan, a graduate student and coach of the women's varsity crew team, told an audience of approximately 50 people,

> We're here to say that gays and lesbians are family. We're every bit entitled to life in family housing as the (heterosexuals) are…. We're not going to let the University Regents determine that this is going to be a bigoted campus.[1]

ROTC was another flashpoint for gay ire at MSU. While any student could enroll in ROTC courses on the MSU campus, students who acknowledged or were known to be gay or lesbian could not go through officer training, the purpose of the courses.[2] Of particular interest were scholarship opportunities for students who completed ROTC; in addition, the federal government had warned college and university administrations that, should ROTC or military recruiting not be permitted on their campuses, research funds and grants from the U.S. DOD would be withdrawn.

In November of 1991, ROTC programs at Michigan State were being reviewed by the Associated Students of MSU Student Board and the Student Council. At an open forum, the chair of MSU's Military Science department, Lt. Col. Donald Schulz, summarized the problematic situation. "'Any student can take four years of military science,' Schulz said. 'ROTC on the other hand is run by federal.'"[3]

As many people across campuses on both sides of the issue lamented, the two choices seemed irreconcilable: ROTC as a program on campus was discriminating against non-heterosexuals; the funding provided to the students in ROTC, as well as to the institution, were deemed necessary.

University of Michigan

The membership of Lesbian and Gay Rights Organizing Committee (LaGROC) had, naturally, changed since Carol Wayman since the 1980s, but the issues it faced were the same: the University of Michigan still did not include sexual orientation in its bylaws. Members felt the task force initiated by the University to study and to make recommendations on the matter was taking too long, that the University was dragging its feet.

In April of 1990, LaGROC resorted to outright sarcasm to demand attention to newly appointed President Harold Shapiro and his administration's lack of progress in satisfying the group's needs and demands. Prompted by the slow pace of the task force charged with assessing the campus climate for non-heterosexuals at Michigan and suggesting remedies or changes, LaGROC called for abolishing the task force, in an attempt to goad the University into action through shame.

LaGROC publicly called upon Michigan's president, Harold Shapiro, to enact the list of demands the group had put forward years earlier, along with three new demands.[4] In addition—and sometimes in direct contradiction—to the nine existing demands, LaGROC wanted:

1. To end the Task Force on Sexual Orientation, which LaGROC found unnecessary; LaGROC had been providing evidence of the campus climate for non-heterosexuals at Michigan for years.
2. To dissolve the Office of Affirmative Action, which LaGROC deemed ineffective and unwilling to serve the needs of non-heterosexual students.
3. To annul the existing presidential policy statement on sexual orientation, which LaGROC viewed as lacking formal mechanisms of redress.

Of course, these demands were made sarcastically.

Nevertheless, the U-M administration did not seem to know how to respond. Mary Anne Swain, Michigan's Associate Vice President for Academic Affairs, told the campus newspaper: "He [Shapiro] is not going to (fulfill these demands). None of these are useful ways of resolving grievances."[5]

That was the point. LaGROC spokesperson Brian Durrance stated the point of their action: the Office of Affirmative Action was only helping some campus minorities. "These demands should call attention to the real problem[,] that the University is not committed to helping us, since they (the office and policies) have no teeth."[6]

"Neutral Counseling"

Regent Deane Baker's years of denigrating gays and lesbians at the University of Michigan boiled over again at the beginning of the 1990–1991 academic year. Despite—or perhaps because of—his staunch Republican conservatism, Baker continued to be elected to the Board of Regents. As he commented in 1990, "The people of Michigan have elected me to represent them and I intend to continue my responsibilities."[7]

At the July, 1990, meeting of the Board of Regents, Baker's called for establishing a "neutral counseling office" that would be "free to present the case for the heterosexual identity to concerned young people." Baker followed up that letter at the July meeting, stating that a neutral counseling center could aid students "who want to come back to the other side."[8] Baker had also previously written to Michigan Provost Charles Vest his disapproval of having non-heterosexual staff counseling students.[9] At age 65, perhaps Baker was only reflecting an earlier generation's perceptions of non-heterosexuals as mentally ill; clearly, though, he was out of touch with the medical profession.

At the August Regents' meeting, Linda Kurtz called for Deane Baker's censure over his anti-gay comments and called upon Duderstadt to include sexual orientation in Michigan's non-discrimination policy.

> Every other Big Ten School and every other Michigan college includes gays in their anti-discrimination policy.... It is your challenge to bring this University into the 21st century.[10]

A number of students, however, spoke in support of Baker, calling LaGROC "hypocrites" for wanting to "silence" Baker.[11] For his part, at the meeting Regent Baker questioned the University's use of state funding to support the Lesbian and Gay Male Programs Office.

In August, Ann Arbor ACT UP organized a "zap"-like protest in response. Over 50 protesters rallied on the steps of the Michigan Union, to stage a kiss-in (no doubt former Union Manager Stanfield Wells would have found their actions improper, too). Prior to kissing, members of the university community (including students as well as staff) spoke about their perceptions of Baker's comments fostering, or amplifying, a hostile environment. Judy Levy, a local union bargaining chairwoman, stated, "The university should publicly condemn his statements and ask him to resign. They are not isolated statements. He went too far this time."[12] Graduate student and ACT UP member Patrice Maurer said, "I feel downright discriminated."[13]

ACT UP issued a series of demands for the University to enact in response to Baker. They included censuring him; asking him to resign; increasing funding for the Lesbian and Gay Male Programs Office; placing gay and lesbian students and staff in charge of the Programs Office; adding "sexual orientation" and "HIV-antibody status" to the University's non-discrimination policy; creating a degree-granting program and department of lesbian and gay studies; creating a gay and lesbian center; implementing "widespread, non-moralistic safer sex education"; free condom and needle distribution; and opening a "worker-controlled" AIDS treatment center at U-M Hospitals.[14]

After presenting their case—and their demands—the protesters embraced and kissed same-gendered partners. Next they marched the short distance to the Office of Affirmative Action; each filed individual grievance complaints against Baker for his most recent comments. Unsurprisingly, Baker did not resign. First elected in 1972, he served as regent from 1973 until 1996.

As in previous years, other configurations of students formed additional non-heterosexual student associations, to increase pressure upon the administration. New Queer Agenda at the University of Michigan continued efforts to change University Bylaw 14.06, to include a clause to prohibit discrimination based upon sexual orientation. Although the presidential policy was still in effect, many in the gay and lesbian community viewed as legally ineffective and personally insufficient. On Valentine's Day, 1991, the group held a kiss-in on campus. According to member Allison Van Norman, "We wanted to gain visibility. It is an excuse to pass out flyers and to show what New Queer Agenda is all about"; another member, Matthew Porter, stated that "Homophobia is the only reason the regents haven't granted (equal rights) to gay men and lesbians."[15]

Despite lingering sentiments such as those expressed by Deane Baker, the climate for non-heterosexual students in Ann Arbor had changed. *The Michigan Daily* article from October of 1991 highlighted two local bars that sponsored "gay nights." The Blind Pig sponsored drag performances on Tuesday nights. The Nectarine had been holding "gay nights" on Tuesdays since 1984; by 1987, demand prompted adding a second, on Friday nights. The Nectarine's general manager noted that straight women enjoyed the "Boys' Night Out" as a respite from "playing the social game."[16] "Some people have the mindset that it's a homo bar and won't come here," the manager stated, adding he would rather those people not patronize his bar. "It helps me weed out the fools."[17]

October brought the 1991 Lesbian and Gay Men's Pride, Awareness, and Commitment Week,[18]culminating with National Coming Out Day rally on the Diag. In many ways, the concept of non-heterosexuals on campus was still as continuous as it was 20 years earlier.

The InterVarsity Christian Fellowship (ICF) held a counterprotest, also on the Diag; the ICF's band, Adam's Brother, played during the Coming Out Day rally, drowning out the speakers. Nonetheless, *The Michigan Daily* noted both rallies proceeded "without a great deal of antagonism."[19] Indeed, an ICF member stated, "We don't hate gay people.... They deserve their rights, too."[20]

For their part, the Coming Out Day speakers decried ongoing discrimination against non-heterosexuals, such as at Cracker Barrel and the University's lack of allowing gay and lesbian couples from access to married student housing. Billie Edwards, long-serving staff member of the Lesbian and Gay Men's Programming Office, read an anonymous letter decrying her office's work. The rally concluded with a march to the ROTC building, to demand ROTC either allow non-heterosexuals to serve or leave the Michigan campus.[21]

INDIANA UNIVERSITY

By 1990, the non-heterosexual student association at Indiana University was styling itself as Indiana OUT.[22] Jeffrey Bass was elected president in January. He and the other newly elected "officers said they want to revitalize the social aspect of the group, which has turned political since its creation three years ago."[23] Duncan Mitchell, a university staff member and external vice president for Indiana OUT, commented upon previous "political" actions by the group and his hopes for more entertaining events.

> We've put more emphasis on new events (Gay Pride Week and the AIDS Memorial Quilt), which is fine.... I'm hoping to boost the social and support aspects of the meetings.[24]

By the fall, more than 40 people were attending weekly meetings; Stuart Schleuse was in as president, and he created two vice-presidential positions—one for men, one for women.[25]

Indiana OUT had been lobbying since October of 1989 to add sexual orientation as a protected class on campus. They had the support of the dean of students, Michael Gordon, who stated,

> We've had enough cases (of gay harassment) on this campus to make it a problem.... The fact is, the clause will say in advance to students that gay-bashing will not be allowed.[26]

Commenting to a statement that such a code would extend protections beyond those offered by state and federal laws, Gordon replied, "There's nothing wrong with adding to the letter of the law."[27]

In August of 1990, Indiana University adopted a revised Code of Ethics for the University, which included sexual orientation for the first time. As so often was the case, the university administration saw no conflict between the code and ROTC being on campus. For the first time, however, the University's non-heterosexual students were able to site a specific act of institutional discrimination in violation of the accepted ethics of the University.

ACT OUT developed as an outlet for the more politically inclined Indiana OUT students. Those inclinations came to the fore during Gay and Lesbian Awareness Week 1992. On October 12, the National Day of Action against the DOD policy, in front of Ballantine Hall, ACT OUT sponsored two kiss-ins, one in the morning and one at noon. Brian Withem, one of the speakers prior to the actual kissing, sounded very much like the GLF students of the 1970s—except with a very different goal.

> "America has declared a moral war on us... And we just want the same rights as everyone else," including "privacy, protection, same-sex marriage and the freedom to show affection in public, without the threat of violence."[28]

With the final direction of "So let the kissing begin," "At least four male couples... embraced and kissed deeply for 15 minutes as supporters cheered and hundreds of passing students looked on."[29]

Negative responses from passersby were all that were reported in the Bloomington *Herald-Tribune*.

> "Get a room. Get a room. And get that shit out of here."
> "Why would they want to do that?," she asked, her hand over her mouth. "That is so gross."
> "It doesn't bother me that they're gay.... I got what they are trying to prove, but I don't think this is the way to do it."
> "They're just going to cause more problems for themselves because people aren't going to respect them for this kind of stuff."
> "I don't like it. I seems like they're throwing this in your face."[30]

Indiana University police officers were among the crowd, not in uniform, because they feared the kiss-in demonstration would prompt physical attacks against the ACT OUT members. "Immediately after each session, they asked the OUT members to disperse, to lessen their chances of becoming victims of physical hate crimes."[31]

Despite the University finally codifying the non-heterosexual students' right to be on campus, the police force of the University would not allow non-heterosexual students to be protected from discrimination and violence. While perhaps protective, the campus police's instructions to disperse demonstrated that even those protecting the speech and association rights of the students also impeded upon those rights.

OHIO STATE UNIVERSITY

In the spring of 1990, Ohio State University (OSU) initiated, after almost 20 years of agitation from its students—and after a presidential committee recommendation—a Gay, Lesbian, and Bisexual Student Services Office.[32] Although not "fully operational" until September of 1991, the office was the fifth of its kind in the United States.[33] Tom Fletcher, the president of Gay and Lesbian Alliance (GALA), noted the progress as well as anticipated negative responses. "I know that there are going to be some people on campus who are going to be very opposed and feel that the university is supporting something that they shouldn't be.... But as an institution of higher learning, Ohio State is trying to make every effort to get rid of things like sexism, racism, and homophobia."[34] It is doubtful Fletcher realized how he personally would need the help of that office.

A few weeks after the *Ohio State Lantern* article announcing the opening of the Gay, Lesbian, and Bisexual (GLB) Student Services Office, the GALA hosted Gay, Lesbian and Bisexual Awareness Week. A candlelight vigil and procession was covered in the campus newspaper on Tuesday, along with information on upcoming events and presentations for the week. A photograph of Fletcher addressing the attendees was published on the front page.[35]

Not listed in the Awareness Week schedule was a rally demanding OSU phase out ROTC programs on campus. May 4, 1990, was the date of a nation-wide day of protest against discrimination against gays and lesbians by the U.S. military.[36] The fact that the day was the 20th anniversary of the shootings at Kent State University was guaranteed to garner some media coverage, coverage that could remind universities of the discrepancy between the words of their non-discrimination statements and the actions of their ROTC programs. Mike Scarce, one of the GALA speakers at the rally, called upon the University to uphold its promise of equal opportunity and access.

> Ohio State tells us that we, as students, have access to everything on campus.... Yet, the ROTC is such a big part of this campus, and they won't let us in. The university is hypocritical and needs to live up to their stated policy of non-discrimination based on sexual orientation.[37]

While the rally was ostensibly about inclusion of gays into the military, the media headlines focused on the rally's secondary goal: removing ROTC

Fig. 5.1 Tom Fletcher leads a protest against ROTC's discrimination policy, Ohio State University, 1990. (*Ohio State Lantern*, courtesy of Ohio State University Libraries University Archives, The Ohio State University)

Tom Fletcher, in military drag, leads protesters in a campus march against OSU ROTC's policy of not allowing gay or lesbian students to join its campus-based programs, May 7, 1990. Fletcher had been elected president of the Gay and Lesbian Alliance at OSU the previous fall.

from campus, as well as any other program that discriminated on the basis of sexual orientation—off campus (Fig. 5.1).

Fletcher was in military drag: "fatigues, boots, and khaki shirt" from the U.S. Army.[38] Fletcher spoke of his choice of attire.

> Gays and lesbians have just as much right to defend our freedoms in the military as anybody else, and that's why I'm dressed like this.... As a person, I don't have a burning desire to be in the military. But I think we need to realize there are a lot of gays and lesbians who are in the military, or want to have the option of military service, who feel less than American because they're either not allowed in or they're kicked out.[39]

Student protesters on at least 25 campuses across the United States staged rallies and marches; students "simultaneously read a statement prepared by a University of Wisconsin-Madison student, demanding ROTC removal from the nation's college campuses." Mike Scarce, GALA vice president, read the speech twice. "We feel that while even one of us suffers under the weight of exclusion, we are all in danger."[40] Indeed, danger struck close to home for Scarce and Fletcher.

Tom Fletcher and Michael Scarce were not just officers in GALA, they were also roommates in Bradley Hall on campus during the 1989–1990 academic year. Since moving in to Bradley Hall, they had endured ongoing harassment. At least three incidents were investigated by the University, resulting in two judicial referrals.[41] In addition, OSU police had monitored the phone line in Fletcher and Scarce's room, to try to determine who was making harassing phone calls to the pair.[42]

Beyond those specific events, the culture of the residence hall was toxic. Scarce described his experiences in a letter to the editor of the *Ohio State Lantern*.

> It has been the single most unhealthy and uneducational environment I have ever experienced. Since late October 1989, we have been verbally abused, threatened, intimidated and harassed because of our sexual orientation.
>
> Our civil rights have been stripped from us by other bigoted, prejudiced, homophobic students who believe they can do these things to us and get away with it....
>
> The University has until 5 p.m. on Tuesday, May 29 to begin educational, disciplinary or legal actions to correct this situation and produce immediate and tangible results to our satisfaction, or we will be forced to implement our own strategy and deal with the situation as we see fit.[43]

On Tuesday afternoon, May 22, the Office of Residence and Dining Halls delivered letters, through campus mail and slid under the doors of all the rooms on the third floor of Bailey Hall, warning that future acts of harassment would result in "serious action."

Late Tuesday night, May 22, 1990, 15 of those letters were made into a poster, taped to Fletcher and Scarce's door; in the middle of the poster were the words "Die Fags." The two students called campus police.[44]

At 12:30 p.m. on Wednesday, the other 32 men living on Fletcher and Scarce's floor were informed that they were being evicted, separated, and moved to different residence halls; if they did not abide by the changes, they would have to find housing off campus, and a few opted to move into fraternity houses.[45] The men had until 10:30 that night to pack their belongings and move; the east-wing floor would be closed. The students were disgruntled.

> "I could see if someone was beating them (Scarce and Fletcher) up. All they (floor residents) are doing is putting stuff on the door. All you do is take it down and ignore it. You don't call the police," Adrian Plesha, a resident of the floor said.
>
> Chris Hadden, another resident, said, "This is really childish. We were not given our say."[46]

Evicted student Eric Poklar indicated that the eviction response was overblown.

> The university is just making a statement because it is coming down to legal action and the reputation of the university is at stake.... There have been incidents all year long and (officials) had names early on but didn't do anything with them.[47]

William Hall, the Housing director, denied that Scarce's letter to the *Lantern* influenced his decision to relocate the students. "The situation has gotten out of hand.... I've given students ample time to come forward and identify offenders. No one did."[48] Fletcher, however, blamed the administration for not initiating educational programming when the harassing activity began. "Their system should have been more effective to deal with this." The Bradley Hall director had produced programs to redress homophobia, but "[t]raditionally people of different opinions steer clear of those actions.... My meetings with students were very negative. I'm not sure being ugly is a solution."[49]

Hall, along with Richard Hollingsworth, Dean of Student Life, met with students, parents, the dean of students, resident advisors, and hall directors of three residence halls on Wednesday afternoon. Hall indicated that the men were not allowed to enter nor to dine in Bradley, Siebert, or Patterson halls. "Mr. Hall told us that if any of us were found on the third floor of Bradley, that it was considered criminal trespassing, and that action would be taken," according to one student.[50]

Hall stated that the residents who did not report information about the harassment were implicated, as well as the perpetrators. "The silence says we support these kinds of things." Hollingsworth stated that the culture on the third floor "was not a healthy environment for anyone on that floor…. There is a clear message being established that if there is a repeated pattern of harassment of anybody that residence halls are going to deal with that and will do whatever is necessary to create positive living environments for everybody who lives there."[51]

Questioned by local press, William Hall concluded, "I think I made the right decision, ethically and morally. It is late in the academic year, but this is also part of their [the other third floor students] education…. It is not going to show up on their grade card, but I really hope they learn and grow from this."[52]

Scarce indicated that although he and Fletcher had intended to stay in their room, they were not returning to residence life in the coming year. "It's just a matter of time before something like this happens again and hopefully the university will handle the situation better from the start instead of letting it get this far."[53] With the closing of the hall, the two were moved into an off-campus apartment, "at university expense," and provided 24-hour protection by OSU police.[54] Nonetheless, Scarce cautioned, even an extensive action as the one taken by the University would eliminate the animus fueling the harassment. "This is definitely not over. Not by a long shot."[55]

Scarce's prophecy was correct. The issue dominated the campus and Columbus news for the rest of the term and was reported upon nationally by *The New York Times* and other media outlets.[56]

On Thursday, close to 50 demonstrators, on both sides of the issue, gathered for an hour in front of Steeb Hall. Both Fletcher and Scarce were accompanied by OSU police officers; it was the first time since the University had "sequestered [them] to an undisclosed location for their safety" in the early hours of Wednesday.[57] As the crowd grew and spilled on to College Road, the OSU police force closed the block (Fig. 5.2).

Lawrence Sumpter, a resident of Steeb Hall (another men's dormitory), organized the protest over the University's summary eviction of the 34 residents, not against homosexuality; asked about the protesters present "who were shouting obscenities, Sumpter said he did not represent them."[58] A freshman said he believed kicking out students two weeks before the end of the quarter violated their rights; he helped hold up a sheet that said, "If homosexuals can co-habitate, we want female roommates."[59]

Fig. 5.2 Protest at Ohio State University after gay threats, 1990. (*Ohio State Lantern*, courtesy of Ohio State University Libraries University Archives, The Ohio State University)

Tom Fletcher and Mike Scarce were roommates at OSU, as well as officers in GALA. After months of enduring harassment and threats of violence, they forced the University to respond. OSU's housing director shut down the floor they lived on, separating the perpetrators by transferring all of the men to other residence halls. Students supporting Fletcher and Scarce, and those supporting their tormentors, held opposing protests, May 25, 1990.

Tom Fletcher believed such sentiments ingenuous, that the protesters were using that argument to conceal their homophobia. "They are focusing the attention on 'the poor people who had to move out of their dorms,' rather than us, who were harassed." Langston Woodruff, a freshman, did not hide his hatred. "Fuck the faggots, really, screw 'em all.... They should basically be dead, I guess."[60]

Speaking to the campus newspaper, Mike Scarce declared that Ohio State needed to become more responsive to the issues of its non-heterosexual students.

> The people in power at the university have realized that while they sit in committees and weigh their options and discuss different tactics, there are people out there who are being victimized.... The university is liable for what happens to those people until direct action is taken.[61]

Tom Fletcher cited specific changes the University could make to redress the issues he and Scarce encountered:

Ohio State must continue educational efforts to address diversity and adapt the curriculum core to give students a broader base of differing educational experience with black, women's and gay studies courses.

Residence and Dining halls should add a clause to their contracts which would discourage discrimination against gays and lesbians, similar to the OSU nondiscrimination policy.

The University needs to actively seek persons to work within the infra-structure who will see that minority concerns are a top priority.[62]

Statements such as that belie Fletcher's and Scarce's claims that they were not engaging, at least in part, as activists in a public protest. Soon after the incident, Scare was quoted as saying, "We are being portrayed as political activists and gay activists, but we are students.... That is why we are at Ohio State University, to get an education."[63] Yet Scarce also stated, "People keep asking us 'Was it worth it?' We say 'It's definitely worth it.'"[64] Fletcher reflected,

Maybe Mike and I are the first two people to decide not to take it any-more.... But regardless of the short-range costs, the long-range advantages of what has happened are going to be worth it.[65]

Fletcher and Scarce were working both sides of the argument: they presented themselves as gay students who were simply victims of anti-gay harassment on campus, but they were also gay leaders capitalizing on the situation for further calls for campus reform. In the same article in which they cited their desire not to be the catalyst for such reforms, Fletcher said, "If my face on the front of a newspaper or on TV helps people, then I'm willing to do that because there are several gays and lesbians on this cam-pus who can't do that," while Scarce noted, "We're making definite changes within the system – real changes."[66]

The University reflected upon the situation and its own actions. Housing Director Hall said,

I think yes, we could have done things faster in the judicial system.... We have trained our residence hall staff so that they're more aware and more sensitive to what these issues are.... Incidents of discrimination and harass-ment are going to get special attention.[67]

Peer mediation groups were established in residence halls, while the uni-versity revised student judicial processes for responses to "hate crimes." In addition, some of the accused harassers "were not allowed to return to residence halls this fall."[68]

In the aftermath of the evictions and protests, six new groups formed at Ohio State: a chapter of ACT UP, a lesbian social support group, and groups for non-heterosexual law students, graduate students, faculty and staff, and peoples of color. Further, the OSU administration funded seven students to attend the annual National Gay and Lesbian Task Force (NGLTF) Making Change Conference.[69]

Scarce and Fletcher opted in the summer not to press charges against the accused students; none of the Bradley Hall residents were prosecuted. "Both the victims... in that case notified us they declined to be involved further in the case."[70]

Minority Consciousness

In January of 1991, as students returned from winter break, Mike Scarce opined in the *Ohio State Lantern*, "The gay, lesbian, and bisexual community here at Ohio State has done more to raise political and social consciousness than any other minority group in 1990."[71]

> The past year seems to have ushered in not only a new decade, but also a new era in gay and lesbian campus activism.... When was the last time the apathetic student body of Ohio State cared enough about anything to rally together by the hundreds?[72]

Scarce's rhetoric harkened back to the positionalities of both the radical and the reformist gay activists of the 1970s. In addition, Scarce acknowledged the duality of non-heterosexuals within American culture, both a part of and apart from society.

> We have also sounded a call to action among ourselves.... [fueled by] the anger and frustration of demanding our equal rights as human beings. We've realized it's OK to go downtown to our safe little bars. It's OK to drink, dance, and have our own fun. But we still remember what is going [on] in the world around us. We cared enough to create change in the world and strive to make it a better place for us all in 1990. Please tell me what is so sick, sinful, or immoral about that?[73]

In May of 1991, Scarce continued GALA's attempts for Ohio State to either enforce its non-discrimination policies against ROTC or to eliminate the military programs. GALA convinced the OSU USG to pass five resolutions charging that the University and the U.S. DOD discriminated against non-heterosexuals. At the time, a total of 186 students at Ohio State received scholarships from the ROTC branch programs on campus, which also over $600,000 in scholarship payments from the military.[74]

Scarce believed that drawing attention to the discrepancy between the non-discrimination policies and the University's acceptance of DOD discriminatory policies might prompt a resolution to the situation. "The university is being hypocritical by saying there is easy access for everyone.... By writing a disclaimer that says ROTC does not comply with university policy, it is a way for the university to be honest.... We are not anti-military, we are anti-military policy."[75]

"The ROTC program is a question of access," Scarce said in response to President E. Gordon Gee's comments. Gee stated, "I think it's a wrong-headed policy, and I've stated it a number of times.... It's an issue of weighing morals. A huge number of students are involved in the ROTC program. The scholarship provides students the chance to get a great education."[76]

Gee was trying to thread a slight needle, making an argument that ROTC was not a part of OSU but rather an arm of the federal government, one that somehow operated independently on OSU's campus.[77] As other university presidents had failed before him, Gee could not reconcile the institution's desire to serve (and receive money from) the military and the institution's pledge to uphold equal rights for non-heterosexual students.

In October of 1991, Marc Contee, GALA vice president, joined Michael Scarce, who had become president of GALA, as members of the homecoming court, in bids for being voted homecoming king. Scarce told the *Columbus Dispatch* that the pair was sincere in their attempts to represent the student body, not "thinking this is purely a media stunt or an activism ploy, [but] partly it is an issue of visibility."[78] Contee noted that "Marc and I are accomplished students who have a right to participate in these events and be recognized for the work we do."[79] One event the two did not participate in was the "tradition at the dance in which the homecoming court enters the ballroom by walking underneath the crossed sabers of ROTC cadets."[80]

In 1993, Ohio State President E. Gordon Gee met with "gay, lesbian and bisexual student leaders" in October of 1993, chosen from a list forwarded by Phil Martin, the director of the GLB Student Services Office.

Gee had proposed allowing domestic partners, including same-sex couples, to live in family housing, only to face opposition to the idea from members of the Board of Trustees.[81] Gee said the issue "did bring out a lot of venom out of people. People don't view this as a civil rights issue, they see it as a moral issue."[82] Whatever the rationale against it, Association of Women Students member Michelle Pearce said, "Because the issue was brought up, it has made the climate here much worse for us. Not just politically but socially, there is a lot more hatred we are seeing on campus."[83]

Gone was the rhetoric of Scarce and Fletcher, replaced with the student leaders decrying the inadequate level of funding for GLB Student Services, compared to other student service program offices. Gone, too, was the self-sufficiency and agency Scare and Fletcher promoted. Kathryn Bernish, a graduate teaching assistant in English, told Gee, "We need people like yourself (Gee) to address the students and more than just you." Gee responded, "I believe it does begin with me. We also need to get people who are just middle-of-the-road, good, solid folks to have an opportunity to spend time meeting in appropriate ways with members of your community."[84]

SOUTHERN ILLINOIS UNIVERSITY EDWARDSVILLE

While student leaders such as Fletcher and Scarce made national news with their actions, demonstrating a sense of public relations and political savvy, students on campuses with less well-organized or well-established gay and lesbian organizations struggled simply to provide the kind of support and/or social organizations evident in the early days of non-heterosexual student campus organizing. For instance, after a two or years in the mid-1970s, non-heterosexual students at Southern Illinois University Edwardsville (SIUE) do not appear to have taken collective action on campus again until the 1990s. In part, this was probably because of the school's proximity to St. Louis, but the commuter-school aspect of the campus at the time no doubt had an effect as well.

The SIUE Student Senate formally approved the Gay and Lesbian Association of Students at SIUE (sometimes referred to as GLASSIUE, but usually just as GLASS).[85] In the constitution provided for Student Senate review, the organization listed three goals for GLASS:

1. Meet on regular basis to discuss common concerns and interests and to relate feelings and experiences.
2. Generally further SIUE's awareness of its gay and lesbian population in an open and receptive fashion.
3. Promote communication between the members of GLASS and the campus community at large.

The constitution stated GLASS' purpose was to "Provide an atmosphere of support for campus gays and lesbians."[86]

Matthew Marco, the group's first president, seems to have been the driving force behind queer student organizing at SIUE. In an interview in the Edwardsville newspaper, Marco said, "For now, GLASS is strictly a social support group for gays and lesbians. Political activism may come later."[87]

GLASS was active prior to campus approval. On March 5, 1991, Marco sent a letter, as the "President of G.L.A.S.S.," to other St. Louis area gay queer student organizations. He wrote, "I believe it could be extremely beneficial to all of us, for each group to come together and form our own group comprised of leader and/or representatives... [for] networking."[88]

In the 1991–1992 academic year, Marco attempted a community-wide "Queerness Eve Ball." The event was held between Christmas and New Year's Eve, on December 28, 1991, in the ballroom of the campus' Student Union. Only 44 tickets were sold.[89] After graduation, Marco moved to Washington, D.C., where he founded the short-lived magazine *Y.O.U.T.H.* (*Young Outspoken Ubiquitous Thinking Homos*).[90]

UNIVERSITY OF MINNESOTA–TWIN CITIES

The 1990s at the University of Minnesota began in late 1989. In October, 1989, an ad hoc group of activists demanded Minnesota Student Association (MSA) President Brian Bergson to resign or face impeachment, over statements Bergson had made about non-heterosexuals in the University of Minnesota ROTC program.[91] Bergson, a white man who was a member of a Greek fraternity as well as member of ROTC, had been quoted on a local radio program that homosexuality was not "conducive to a good morale and a good strong structure within the military,"[92] echoing comments he had made to the *Minnesota Daily* editorial board before his election, where he had also complained about affirmative action.[93] The group, eventually named the Ad Hoc Coalition for Equal Opportunity, consisting of 50 members, included David McPartalin and Robert J. Jacobson. Both were members of the University Gay Community, the Minnesota non-heterosexual student organization for men.[94] Jacobson was also a member of the University's student Senate.

Similar to the cross-minority alliances built at the University of Kansas during these years, Jacobson and McPartalin made political alliances with ethnic and racial minority student populations on campus. Bergson had made public comments against affirmative action during his campaign for student body president in the spring of 1989. Together, they formed a coalition with members from several student organizations from across the University. They demanded an apology and were dissatisfied with Bergson's statement that included, "If any of the comments that were taken out of context during last week's media show hurt anyone, I am very sorry.... But my personal opinion has not changed."[95]

Unsatisfied with Bergson's comments, the coalition called for an impeachment within a week. For the University Gay Community, Bergson was a symptom, not a cause, of the larger issue of inequitable access and opportunity for non-heterosexuals on campus. McPartalin indicated that Bergson's removal would be the first step in an attempt to change ROTC policies on a national level. "We are aware that everything cannot be changed on a local level.... But we have to start somewhere."[96]

A rapprochement was reached on November 1. Bergson signed an apology to any offended gays and lesbians, along with a reaffirmation of his commitment to civil rights.[97] The ad hoc coalition renamed itself the Coalition for Equal Opportunity. Robert Jacobson remained a spokesperson for the group, which focused on ROTC programs on campus, lobbying university officials and trying to build support in the Faculty Senate. "We're not a bunch of meanies who are out to get rid of ROTC," [Jacobson] said. "We just want to end the blatant discrimination within the institution. We want to give them a clear choice."[98]

In April of 1990, Jacobson announced his candidacy for MSA vice president at a University Gay Community rally against ROTC's discrimination and for the program's removal from campus. Jacobson's campaign focused on a student government report that the University provided $330,000 in unreimbursed expenses, along with over $8 million worth of facility use each year.[99] Jacobson, who was publicly out as gay at the time, was soon overshadowed by someone who was not.

Suzanne Denevan

To the press, Suzanne Denevan called herself a "social architect."[100] What she did not call herself publicly, during the election, was lesbian.[101] Denevan maintained that it was the press (and her opponents') choice not to bring up her sexual orientation, so she did not, either.

> The Daily didn't print it and they knew. The University DFL endorsed me and they knew it. And when the greek system endorsed me they knew it. When the Greens endorsed me they knew it too.
>
> They still chose to endorse me even with my history of being arrested in protests, being a lesbian and not having greek system background. They endorsed me over Bergson who was in the ROTC and in the greek system.[102]

While her sexuality might not have been well known on campus, Denevan certainly was. After graduating high school in Sioux Falls, she matriculated to Minnesota wanting to be an astrophysicist, but eventually majored in political science and women's studies.[103] Denevan first became involved in campus politics in 1989, when she ran for a student Senate as a member of the Coalition for Student Unity; the Coalition had launched a campaign to enhance the participation of women students, students of color, and gay and lesbian students in campus politics.[104] Thirteen of the 14 students on the Coalition's slate of candidates—all except president— won in 1989, and Denevan became a student senator.[105] By the spring of 1990, Denevan had decided the MSA needed reform, and in order to rebuild it, she ran for president of the student body.

In February of 1990, Denevan was one of six students arrested for protesting against budget cuts the University was proposing to the Restore Sexual Violence Program (RSVP), particularly the reduction in the budgets of the peer counseling and crisis hotline services. On February 9, the University of Minnesota Regents met to discuss the upcoming year's budget.

Denevan and her colleagues attempted to enter the locked room in which the Regents were meeting. University police then ordered the protesters to leave the building. When the students did not comply, the officers arrested them, escorting them out of the building in handcuffs. They were charged with misdemeanor charges of disorderly conduct and had to appear in Hennepin County District Court on May 16, 1990.[106]

Denevan viewed the actions as an attempt by the University to curtail student voice about issues of importance, and that became another focus of the work she wanted to do as student body president. "I am of the belief that the reason they have so many police officers at these demonstrations is not for keeping anyone safe, but to intimidate people out of protesting.... I won't bow to that."[107] At the May 16 court hearing, charges against all of the students were reduced to petty misdemeanor disruption of a meeting, due to insufficient evidence.[108]

While feminist issues served as the basis for her public activism, her campaign focused on reconstructing the MSA, to make it more responsive to student values and needs. "In her campaign, Denevan advocated changing the focus of MSA from governing to an activist role – a similar role to the one she played in leading the protests to restore the cuts in the Sexual Violence Program."[109] To the role, she brought feminist approaches to leadership and decision-making.

> My campaign emphasized co-leadership.... We made decisions on a consensus basis. I emphasized the kind of non-hierarchical leadership that I think is really needed all over the country in order to regenerate our leadership skills.[110]

Denevan also campaigned on giving ROTC six years to change its policy to comply with the University's Affirmative Action policy or face exclusion from campus.[111]

First Lesbian Student Body President

Denevan received 1793 votes, while her opponent received 739. While in terms of percentage of the vote, Denevan won by a landslide, it is important to remember how unimportant the election seemed to most Minnesota students. Almost 37,000 students were eligible to vote.[112] That apathy within the student body is strikingly evident in a photograph of Denevan presenting her state of the campus address in October. About 130 people attended that event in the Coffman Memorial Union. But as Denevan spoke, just behind her, on a bank of couches, a student took a nap.[113]

Denevan's rhetoric was a clarion echo from the 1970s liberation movements. "The attitude of administration toward students is patently anti-student from the word go.... We don't govern anything. We don't have power in anything."[114] Denevan argued that students were "shareholders" in the University and students should fight for their rights and responsibilities as such. Her presentation was well-received by many in attendance, including Student Senator Robert Jacobson. "Last year we were a bureaucratic organization – passing resolutions with no action.... There is a whole transformation of MSA to be more activist."[115]

A few days after her election, University officials charged Denevan and her five fellow protesters with violating the Student Conduct Code, specifically not complying with a police order to leave Morrill Hall and disrupting university business. The campus newspaper ran a large photograph (albeit on page 11) from February 9 of Denevan being arrested and taken to jail for processing.[116] In theory, she could have been expelled and, unable to register for six credit hours, would not be allowed to serve as student body president (just as had happened to Jack Baker in 1973). As the charges were reduced, the University did not punish the protesters; perhaps the University did not want to being attention to its newly elected student president having been arrested protesting her very university.

No doubt, the Regents were none too thrilled at one of Denevan's protest at the state capitol. Less than two weeks after taking her oath of office, she joined in a rally against ROTC discrimination, organized by ACT UP. In a short speech, she called for the Big Ten universities to join together to oppose ROTC's policies. Wearing a black ACT UP MINNESOTA T-shirt, Denevan also said, "I am a lesbian, and I am proud of it.... And I am (student-body) president of the largest university in the nation" (Fig. 5.3).[117]

Local gay community press had pointed out the apparent inconsistency of a comment Denevan made in the *Minnesota Daily* on May 3, in a column on outing. That article was the first mention, it would seem, of Denevan being a lesbian; in it, she claimed to oppose outing but thought that gays and lesbians should make themselves visible; reporter Tim Campbell noted Denevan had not come out during any of the ROTC debates, nor during her supporting a boycott on campus of Burroughs-Wellcome products because of the company's anti-gay policies.[118] Nonetheless, she was out after the election. At the ACT UP rally against ROTC, Denevan also called upon the University for a gay and lesbian cultural center, a gay and lesbian studies program, and more tenured lesbian and gay faculty (Fig. 5.4).[119]

The National Gay and Lesbian Task Force's annual conference, Creating Change, was held in Minneapolis in November of 1990. The University's non-heterosexual students availed themselves of the estimated 700 gays and lesbians descending upon the Twin Cities as an opportunity to press

Photo Courtesy University of Minnesota Archives

Fig. 5.3 Suzanne Denevan, University of Minnesota–Twin Cities, ACT UP Minnesota protest, 1990. (*Minnesota Daily*, courtesy of University of Minnesota Archives, University of Minnesota–Twin Cities)

Suzanne Denevan was elected student body president at the University of Minnesota–Twin Cities in 1990. Although not publicly out when elected, she soon declared her lesbianism at this protest in June, 1990, speaking out against ROTC and DOD policies at a demonstration sponsored by ACT UP Minnesota. She wears one of their T-shirts.

for reforms on campus. Queer Nation, "a newly formed gay and lesbian group," arranged a kiss-in demonstration in front of the Armory Building on campus, to protest the ROTC's policy of not allowing non-heterosexuals into its programs. Robert Jacobson served as Queer Nation's spokesperson for the event; he proclaimed, "We are queer and we are proud."[120] Also while the Creating Change conference was in Minneapolis, in conjunction with local gay and lesbian leaders, non-heterosexual campus

Fig. 5.4   Queer Nation kiss-in against ROTC discrimination, Armory Building at University of Minnesota, November 12, 1990. (*Minnesota Daily*, courtesy of University of Minnesota Archives, University of Minnesota–Twin Cities)
Held in conjunction with the National Gay and Lesbian Task Force's "Creating Change" conference in Minneapolis that year, this kiss-in was the first public action of Queer Nation, which had just formed a campus chapter. Some critics of the time wondered how public displays of affection related to issues of gay and lesbian service in the military; the public displays were to demonstrate how unquestioning the straight population was of its own social entitlement and privilege in all aspects of U.S. society.

leaders held a rally to promote equal rights and benefits for domestic partnerships of non-heterosexual couples. Suzanne Denevan spoke to the approximately 80 attendees. "Yes, we are family, too, and we desire domestic partner benefits."[121]

Back on campus, Denevan found that her plans for restructuring the student government were not as simple in execution as in idea. "It's a difficult process," she said in September.[122] In October she observed that the bureaucratic functions of being MSA president were very demanding. "I wasn't prepared for the phone calls and business.... I've inherited an organization that needs housekeeping. It's frustrating." The daily duties, Denevan said, kept her from giving adequate attention to her goal of encouraging student empowerment, specifically issues of tuition rates, academic and student service program retrenchment, and access to information about the university's budget. The *Minnesota Daily* reporter noted that "Endless committee meetings, ROTC issues and the split of the Graduate and Professional Student Association from MSA are continuing problems for Denevan," but ended with Denevan's encouragement for students to become active in university governance. "It's worth taking charge of your education at the University – and your life."[123]

University of Kansas

Like the University of Minnesota, KU had no problem supporting organized gay and lesbian students on its campus. KU had, for a brief time in between 1989 and 1991, active ACT UP and Queer Nation groups. The memberships of the ACT UP and Queer Nation were substantially the same; neither was a registered campus organization, in order to avoid culpability for potential disruptions. Both group's members were also involved in Gay and Lesbian Services of Kansas (GLSOK), the umbrella social and service organization for the campus. While the more radical student organizations drifted into inaction as many of their founders left campus (much like the early Gay Liberation campus organizations), GLSOK not only survived but also thrived.

Protests over military recruiting and ROTC courses offered on campus continued after Queer Nation and ACT UP faded away at KU. GLSOK corresponded regularly during these years with campus leaders, pointing out the discrepancy between non-heterosexual inclusion on campus and the ban on gays and lesbians serving in the military. In addition, GLSOK staffed information and protest tables, including on the main floor of the Kansas Union.[124]

But perhaps most important, during the 1990–1991 academic year, were the alliances GLSOK forged with the Black Men of Today (BMOT), the Black Student Union, the Native American Student Association, Women's Student Union, Hillel, and the Hispanic American Leadership Organization. Most of these organizations shared office space in a short hallway in the Kansas Union; most were also dissatisfied with how they viewed the University's response to the needs (and demands) of diverse students. By 1991, all recognized each other as minority students on the KU campus.

A Year of Protests

In reviewing the year 1990, the Lawrence, Kansas, newspaper declared that "April was a month of protests."[125] Indeed, the entire year was filled with student demonstrations on campus. Some of the demonstrations centered on specific acts of violence, or threats of violence; all of the actions, however, concerned lack of response by the KU. KU's GLSOK were extensively involved in the simmering campus issues that boiled over in 1990. To understand the experiences and actions of gay students at KU at the beginning of the 1990s, one must appreciate the campus cultural climate in which they occurred.

While campus protests developed regularly in 1990, the underlying issues were on display earlier. For members of GLSOK, public proclamations of hatred were evident in the late 1980s. Although the organization was successful in securing funding both for their operations on campus and Gay and Lesbian Awareness Week program, the viability of its programs depended upon a student-elected government. In March of 1988, after an hour of deliberation about the final amount to include for publicity expenses, the KU Student Senate allocated $1550 for the April Gay and Lesbian Awareness Week. The need for it was evident, as were changes in the attitudes of serving senators: one stated, "The whole homophobia issue is in style again with AIDS going around.... It is important to have it [GALA Week] because there is an incredible amount of ignorance on campus."[126]

Such ignorance was on display the next spring. In an alley in downtown Lawrence, someone had spray-painted graffiti: "Fat dyes will die," "Fat dykes don't make, this means you!," and a swastika. Liz Tolbert was a junior at KU and director of GLSOK. She said, "I feel scared because the graffiti comes out of nowhere, because I know that the graffiti comes from a person and is aimed at a person, and that violent thoughts cause violent words (that) cause violent acts." She noted increasing incidents of "gay and lesbian harassment in Lawrence."[127]

Such anti-gay animus seemed to be part of a growing incivility and discrimination felt by minority students in town and at the University. Black and Hispanic students had been advocating for stronger minority student recruitment and retention. Native American students, who had close ties to students at Haskell Indian Junior College (located on the outskirts of Lawrence), were concerned about four Native Americans found dead in Lawrence over the past few months, with seemingly little progress on determining the circumstances of their deaths. Women had been arguing for more security, even more lighting, on campus, out of fear of physical harm.

The issues all coalesced at the end of March 1990. On March 30, a black, female undergraduate student was working as a pizza delivery driver in Lawrence. On a delivery trip to the Sigma Alpha Epsilon house, a fresh-man fraternity member answering the door insulted her with racial slurs, throwing one pizza on the ground and another at her. While this was happening, her vehicle was burglarized, resulting in the loss of other pizzas to be delivered as well as personal items.[128]

For the African-American students at KU, who had been expressing their own concerns to administrators, this action was the epitome of the discrimination they felt on campus. Hispanic students, less of presence on campus than even the black students, viewed a need for more Hispanic students on campus, hoping for more safety and strength in numbers. Jewish students saw frightening harbingers of potential violence. For budding feminists (men and women), this action showed the need for a bringing notice and responses to issues they had been complaining about for some time. And for gay and lesbian students, represented in all the other minorities on campus, this was an opportunity to illuminate the connections between the forms of discrimination and their common cause.

The students articulated a common impression of their experiences on campus: incivility, hostility, fear, objectification, and an administration that did not hear their complaints, understand their issues, or—worse—did not care to respond in ways the students felt effective. What would later be termed by scholars as "intersectionality" allowed the groups to unite.

Students demanded the University take action to improve security on campus, to expel the fraternity chapter and the freshman student, and to state clearly that the University would not tolerate discrimination. Initially, the administration was reluctant to respond. Finally, on April 11, over 500 "student demonstrators" protested in front of the administration building, Strong Hall. The students, organized by BMOT, eventually entered the building and occupied the first-floor rotunda, while a group of students from BMOT occupied the chancellor's suite of offices (Fig. 5.5).[129]

Photography By
Ben Bigler
The Lawrence Journal World

Fig. 5.5 Protesting students occupy Strong Hall Rotunda at University of Kansas, 1990. (Kenneth Spencer Research Library, University of Kansas Libraries, The University of Kansas)

A coalition of student minority groups and their supporters occupy the Rotunda in the administration building, Strong Hall, April 13, 1990.

Gene A. Budig, the chancellor, was on the Medical School campus in Kansas City; Dean of Students Caryl Smith initially told the students in the administrative suite that the chancellor "preferred to meet with only a few of the protestors and not the entire crowd."[130] The protesters were skeptical. In the words of Marc McClure of BMOT,

> We've had meeting after meeting after meeting, and nothing has happened.... If four of us sit down, nothing would happen. He will address this entire body of people first. He's been putting us off all year.[131]

Nonetheless, the chancellor did not appear. After three and a half hours, the protesters dispersed. The chief of the Lawrence police noted, "The crowd was extremely cordial and just wanted to express their right of free speech.... It was a very, very good crowd."[132]

On April 12, Budig did make a public statement, in front of many of the same protesting students. He apologized for the incident, which he said made him "ashamed for the university," and he announced the release of a new minority affairs plan for campus. He said, "We have done a miserable job communicating what we are doing.... to the total campus community. I apologize."[133]

The students, many of whom interrupted Budig's address, seem less than thrilled. Andrea Katzman, a member of Hillel and also spokesperson for the new Students Concerned About Discrimination, said the attack and the institutional response

> represents how people feel towards minorities on campus. We have an administration that is allowing an environment that is not welcoming to minority on campus.... I think all of us here have to stand up and say, "It's not OK."[134]

Kristin Lange, an undergraduate student who founded Women's Student Union after the attack at the Sigma Alpha Epsilon fraternity house,[135] opined that the incident had as much to do with racism as with "the kind of violence toward women that we accept as a society."[136]

On April 12, 1990, a group of KU administrators—Budig, Executive Vice Chancellor Judith Ramaley, and David A. Ambler—met with student leaders from the various protesting groups. According to Ambler, "It was a fairly widespread group." Nonetheless, the only outcome was to continue conversations. After this meeting, the administration's attempts to disaggregate the student organizations became a strategy it would continue to deploy for the rest of the year.[137]

It was in this fortnight of demonstrations that the national day of protest against the DOD's policy of excluding homosexuals for service in the military occurred. On April 13, a group of 50 students demonstrated during the noon hour against the policy and KU's capitulation to it. The group, including members of other student minority organizations, gathered in front of Watson Library, carrying signs and making proclamations (Fig. 5.6). The university's assignment of office space to the minority groups, including GLSOK, in the same hallway of the Organizations and Activities Center in the Kansas Union, facilitated sharing of information and garnering support from students who happened to be in their organization's office at any particular moment.

Fig. 5.6   Protest in front of Watson Library, University of Kansas, 1990. (Kenneth Spencer Research Library, University of Kansas Libraries, The University of Kansas)

From one of several campus protests at the University of Kansas over lack of attention to minority student issues, July 18, 1990. Members of GLSOK are prominent in this photograph, including those holding the banner reading "No Bigots on My Campus," as well as those directly behind, in front of, and aside them.

Days after the DOD protest in front of Watson, GLSOK sponsored its annual Gay and Lesbian Awareness Week. According to GLSOK member Henry Schwaller, "By doing this, we try to show that gay and lesbian people don't fit the stereotypes.... We try to end discrimination by showing who we are."[138] GLSOK was firmly aligned with other minority student organizations fighting discrimination at the University.

The spring 1990 semester ended with concerns yet again about who had a voice at the administrative table. Ambler had for years sponsored a monthly Presidents' Round Table, an informal meeting of campus organization leaders, to provide a conduit of communication between students and the administration. The Round Table had traditionally been composed of mainly "majority" students, although African-American students had recently been added to it. Wendy Griswold, a member of GLSOK, wrote to Ambler, declaring that the group should be represented in the Round Table. Ambler responded to Griswold, "I do plan to expand the group, and I want to include additional student organizations that would not otherwise be represented in the group." Nevertheless, an answer to her request would not come before summer, at the earliest. Griswold told the press, "I was not very happy with the fact that he didn't feel that he could commit to a definite answer."[139]

Liz Tolbert helped organize an event just before final week, to protest the University's continued support of ROTC and military recruiting on campus. KU had amended its equal opportunity statement in 1987 to include sexual orientation, except where the military was concerned. The newly elected Student Senate leadership spoke in support of changing the University's practices to match its policies. Amie Hall, the incoming student body vice president, said, "It would be hypocritical for Chancellor Budig not to support [ending] the [DOD] policy, because of the strong non-discrimination policy." Mike Schreiner, the new student body president, said, "The exclusion of gay men, lesbians and bisexuals from military service violates a fundamental trust that we place in our society. It is... a very artificial barrier."[140]

The academic year ended with the KU student body president speaking out in support of gay rights—actually using the term "gay men, lesbians and bisexuals"—while KU's chancellor had yet to say those words (Fig. 5.7).

Photograph By
SCOTT CARPENTER
Lawrence Journal-World

Fig. 5.7 Amy Myers, Gay and Lesbian Services of Kansas, Gay and Lesbian Pride March, 1989. (Kenneth Spencer Research Library, University of Kansas Libraries, The University of Kansas)

Gay Pride Week march, Summer 1990. Amy Myers, recently elected as director of Gay and Lesbian Services of Kansas, holds the sign reading "Save the Gay Whales."

The Autumn of Discontent

The autumn of 1990 provides an example of how old liberation and new queer activism merged at KU. Members of GLSOK, along with members of the Student Senate's Executive Committee, had been lobbying the university administration to press the National ROTC to change its policies concerning sexual orientation. Non-heterosexuals were by then nominally protected against discrimination at KU, in direct contrast to the DOD's and ROTC's policies of not allowing homosexuals to serve within their programs.

The 1990–1991 academic year also started with simmering unresolved discontent among most of KU's minority student organizations. Within GLSOK, along with the traditional programming for socialization and coming out, some members pushed for political demonstration to force the university to enact its ideals.

The night of September 20, ACT UP/KU held a candlelight vigil in front of the chancellor's residence on campus. As in the past with other campus-based gay-related organizations, the membership of the ACT UP/KU overlapped to a great extent with that of GLSOK. However, ACT UP/KU was not an officially registered student organization. Around 75 members, from several campus organizations, protested not AIDS but rather the University's allowing ROTC to remain on campus, in apparent violation of KU's equal opportunity statement. Flyers and posters had appeared on campus, stating "No Fags in My Foxhole!" The GLSOK members in ACT UP/KU were older, and had been on campus longer, than GLSOK's new director, Amy Myers; they took charge of the event. The vigil was rather quiet, but it set the chancellor's residence as the stage for campus protesting for the rest of the year.

The second public GLSOK protest of the year began at 8:00 p.m. the next Tuesday, September 25, in response to a vote of the faculty not to eliminate academic credit for ROTC courses. The more political members of GLSOK, who had been active with the organization on campus for some time, were particularly angry at the lack of response from Budig. They likened it to his ill-crafted statement in 1983 that was prompted by anti-gay violence and harassment on campus but in which the chancellor never used the words "gay and lesbian," instead relegating them to the phrase "and the like." The group was also angry over, though not surprised by, the vote of the KU faculty to continue to grant academic credit for ROTC classes, despite the fact the DOD still banned homosexuals for serving in the military.

Approximately 70 demonstrators trooped from the Kansas Union to the chancellor's home. Many of the marchers held hand-painted signs, with saying such as "Liberty and Justice For All – Offer Not Yet Available at KU"; they chanted as they walked up Jayhawk Boulevard: "We're here, we're there, we're everywhere, and we're not going away." At their destination, they shouted, "Shame General Gene," pointing out the potential conflict of interest the chancellor might have had, given his rank as a major general in the Air National Guard.[141]

At the residence, the protesting students held a short candlelight vigil for those affected by anti-gay discrimination and violence. They read a statement, "condemn[ing] the apathetic attitude of the University of Kansas towards its gay and lesbian students." In addition, the statement outlined their position and their expectations for the University to address.

> Over the past few months, several minority groups and student organizations have attacked the administration of the University of Kansas for its inherent insensitivity to minority concerns.... We are dismayed by the Chancellor's stance on specific issues which affect gay and lesbian students. Furthermore, his inability to simply state the words "gay and lesbian" in public speeches or statements regarding minorities clearly demonstrates that he is indifferent or hesitant to take a firm position against sexual orientation discrimination.[142]

Three points comprised GLSOK's requirements: a strong message that discrimination on sexual orientation would not be tolerated, attention to and recruitment for gay and lesbian academics and scholarship, and an end to ROTC on campus. GLSOK had also developed detailed position papers on each of these topics.[143]

Although Budig (nor his family) was not at home, three KU administrators spoke to the students: Ann Eversole, Director of Organizations and Activities; Danny Kaiser, Assistant Dean of Student Life; and David Hardy, Assistant Director of Organizations and Activities. The three agreed to come to the next night's general GLSOK meeting. Hardy, a GLSOK member and student senator in the 1980s, attempted to pacify the students, saying, "I'm openly gay, and I'm openly an administrator.... I wouldn't work in an organization that was too homophobic to discuss it."[144] The tenor among the protesters, however, would not be placated; Liz Tolbert summarized the mood.

> People are rockin' now.... I think students are tired of sitting down and waiting, and they're tired of statements of placation. We want KU to take a pro-active stand for lesbians and gays.[145]

The administration, however, did not seem to be "rockin'." The next day, Kaiser summarized the situation to the local media. "Their concerns are not being ignored.... They may not like the responses they have received, but they are not being ignored."[146]

Kaiser, Hardy, and Eversole were joined at that September 27 meeting by Interim Executive Vice Chancellor Delbert Shankel. Shankel had stepped in to replace Judith Ramaley. Ramaley had known in April, when declaring she would meet with demonstrating students, that she was leaving the University. Shankel had been a faculty member at KU for decades and served as the University's chancellor in 1980–1981. Shankel was very receptive to gay and lesbian issues in the 1980s, and he was supportive of the students' requests. Were it up to Shankel, the policy discriminating against gays in the military could be changed, but as it was, he was limited as to his scope of power. Nonetheless, he and other administrators were planning to go to the Pentagon to lobby for a change.

Shankel hoped that conversations between GLSOK and the administration could continue. Chris Craig, former student and long-time GLSOK Peer Counseling Coordinator, and Liz Talbot decried the creation of committees in place of action. Craig stated he doubted that the University and GLSOK shared the same goals.[147] Nonetheless, GLSOK and the administration agreed to a 30-day timeframe to discuss the issues and responses to them.

On Friday, September 28, the Women's Student Union sponsored a Rally Against Discrimination and Sexism. Over 200 members from the groups actively protesting discrimination on campus met in front of Watson Library before proceeding to the rotunda of Strong Hall. The protesters called for better and more minority recruitment of students and faculty, better campus lighting, end to discrimination, and non-sexist student health care. Aaron Andes, a former director of GLSOK, spoke to the demonstrators and approximately 100 faculty and student onlookers (Fig. 5.8).[148] This event could be noted as the first GLSOK rally that drew substantial support from non-heterosexuals: the groups had found strength in supporting each other. The Friday afternoon protest, large as it was, would be overshadowed by the events of that night.

Angela Davis Comes to the University of Kansas

Friday night, African-American feminist philosopher Angela Davis gave a speech on campus; over 2700 attended. Davis began by acknowledging the incidents of 1990. For over two hours, Davis spoke and answered questions. She stressed that injustice must be confronted and encouraged students to work together across racial, gender, sexual, or other lines that too often kept them apart. Perhaps her most resonant comment was a call to action: "This institution is not going to change unless you demand it."[149]

Fig. 5.8   Aaron Andes speaks at rally for minority student issues, University of Kansas, 1990. (Kenneth Spencer Research Library, University of Kansas Libraries, The University of Kansas)

Aaron Andes, KU student and former GLSOK director, speaking from the steps of Watson Library at the Rally Against Discrimination and Sexism, September 28, 1990.

Students in the hallways of the Organizations and Activities Office asked each other all week: would there be a protest after Davis' speech? As they walked out of Hoch Auditorium, audience members strolled toward the chancellor's house. No formal notice had been given, no plans shared; at least to many students, the gathering seemed a spontaneous event.[150]

At least 200 students converged at the house, many of the African-American but also including a substantial number of members of GLSOK and Women's Student Union. Caryl Smith, the Dean of Students, David Hardy, and Danny Kaiser hid in the shrubbery, "observing" they said, in response to questions as to what they were doing. As more people joined the protest, the group expanded from the portico, extending around the building, periodically calling for the Chancellor, who was thought to be in residence, to address the crowd. After more than an hour, students were not leaving; by midnight, they were joking about ordering pizza to be delivered. Davis eventually appeared to congratulate the demonstrators but also to protect them. She told the protesters we had made our point; now we needed to go make our plans.

The administration did not wait long to plan their next steps. On Saturday, September 29, University staff called students whom they identified as "leaders" of "concerned student groups," those protesting students together at the Chancellor's house. The staff called the students to meetings on Sunday afternoon; they also told the students not to speak to the other groups' students. On an undated memo from KU's Department of Student Life, the points to make at the meetings were given (and edited by what appears to be two individuals, one in typeset, one in ink).

(a) Three demonstrations... during this past week have disrupted the privacy of the Chancellor and his family (including an eight-year-old daughter), this cannot continue.

(b) The University will not tolerate disruption of teaching, research, or administration (see CODE, article 17).

(c) The issues of concern to various student organizations have gotten "muddy" (struck out and replaced in the edits by "so numerous"), and student behavior is now becoming the focus, not the problems that the students are wanting to discuss.

(d) (Starred) Many in the university administrative structure and in the faculty are willing to meet with you and to help with considerations of your concerns, with understanding the current situations, and with working toward a plan of action for the future.

(e) Will you please (change to typescript) assist by communicating these concerns to the membership of your organization and perhaps, more importantly, by keeping the issues well defined?

(f) (Added in typescript) Call us if we can be of assistance, at anytime.[151]

Student leaders who attended those meetings told me at the time they felt as if they were being pitted against one another. The administrators distributed copies of the KU Student Handbook, with pages marked to section regarding activities that might prompt arrest. Scott Manning of GLSOK was one of the students called to a meeting; he told me that GLSOK—and by implication, that he specifically—was implicitly threatened with university and legal sanctions. Manning said he looked at the attorney staff member represent the University—former ROTC student, student senator, and GLSOK member David Hardy—and replied that the University knew that was a hollow threat, as the demonstrations did not violate any law or University bylaw.

Hardy was in a difficult spot, to be sure: a one-time ROTC student, Hardy resigned from the program and began his own coming out process in the early 1980s. As a graduate student, he joined Gay Services of Kansas and was elected to the Student Senate. After law school, he accepted a position as an assistant director of student activities. Hardy conveyed to the *University Daily Kansan (UDK)* that he viewed his time as a graduate student as one of rebellion: "I was a radical student on this campus," he said, although his definition of "radical" certainly would not match that of the early Gay Liberation Movement members. He reflected on being asked to be an observer at the GLSOK protests at the Chancellor's residence: "I was torn.... I looked out there, and that used to be me."[152] Responding to complaints of the University's inaction on the ROTC issue, Hardy said, "This issue is so complex.... It bothers me that people say we are not doing enough. There are a number of us that have remained committed."[153] Nonetheless, Hardy followed his instructions from the chancellor to threaten legal action against the individual members and the student groups protesting.

By attempting to disaggregate the protests into individual issues specific to different student populations, the administration seemed to believe that the student coalition would dissipate. The student leaders said that of course they spoke to one another, before and after the meetings, and agreed that unified around common issues of lack of response to minority student needs, they had more power. The student organizations had come to the meetings with their own list of concerns and demands for redress. GLSOK's ended with a demand for Chancellor Budig to "issue a statement demonstrating and articulating the University's committment [sic] to the well-being of it's [sic] lesbian and gay students and staff." Another was to initiate a data-based campus climate report.[154]

Continuing Protests

After the October 29 meetings, the protesting student organizations were more unified than ever. GLSOK, Women's Student Union, February Daughters, Hispanic American Leadership Organization, BMOT, Changing Men of Lawrence, Students Concerned About Diversity, KU-ACLU, Students Against Violence Against Women, People Stopping Rape, and other organizations planned their next on-campus action. An October 2 sit-in at the Military Science building was planned, but organizers decided that morning to forego the occupation and instead have an hour-long rally in front of Watson Library, focusing on the University's non-discrimination clause and its incompatibility with DOD policy.[155]

The substitute rally would be more visible, on the central part of campus, ensuring a greater audience. About 50 students protested on the steps of the main library, joined by 100 students and faculty onlookers, in addition to those walking along Jayhawk Boulevard during the noon hour. Conveying an official response to the issue from the administration, Michael Schreiner, KU's student body president, read a statement from Chancellor Budig, indicating that those seeking change to the military's policies should work through Congress and national educational organizations.[156]

GLSOK members were less than receptive to Budig's suggestions, reflecting that inaction to minority student needs seemed to be KU's modus operandi. Referring to the "Fagbusters" events of the 1980s, Christopher Craig stated that "Six years ago, KU and (Chancellor Gene A.) Budig were critically aware of violence towards gays and lesbians." Henry Schwaller "said the KU protests represent a movement toward eliminating discrimination on a larger scale."[157] Jay Johnson, serving as spokesperson for the new coalition of minority groups, told the campus, "Together we are not a minority."[158]

Together, the students made some administrators, if not necessarily Budig, respond. Campus administrators initiated another round of meeting with the leaders of the student organizations, this time without implications of arrest. Among the university leadership at those meetings was Executive Vice Chancellor Del Shankel. Shankel wrote to the president of GLSOK the week after the Sunday meetings, addressing each of the points on the position paper. He agreed to initiate a committee "to study the problems of gay and lesbian students on this campus.... I will work with the leaders of the Student Senate, faculty governance and with the Vice Chancellors regarding the membership and charge for this committee. I would welcome your suggestions on the committee as well."[159]

Shankel also agreed "immediately" to provide funding for a graduate assistantship for gay and lesbian concerns in the Division of Student Affairs.[160] Additionally, Shankel gave $1000 to assist in the costs for sending student delegates to the National Gay and Lesbian Task Force's annual Making Change Conference in Minneapolis.[161]

Pursuit of Happiness

A complement to Gay and Lesbian Awareness Week in the spring, Gay and Lesbian Pride Week was a relatively new event on the KU campus. Similar to GALA Week, guest speakers, educational panels, social events, and campus visibility were goals for Pride Week. GLSOK ordered posters from national gay organizations, including a set that depicted two young men, apparently naked but wrapped in a U.S. flag; they were smiling, and one was holding up a condom. Along the side and top of the poster were the words, "Life, Liberty, and the Pursuit of Happiness." GLSOK members had reserved the glass "information booth," at the intersection of the two main roads on campus, roughly halfway between Strong Hall and the Watson Library, for the week, and installed the posters (along with others) in the booth.

On October 9, during a Pride Week event nearby, a vocal confrontation between GLSOK supporters and detractors broke out in front of the booth.[162] The next day, two men, presumably students, attempted to jimmy the locks to the booth and succeeded in ripping one of the "flag" posters. The incident was observed by GLSOK member Aaron Andes, who approached the men. Andes told the pair, "I wouldn't do that if I were you." One of the men responded, "I wouldn't worry about it, if I were you." After their work was aborted, the men left, headed toward Watson Library. Andes followed them, repeatedly asking their names, but eventually lost track of the men.[163]

At the end of Pride Week, the booth was vandalized, the glass broken, and the posters torn and removed. The GLSOK members were dismayed and felt in danger for their physical well-being.[164] Much later that night, Rodney Soldier, a Native American graduate of Haskell Indian Junior College who was gay, was found behind Watson Library, the apparent victim of a violent assault; GLSOK members wondered if the attack, which resulted in Soldier being in a coma for three weeks, was motivated by homophobia.[165]

GLSOK quickly organized a candlelight vigil at the Campanile. Over 120 attended, including members from Native American Student Association and representatives from other minority groups on campus. The congregants first recognized a minute of silence for Soldier, followed by denunciations of the lack of administrative response to both Soldier and the general anti-gay prejudice on campus. Liz Tolbert was angry at KU's silence about the danger apparently facing its non-heterosexual students. "No action has been taken to inform the students about what happened" in regard to the circumstances around Soldier's attack. Chris Craig relayed a recent incident at Kansas State University (KSU), in which vandals spray-painted "Kill the Fags" on campus property. At KSU, "The administrators spoke out immediately.... At KU, there is silence." Scott Manning, identified as a member of ACT UP but also a GLSOK member, summarized the dejection and fear that now tinged the gay students' interactions with their campus. "I tried to pretend that those who destroyed the booth didn't get a part of me.... But they did."[166]

After Pride Week, Amy Myers, the GLSOK director, resigned. She indicated to the members that she was not comfortable being as visible and as political as the group was making her feel, and that the amount of time and energy she was contributing to the organization was interfering with her academics and her personal relationships. Myers later reflected to the *UDK* that in GLSOK, "There is a small group that wants to be as political as it can, and there is a rather larger group that is more interested in providing services for the members."[167]

After the Fall

Year 1990 ended much as it began: an attack against a minority, administrative silence for days, unified student protests, and a unified minority student body. But for GLSOK, through the personal efforts of Executive Vice Chancellor Shankel, some changes were on the horizon. In early

1991, Shankel impaneled the executive vice chancellor's Concerns Study Committee, the membership of which GLSOK had significant input; two years later, the committee would issue its final report, including a campus climate survey conducted in 1991. After a brief interim in January, Michael Sullivan was elected director of GLSOK. In February, Tom Emerson, a student in the Law School, was selected as KU's first gay and lesbian advocate, a part-time graduate student position funded by David Ambler's Division of Student Affairs.

In April, KU changed the wording of its equal opportunity policy from "sexual preference" to "sexual orientation." GLSOK sponsored a rally that drew from the informal coalition of minority organizations for the national day of action against the DOD policy, where the student body president read a statement from the University Council against the policy.[168] The April 15th DOD protest was held as one of the events of Gay and Lesbian Awareness Week. Perhaps nothing demonstrates the change in the relationship between protesters and the protested as much as the correspondence over the April 15th demonstration. Michael Sullivan wrote to the office of Del Shankel, the executive vice chancellor, to inform his office of GLSOK's plans for a "peaceful demonstration." Shankel responded by saying, "I appreciate the way that you and your colleagues are working with the university administration to try to address the discrimination concerns that we all share."[169]

Also in April, Sullivan, Arthur Satterfield, and I were elected to the Student Senate. We, along with Kristin Lange from Women's Student Union, Angela Cervantes from Hispanic American Leadership Organization, and other campus activists from the previous year, were part of the Impact! Coalition. Darren Fulcher, who would be elected KU's first African-American student body president, and Alan Louden, an Asian-American fraternity member who was elected vice president, had put together a diverse slate of candidates. As Fulcher related later,

> I wanted to bring people together that had never been put together before. I wanted to put the white Greek organizations into a coalition with the minority organizations. I wanted the gay and lesbian organizations and the Women's Student Union. I just wanted to include everyone in a broad-based coalition where everyone felt like they had a part.[170]

The student alliances formed during 1990 forged political alliances among the students. Many of the "majority" senators that year indicated they had never worked—nor known—so closely with gay people. Further, the multicultural nature of the 1991–1992 Student Senate allowed other students elected to begin their own coming out process.

The 1990–1991 academic year, in some ways, was no different from the previous. The University had not enacted any of GLSOK's demands; there was no change on ROTC, or a sense of safety for non-heterosexual students on the KU campus. Other aspects of campus climate had changed. GLSOK had more official conduits to policy-making members of the administration and the student government. Non-heterosexual students had recognized as a minority with recognizable similarities to ethnic minorities. Perhaps most important, they had become a political force on campus.

CONCLUSION

By the end of the 1990s, non-heterosexual students at the KU were categorized, at least by the Student Senate, as a minority constituency. On March 11, 1998, the KU Student Senate approved a bill submitted by its Student Rights Committee to amend the Student Senate Rules and Regulations to include student senators, "elected or appointed," from minority constituency groups: Black Student Union, Hispanic American Leadership Organization, Native American Student Association, Native American Student Association, and Queers & Allies. These were the student organizations that banded together in the early 1990s.

Such designations were common in student governments by that time. The coalitions between ethnic minority students and non-heterosexual students, aspired to by the radical GLF members of the 1960s and 1970s, came to political maturity in the 1990s. This alliance made by recognizing the similarities of the other's socially constriction and discrimination, however, did not rend asunder U.S. social order; rather, the groups recognized that by combining their forces and resources toward a common goal of campus inclusion, access, and support (both monetary and social), both groups stood a better chance of succeeding.

In the Midwestern state universities, the minority status recognition begun in the 1970s through the registration of gay and lesbian student organizations had slowly, by the 1990s, become accepted as a status for non-discrimination and equal opportunity on campus. It was a slow result made possible by successive cohorts of non-heterosexual student activists, most of whom would not be on their campuses when the changes for which they fought would finally take effect.

Non-heterosexual students were less successful, however, in their attempts to force larger political policy changes. At least, that is, in one regard. The DOD did not change its policies about not allowing non-heterosexuals to serve in the military because of the demonstrations and rallies of the university students. What did change, though not as quickly as the student activists had hoped, was the understanding of lawmakers and policy makers in the U.S. government. The infamous "Don't Ask, Don't Tell" policy of the Clinton Administration went into effect in February of 1994, the first of the small steps toward allowing non-heterosexuals to serve in the military. The non-heterosexual activists lost the battles, but they won the war of public opinion.

NOTES

1. Joshua Mecklen, "Lesbians and Gay Males Hold Rally Against 'U' Housing Policy," *The Michigan Daily*, October 16, 1991, 1, 2: 1.
2. Areeya Chumsai and Jean L. Bonnette, "ROTC Program Still Under Fire," *State News*, November 13, 1991, 3.
3. Chumsai and Bonnette, "ROTC Program Still Under Fire."
4. Frank Krajenke, "LAGROC Adds to Existing Demands," *The Michigan Daily*, April 17, 1990, 1.
5. Krajenke, "LAGROC Adds to Existing Demands."
6. Krajenke, "LAGROC Adds to Existing Demands."
7. S. Jhoanna Robledo, "Gay Activists: Baker Must Quit Over Comments," *Ann Arbor News*, August 1, 1990, A1, A7: A7.
8. Robledo, "Gay Activists: Baker Must Quit Over Comments."
9. Robledo, "Gay Activists: Baker Must Quit Over Comments."
10. Daniel Poux, "Students Speak Out to Regents," *The Michigan Daily*, September 21, 1990, 1, 8: 1.
11. Poux, "Students Speak Out to Regents," 1.
12. Poux, "Students Speak Out to Regents."
13. Poux, "Students Speak Out to Regents."
14. Poux, "Students Speak Out to Regents."
15. Henry Goldblatt, "Students Rally on Diag in Support of Lesbian, Gay Rights," *The Michigan Daily*, February 15, 1991, 1.
16. Karen Sabgir, "Gays, Straights Party Together," *The Michigan Daily*, October 7, 1991, 7.
17. Sabgir, "Gays, Straights Party Together."

18. The 1990s wrought as many changes in nomenclature in the student organizations and their activities as did the 1970s.
19. Mary Lederman, "Rallies and Dance Conclude National Coming Out
Week," *The Michigan Daily*, October 14, 1991, 1, 2: 2.
20. Lederman, "Rallies and Dance Conclude National Coming Out Week," 1.
21. Lederman, "Rallies and Dance Conclude National Coming Out Week."
22. Christy Powell, "OUT Elects New Officers, Forms Semester Agendas,"
Indiana Daily Student, January 22, 1990, 2.
23. Powell, "OUT Elects New Officers, Forms Semester Agendas."
24. Powell, "OUT Elects New Officers, Forms Semester Agendas."
25. Leslie Leasure, "OUT Meeting Attendance Grows," *Indiana Daily
Student*, September 30, 1990, 3.
26. Christy Powell, "Activists Call for Code Reforms," *Indiana Daily Student*,
October 24, 1989, 1, 8: 8.
27. Powell, "Activists Call for Code Reforms."
28. Rochell Denise Thomas, "Kiss-In Held to Demand Rights," *Indiana
Daily Student*, October 13, 1992, 1, 12: 1.
29. David Thompson, "Campus 'Kiss-In' Draws a Reaction," (Bloomington)
Herald-Tribune, October 13, 1993, A1, A2: A1.
30. Thompson, "Campus 'Kiss-In' Draws a Reaction," A2.
31. Thompson, "Campus 'Kiss-In' Draws a Reaction," A2.
32. Chris Devito, "Minority Group Receives Office," *Ohio State Lantern*,
April 16, 1990, 1.
33. Mike Scarce, "Gay and Lesbian Consciousness Raised During 1990," *Ohio
State Lantern*, January 7, 1991, 4.
34. Scarce, "Gay and Lesbian Consciousness Raised During 1990."
35. Chris Devito, "Events to Educate Public About Sexual Preferences," *Ohio
State Lantern*, May 1, 1990, 1, 2.
36. Randy Shilts, *Conduct Unbecoming: Lesbians and Gays in the U.S. Military,
Vietnam to the Persian Gulf* (New York: St. Martin's Press, 1993), 702.
37. Tim Doulin, "Gay Students Want ROTC Ended at OSU," *Columbus
Dispatch*, May 6, 1990, 2B.
38. Jim Criswell, "Rally Demands End to ROTC," *Ohio State Lantern*, May 7,
1990, 1, 2: 1; Tim Doulin, "Gay Students Want ROTC Ended at OSU,"
Columbus Dispatch, May 6, 1990, 2B; Tom Dodge, "Group Demands
ROTC Ouster," *Columbus Dispatch*, May 6, 1990, 1.
39. Criswell, "Rally Demands End to ROTC," 2.
40. Criswell, "Rally Demands End to ROTC," 1.
41. Kurt L. Leib, "Controversy Over Gay, Lesbian Issues Continues," *Ohio
State Lantern*, May 25, 1990, 2.
42. Tim Doulin, "OSU Police Try to Find Who Threatened Gays," *Columbus
Dispatch*, May 25, 1990, 1C.

43. Michael Scare, "Letter to the Editor, Homophobic Values Condoned by OSU," *Ohio State Lantern*, March 23, 1990, 5.
44. Kurt L. Lieb, "Residents Ousted for Threats to Gays," *Ohio State Lantern*, May 24, 1990, 1.
45. Lieb, "Residents Ousted for Threats to Gays"; Doulin, "OSU Police Try to Find Who Threatened Gays"; Tim Doulin, "Homosexual Harassment Isn't Unusual at OSU," *Columbus Dispatch*, May 28, 1990, 1D, 2D.
46. Lieb, "Residents Ousted for Threats to Gays."
47. Lieb, "Residents Ousted for Threats to Gays."
48. Leib, "Controversy Over Gay, Lesbian Issues Continues."
49. Leib, "Controversy Over Gay, Lesbian Issues Continues."
50. Leib, "Controversy Over Gay, Lesbian Issues Continues."
51. Leib, "Controversy Over Gay, Lesbian Issues Continues."
52. Doulin, "OSU Police Try to Find Who Threatened Gays."
53. Doulin, "OSU Police Try to Find Who Threatened Gays."
54. Rex Wockner, "Ohio State Closes Anti-Gay Dorm Wing," July 1990, *Baltimore Alternative*; Doulin, "OSU Police Try to Find Who Threatened Gays."
55. Doulin, "OSU Police Try to Find Who Threatened Gays."
56. "Campus Life: Ohio State; Students Moved for Harassing Gay Roommates," *The New York Times*, June 3, 1990, 43, 44.
57. Jim Criswell, "Gays Look for Change in RDH Bureaucracy," *Ohio State Lantern*, May 29, 1990, 1.
58. Larra Reed, "Students Clash Over Resident Rights," *Ohio State Lantern*, May 25, 1990, 1, 2: 1.
59. Reed, "Students Clash Over Resident Rights," 2.
60. Reed, "Students Clash Over Resident Rights," 2.
61. Criswell, "Gays Look for Change in RDH Bureaucracy," 1.
62. Criswell, "Gays Look for Change in RDH Bureaucracy," 2.
63. Doulin, "OSU Police Try to Find Who Threatened Gays," 1C; also Leib, "Controversy Over Gay, Lesbian Issues Continues," 2.
64. Leib, "Controversy Over Gay, Lesbian Issues Continues," 2.
65. Criswell, "Gays Look for Change in RDH Bureaucracy," 1.
66. Criswell, "Gays Look for Change in RDH Bureaucracy," 1.
67. Sherry Beck Paprocki, "At OSU, Response to Bradley Hall," *Columbus Monthly*, November 1990, 95–98; 97.
68. Paprocki, "At OSU, Response to Bradley Hall," 97.
69. Scarce, "Gay and Lesbian Consciousness Raised During 1990."
70. Paprocki, "At OSU, Response to Bradley Hall," 97.
71. Scarce, "Gay and Lesbian Consciousness Raised During 1990."
72. Scarce, "Gay and Lesbian Consciousness Raised During 1990."
73. Scarce, "Gay and Lesbian Consciousness Raised During 1990."

74. Dona S. Klinger, "USG Charges Military, University with Open Discrimination Policy, Continues to Support OSU ROTC," *Ohio State Lantern*, May 2, 1991, 1, 2.
75. Klinger, "USG Charges Military, University with Open Discrimination Policy, Continues to Support OSU ROTC," 2.
76. Shannon Jackson, "Gays Call for Stand Against ROTC," *Ohio State Lantern*, May 29, 1991, 1, 2.
77. Jackson, "Gays Call for Stand Against ROTC."
78. Tim Doulin, "Gay Men Part of Homecoming Court," *Columbus Dispatch*, October 23, 1991, 2C.
79. Doulin, "Gay Men Part of Homecoming Court."
80. Doulin, "Gay Men Part of Homecoming Court."
81. H. J. Chiu, "OSU To Let Gay Partners Live Together on Campus," *Ohio State Lantern*, May 7, 1993; Aimee Trimarche, "Housing Just Beginning of Equality Goals for OSU Gays," *Ohio State Lantern*, July 8, 1993, 1, 2.
82. Amy Wilkin, "Gay Students Talk with Gee," *Ohio State Lantern*, October 12, 1993, 1.
83. Wilkin, "Gay Students Talk with Gee."
84. Wilkin, "Gay Students Talk with Gee."
85. John D. Simmons, Student Body President, to Matthew Marco, President, GLASSIUE, 4/2/91. Gay and Lesbian Association of Students at SIUE, GLASS, Accession A94:34, Student Organization Records Collection, Louisa H. Bowen University Archives, Lovejoy Library, Southern Illinois University Edwardsville.
86. GLASSIUE Constitution, Gay and Lesbian Association of Students at SIUE, GLASS, Accession A94:34, Student Organization Records Collection, Louisa H. Bowen University Archives, Lovejoy Library, Southern Illinois University Edwardsville.
87. Steve Arney, "Gay-Lesbian Group Plans Campus Party," *Edwardsville Intelligencer*, December 18, 1991.
88. Matthew John Marco to Dear St. Louis Student Organization, March 5, 1991. St. Louis Lesbian and Gay Archives (1987–) Collection (1972–1992), S0545, Series 1, Box 3, File 99: Gay and Lesbian Students at SIU-Edwardsville, (G.L.A.S.S.), 1991, State Historical Society of Missouri, St. Louis.
89. "Turnout for Gay Ball Was Small," *Edwardsville Intelligencer*, January 8, 1992.
90. Wayne Hoffman, "Magazines for Lavender," *Bay Area Reporter*, May 5, 1994.
91. Lori Janies, "Quit Within a Week, Group Tells Bergson," *Minnesota Daily*, October 10, 1989, 1, 10.
92. Janies, "Quit Within a Week, Group Tells Bergson," 11.

93. Blake Morrison, "Paying His Penance?," *Minnesota Daily*, February 13, 1990, 1, 3.
94. The University Gay Lesbian Community organization had split by gender in 1982, and University Lesbians formed their own organization. In 1991, the two joined, along with other, smaller non-heterosexual student groups, as the Association of GLBT Student Organizations and Their Friends (International Communities of Color, Progressive Student Organization G/L/B Caucus, Delta Lambda Phi Fraternity, University Friends of Lesbians and Gays, University Bi Community, and L/G/B Medical Students) as the Association of GLBT Student Organizations and Their Friends, an umbrella coalition.
95. Janies, "Quit Within a Week, Group Tells Bergson," 1.
96. Janies, "Quit Within a Week, Group Tells Bergson," 11.
97. Morrison, "Paying His Penance?," 3.
98. Margaret Taus, "Refusal Won't Deter Students," *Minnesota Daily*, February 28, 1990, 1, 16: 16.
99. Marie Kornak, "Report Calls on U to End ROTC Affiliation," *The Michigan Daily*, April 4, 1990, 3.
100. Jerry Daoust, "Denevan Wins in Election Landslide," *Minnesota Daily*, April 27, 1990, 1, 8: 8.
101. Tom Cushman, "MSA President Suzanne Denevan Discusses Her Agenda at U of M," *Twin Cities GAZE*, 6 June 28, 1990, 1, 5.
102. Cushman, "MSA President Suzanne Denevan Discusses Her Agenda at U of M," 1.
103. Cushman, "MSA President Suzanne Denevan Discusses Her Agenda at U of M," 1.
104. Tim Campbell, "Lesbian Feminist Elected President of U of M Student Association," *GLC Voice*, May 21, 1990, 1.
105. Campbell, "Lesbian Feminist Elected President of U of M Student Association."
106. Wayne Nealis, "Denevan Cited in Code Violation," *Minnesota Daily*, May 1, 1990, 1, 11; Wayne Nealis, "Denevan's Charges Reduced," *Minnesota Daily*, May 17, 1990, 1, 5; Jerry Daoust, "Denevan: I Won't Be Deterred By Charges," *Minnesota Daily*, May 16, 1990, 1.
107. Daoust, "Denevan: I Won't Be Deterred by Charges," 1.
108. Nealis, "Denevan's Charges Reduced."
109. Nealis, "Denevan Cited in Code Violation."
110. Cushman, "MSA President Suzanne Denevan Discusses Her Agenda at U of M," 1.
111. Jerry Daoust, "Denevan Wins in Election Landslide," *Minnesota Daily*, April 27, 1990, 1, 8: 8.
112. Daoust, "Denevan Wins in Election Landslide."

113. Marie Beunaiche, "Denevan Takes Administration, Students to Task," *Minnesota Daily*, October 18, 1990, 1, 4: 1.
114. Beunaiche, "Denevan Takes Administration, Students to Task," 1.
115. Beunaiche, "Denevan Takes Administration, Students to Task," 4.
116. Nealis, "Denevan Cited in Code Violation."
117. Jennifer Corbett, "Denevan: U Must Fight ROTC Homosexual Ban," *Minnesota Daily*, 6/25/90, 4.
118. Campbell, "Lesbian Feminist Elected President of U of M Student Association."
119. Corbett, "Denevan: U Must Fight ROTC Homosexual Ban."
120. Molly Guthrey, "Weekend Events Look at Gay/Lesbian Issues," *Minnesota Daily*, November 20, 1990, 1, 2: 2.
121. Guthrey, "Weekend Events Look at Gay/Lesbian Issues," 1.
122. Wayne Nealis, "MSA President Focuses on Changes," *Minnesota Daily*, November 17, 1990, 1.
123. Marie Beunaiche, "MSA Presidency Overly Bureaucratic," *Minnesota Daily*, October 18, 1990, 4.
124. Patrick Dilley, *Queer Man on Campus: A History of Non-Heterosexual Men in College, 1945–2000*. New York: Routledge Falmer, 2002.
125. "1990: A Look Back at the Year in Lawrence," *Lawrence Journal-World*, December 31, 1990, 8A, 9A: 8A. 2/31/90.
126. Jeff Moberg, "Gay Awareness Week Gets Senate Funds," *University Daily Kansan*, March 10, 1988, 3.
127. Marian Weeks, "Group Wants Amendment for Gay Rights Passed," *University Daily Kansan*, February 2, 1989, 1, 12: 1.
128. Deb Gruver, "Protest Leaders Say They'll Keep Pressuring KU for Action," *Lawrence Journal-World*, April 12, 1990, 1A, 10A.
129. Gruver, "Protest Leaders Say They'll Keep Pressuring KU for Action."
130. Gruver, "Protest Leaders Say They'll Keep Pressuring KU for Action," 10A.
131. Gruver, "Protest Leaders Say They'll Keep Pressuring KU for Action," 10A.
132. Gruver, "Protest Leaders Say They'll Keep Pressuring KU for Action," 10A.
133. Tim Carpenter and Deb Gruver, "KU Officials Meet with Protest Leaders," *Lawrence Journal-World*, April 12, 1990, 1A, 9A: 1A.
134. Carpenter and Gruver, "KU Officials Meet with Protest Leaders," 9A.
135. Deb Gruver, "KU Group Voices Women's Concerns," *Lawrence Journal-World*, October 8, 1990, 8A.
136. Carpenter and Gruver, "KU Officials Meet with Protest Leaders," 9A.
137. Deb Gruver, "KU Officials Meet with Students," *Lawrence Journal-World*, April 13, 1990, 3A.

138. "Gay and Lesbian Awareness Highlighted in GALA Week," *University Daily Kansan*, April 16, 1990, 14.
139. Carol B. Shiney, "GLSOK Members Ask for Placement on Advisory Board," *University Daily Kansan*, April 24, 1990, 3.
140. Tim Carpenter, "KU Groups To Protest ROTC Policy," *Lawrence Journal-World*, May 5, 1990, 3A, 13A.
141. Deb Grover, "Students Protest Over ROTC Vote," September 26, 1990, 3A, 9A.
142. University of Kansas Student Organization Records, University Archives, RG-67, Kenneth Spencer Research Library, University of Kansas, 67/66, Queers & Allies, Box 1.
143. Copies of position papers were included with statement; attached to letter from David A. Ambler to Executive Vice Chancellor Shankel, September 14, 1990. University of Kansas Student Organization Records, University Archives, RG-67, Kenneth Spencer Research Library, University of Kansas, 67/66, Queers & Allies, Box 1.
144. Ibid.
145. Grover, "Students Protest Over ROTC Vote," 9A.
146. Grover, "Students Protest Over ROTC Vote," 9A.
147. Monica Mendoza, "Four Administrators Meet with GLSOK," *University Daily Kansan*, September 28, 1990, 11.
148. "KU Students Protest Incident," *Lawrence Journal-World*, April 15, 1990, 7A.
149. Steve Buckner, "KU Students To Keep Up Pressure," *Lawrence Journal-World*, September 29, 1990, 3. I was in the audience for Davis' speech; my recollections of the events of that night, which are not necessarily reflected in the extant newspaper accounts, are shaped in some part by my involvement in the events and the organizations of the time.
150. I remember asking my friend, Gaywyn Moore, if she would like to go to the chancellor's house; we walked arm-in-arm on the sidewalk alongside Jayhawk Boulevard, and I sang songs from the film *Cabaret*. Sometime after midnight, a cry came from those on the north side of the house that someone should order pizza to be delivered. It seemed more a party than a protest.
151. I am in possession of copies of two different individual's edited copies of this memo. I am not certain the edited memos are in any official archive.
152. Monica Mendoza, "Gay Former Student on Both Sides of Issue," *University Daily Kansan*, September 28, 1990, 1, 9: 1.
153. Mendoza, "Gay Former Student on Both Sides of Issue," 9.
154. I am in possession of a copy of this statement. I am not certain it is in any official archive.

155. Deb Gruver, "KU Students Join Forces To Protest," *Lawrence Journal-World*, October 2, 1990, 1A, 11A; Karen Park, "Protestors Cancel Sit-in, March in Front of Watson," *University Daily Kansan*, October 3, 1990, 1.

156. Park, "Protestors Cancel Sit-in, March in Front of Watson."

157. Monica Mendoza, "Students Find Protests Effective," *University Daily Kansan*, October 3, 1990, 3.

158. Gruver, "KU Students Join Forces To Protest."

159. Delbert M. Shankel to Amy K. Myers, October 5, 1990. University of Kansas Student Organization Records, University Archives, RG-67, Kenneth Spencer Research Library, University of Kansas, 67/66, Queers & Allies, Box 1.

160. Delbert M. Shankel to Amy K. Myers, October 5, 1990. University of Kansas Student Organization Records, University Archives, RG-67, Kenneth Spencer Research Library, University of Kansas, 67/66, Queers & Allies, Box 1.

161. Monica Mendoza, "Office to Add Position," *University Daily Kansan*, October 22, 1990.

162. Monica Mendoza, "GLSOK Display Prompts Confrontation on Campus," *University Daily Kansan*, October 10, 1990, 1, 3.

163. Monica Mendoza, "GLSOK Poster Display Causes Second Campus Confrontation," *University Daily Kansan*, October 11, 1990, 1.

164. Monica Mendoza, "Display Vandalized," *University Daily Kansan*, October 15, 1990, 1.

165. Monica Mendoza, "Candles Denounce Violence, Prejudice," *University Daily Kansan*, October 16, 1990, 3; Deb Gruver, "Man's Injury Still Puzzles KU Police," *Lawrence Journal-World*, November 3, 1990, 3A, 11A.

166. Mendoza, "Candles Denounce Violence, Prejudice."

167. Monica Mendoza, "GLSOK Director Quits, Cites Personal Reasons," *University Daily Kansan*, November 12, 1990, 1.

168. Patricia Rojas, "GLSOK To Rally for National Day of Action About ROTC," *University Daily Kansan*, April 10, 1991, 3; Patricia Rojas, "GLSOK Protest Military Ban," *University Daily Kansan*, April 11, 1991, 1.

169. Delbert M. Shankel to Mike Sullivan, April 15, 1991. University of Kansas Student Organization Records, University Archives, RG-67, Kenneth Spencer Research Library, University of Kansas, 67/66, Queers & Allies, Box 1.

170. J. Duncan Moore Jr., "A Political Prairie Fire," *Los Angeles Times*, October 22, 1991.

CHAPTER 6

How Non-heterosexual Student Groups Utilized Liberation to Achieve Campus Assimilation

In November of 1993, the student newspaper at the University of Northern Iowa profiled Adam Buchanan, a member of the tennis team. Buchanan had just publicly revealed to his team that he was gay. Although at least one of his teammates did not "like" Buchanan's sexual orientation, he (and the rest of the team, a reader of the article would suppose) looked past Buchanan being gay; Buchanan was a good player. Buchanan registered the difference for the paper: "A lot of people think that when you say you're gay, they define it by who you do, not who you are."[1]

Buchanan's experience, along with his conceptualization of his identity vis-a-vis his sexuality, represented many of the changes U.S. non-heterosexual college students experienced between 1969 and 1993. An abject approbation turned into acquiesce, at least if the non-heterosexuals accepted the structures and values of the campus. In other words, if the non-heterosexual students accepted the minority role (which the campus might begrudgingly grant), even in how they thought of their personal identities, non-heterosexual students could by the 1990s engage in campus activities and cultural events. Non-heterosexual collegians could do so as long as they stressed how similar to heterosexuals they were, as long as they were not "too gay" in their self-identities or their campus activities, as long as they were not too outlandish in their affect or behavior.

© The Author(s) 2019
P. Dilley, *Gay Liberation to Campus Assimilation,*
https://doi.org/10.1007/978-3-030-04645-3_6

OPPORTUNITIES AND STRUCTURES

I find three areas in which to understand the nature of non-heterosexual student organizations on U.S. campuses during those years. First is the focus on providing opportunities and structures for non-heterosexual collegians to participate more fully on campus; in this regard, non-heterosexual collegians were making an argument about student rights of access and inclusion that either paralleled earlier ethnic and racial minority students' arguments. Buchanan's ability as a member of a campus sports team to be open about his sexuality—and the response of his teammates—is evidence of that change.

Developing a non-heterosexual identity—particularly proclaiming a specifically "gay" identity—was paramount to the founders of the early Midwestern non-heterosexual college student organizations. The action had political as well as personal motivations; it had cultural connotations beyond describing one's sexual orientation, as one might consider it today.

> Adopting a gay identity in 1969 meant more than simply affirming one's same-sex orientation by declaring oneself "a homosexual"; it meant positioning oneself in relation to a clearly articulated set of commitments and ideals associated at the time with radical politics. First and foremost, being gay in 1969, 1970, or 1971 meant being out of the closet and against the Vietnam War.[2]

The overlap between civil rights, women's rights, gay rights, and the anti-war movement provided energy, encouragement, and example for non-heterosexual student activists.

FORMAL RECOGNITION

The second area of understanding needed for making sense of the changes between 1969 and the early 1990s encompasses the effect of formal recognition of non-heterosexual student campus organizations. Recognition had been the major struggle for the pioneering Midwestern gay and lesbian campus groups. Achieving recognition allowed a foundation to advocate for other campus changes; in addition, it paved the groundwork for establishing understandings (of both students and administrators) of the commonality of non-heterosexual minorities with ethnic and racial minorities.

Mary Bernstein posited that early gay activists found ideological absolutes trumped potential practical gains.

Radicals considered seeking the attainment of minor concession from the existing political structure to be an implicit acceptance of a flawed regime; efforts would be better spent allying with racially and ethnically based revolutionary liberationist movements.[3]

The association of the gay liberationists to other "radical" groups transmogrified as the wider society began to include more non-white, non-heterosexual social- or identity-based populations within the "radical" groups. When and where the organizations had "gained community respect... tactics were moderate. Where access to the polity was limited, however, activists became more militant."[4]

This seems to be true on university campuses in the Midwest between 1969 and 1993. The power of the administration (or the student government) to restrict access to campus rights and privileges inadvertently empowered non-heterosexual students (and other minority students) to organize around radical and militant ideals—or around actions that seemed radical only because someone not of the majority was doing the acting. As the students gained more "respect," more access, and more rights to campus, their ideals changed from one of revolution (breaking the system) to reformation (allowing new entrants to the system). Being "who you are," as Buchanan phrased it, became possible because the concept of "who you are" as a non-heterosexual improved over 25 years, thanks to the efforts of the early campus organizations to provide speakers' bureaus, peer counseling, and, most important, visibility among college students on campuses.

Among the other changes advocated for was inclusion in a university's non-discrimination or protected category status statements. While anti-gay bias was often difficult to document (and without documentation, few administrators seemed too timid to propose such inclusion), one major partner of postsecondary institutions had a specific, codified discrimination statement against non-heterosexuals: the US military. The efforts toward policy reform regarding non-heterosexuals on college campuses during the 1980s and early 1990s centered on forcing universities to honor their non-discrimination statements, either by forcing the military to change its policies or by banning recruitment and training on campuses. Eventually, national policies changed to allow reconciliation, of sorts, between the conflicting university stances.

CHANGING IDEOLOGY

The final area I would highlight is a shift in ideology of the campus organizations: the ethos for the majority of students between the mid-1970s and late 1980s was less revolutionary, more assimilationist, than it had been in the first half of the 1970s. Even as non-heterosexual activists on campus during the late 1980s and early 1990s were more confrontational, even radical, in their tactics, their goals still centered on assimilation into campus (and larger social) structures. Unlike some of the earliest Gay Liberation Front (GLF) founders, later students wanted a seat at the proverbial table of the campus, along with a piece of the pie that was student funding.

A Short History of Early Midwestern Non-heterosexual Student Organizing

I use these three general areas of change to scaffold a condensed version of the 25 years covered in the earlier chapters of this book. The earliest organizing of non-heterosexual students into campus groups began in the late 1960s, and by the mid-1970s, most state universities in the Midwest had at least one, if not more, such organization. The organizers of the earliest groups were influenced greatly by the Gay Liberation Movement (GLM), as well as other movements that had significant campus presences (specifically the women's movement, the Black Power movement, and the anti-war movement). Mary Bernstein noted that "Liberationists sought recognition for a new transformative identity that challenged dominant understandings of both heterosexual and homosexual identity."[5] Not surprisingly, the pioneering founders shared in the liberation ethos of the time, espousing questions of—and desires to deconstruct—heteronormative social constructs, such as marriage and gender roles. As early Philadelphia GLF member Tommi Avicolli Mecca noted,

> Despite its shortcomings, gay liberation succeeded in making coming out a queer rite of passage. It was a political strategy that affirmed the feminist adage that the personal is political. It was also a revolutionary act at a time when polite company didn't discuss sex, let along [sic] someone's sexual orientation.[6]

After this initial organizing on college campuses,[7] gay and lesbian student organizations transitioned from models of direct campus activism for Gay Liberation to providers of campus services.[8] In part, this seems a response to the limited utility of Gay Liberation, as a concept, to prompt the revolutionary change upon which it was predicated, not the least of which was on university campuses, a culture notoriously slow to change.

Hal Tarr, a GLF member at the University of Pennsylvania in the early 1970s, observed the GLF's effectiveness.

> GLF was created with the idea that the country would experience a revolution of some sort. As that did not seem to be taking place, the framework of GLF seemed more and more separated from reality.[9]

The defining elements of gay and lesbian activism became less grounded in "Gay Liberation,"[10] but more in creating structures of "gay culture,"[11] particularly through crafting "respectable" public images.[12]

In conjunction with this, and perhaps in contradiction to this, many of those non-heterosexual student leaders sought to establish structures and services on campus to support non-heterosexual students participate on campus. Such efforts included changes in campus counseling services, medical services (particularly for women), and campus, town, and state rules and laws prohibiting non-heterosexuals from congregating or having sex.

Organized Dancing

Dancing—and sponsoring dances—was a central activity of non-heterosexual student organizations across the Midwest. A survey of "a broad cross-section of campus gay groups throughout the U.S. and Canada" conducted by the national gay newspaper *The Advocate* in 1976 documented "that dances are the most popular activity of the campus gay groups."[13] As simple as it might seem in retrospect, dancing with someone of one's own gender was a consistent goal among the membership of non-heterosexual student organizations across the country in the last quarter of the twentieth century. The act of dancing was seen in the last half of the twentieth century as a rite of youth as well as in some instances a political action.[14] Further, in the early 1970s most Midwestern states had changed drinking laws, even those allowing for consumption of beer, raising the drinking age. Non-heterosexual college students under age 21 were thus barred from dancing in social establishments off campus. Both aspects of teenage life were denied to non-heterosexual youth, not only by social custom but also by codified discrimination in city and state laws.

Having a space to dance meant having a space in which to enact a form of sexuality. The inherent sexuality of dancing had been clear, if not often spoken of, by straight college students (and administrators) for decades[15]; nonetheless, both formal and informal dances were allowed by, even sponsored by, postsecondary institutions. Prior to the early Gay Liberation student activists, however, even same-gender dancing in private rooms was not allowed. Gay Liberation and its successor organizations changed that on campus.[16]

In addition, dances sponsored by the campus organizations provided visibility of the group (both the number of non-heterosexual attendees and the number of straight people in the area who were willing to associate with non-heterosexuals). The dances were first held off campus but later became offered on most of the campuses in this study. The dances also provided an opportunity for the student organizations to raise funds for their campus activities, which until the late 1980s were often not funded either by the institution or its student government, and when funded usually poorly and with no guarantee of future funds.

University of Kansas (KU) student leader Ruth Lichtwardt remembered hundreds of people would attend dances there,

> including many from Kansas City who would normally have been at the bars.... People were dressed in everything from street clothes to gender-fuck.... People we talked to had come in from Manhattan, Wichita, Topeka, and even Omaha for this dance....
>
> None of us in Kansas City knew much about the gay organization at KU except it was a student group that held the dances to raise money. Because I knew of GLSOK's existence through the dances, however, one of the first things I did when I became a KU student in the Spring of 1981 was try to look them up.[17]

The queer dances at Kansas, as well as Indiana, Illinois, Minnesota, Iowa State, and other universities, served as a visible announcement of non-heterosexuals on campus, to those on and off campus.

Campus Services

Beyond dancing, during the mid-1970s through the 1980s, the efforts of non-heterosexual campus student organizations centered on providing other services, as well as advocating for institutional support or administration of those services. Gay and lesbian students were providing the vast majority of the education on college campuses about non-heterosexual issues and identities; by the late 1980s, they were also providing the vast majority of the education on HIV and AIDS. They were ensared in what Maia Ettinger termed the "Pocahontas Paradigm," in which a dominated population allowed into a culture while simultaneously being made to both to educate about itself to the majority population while also expected to absolve and forgive the dominators.[18] Other minority populations on campus were in similar straights, so to speak. Alliances with—and following proven strategies of—racial- and gender-based identity student protesters and organizers provided a model of identity and campus initiative for non-heterosexual students. Similarly, Bernstein, in analyzing the political alignment of non-heterosexual state politics, noted a shift in gay and lesbian organizing that is also evident in the Midwest student campus groups.

> By the end of the 1970s, the lesbian and gay movement had undergone profound internal change. Activists no longer placed the same emphasis on challenging gender roles and the construction of heterosexuality.... [A]n ethnic- or interest-group model that sought achievement of rights replaced the liberation model that sought freedom from constraining gender roles and sexual categories.[19]

Gay and lesbian students might be only tangentially involved in a campus organization, but the student leaders of those organizations were often very heavily involved in issues and circumstances that called upon them in ways straight students would probably never feel.

Having to deal with coming to terms with their own sexuality, their own changing identities, academic coursework, fighting for inclusion on campus, sometimes becoming part of the campus governance system, and providing the education for enlightenment of the straight students on campus could burn out undergraduates. Sometimes it did, and the campus organizations' institutional memories suffered for it, while the administration usually gained.

The organizations included students with varying identities, genders, ages, membership in other populations and organizations, and experiences of coming out; tensions over ideologies, identities, and strategies were bound to result. Bernstein is again helpful in understanding this part of the history from an organizational-action perspective. Dissent within the population—between those who exercise agency within other organizations and those who feel they have no agency—"will lead to factionalization and will produce moderates who will focus more on education and traditional lobbing tactics and radicals who will focus on criticizing dominant values."[20] Certainly this seems to have been the case for at least two students from KU: Amy Myers, who resigned from being director of Gay and Lesbian Services of Kansas (GLSOK) in 1990 because of disagreements over whether and how the group should "be" political, and David Hardy, who moved from activist to administrator, gaining "insider" access and counsel to those who could make change while giving up some of his "outsider" agency to prompt such change to be made.

RE-QUEERING ACTIVISM

By the end of the 1980s, most Midwestern non-heterosexual college organizations had established the foundations of their efforts on campus. Most held some form of campus-wide or city-wide celebration of National Coming Out Day in the fall semester (often encompassing a whole week) and a Gay Pride Week (usually in late spring, although sometimes in the summer, to coincide with the anniversary of the Stonewall riots). Almost all of the Midwestern campus non-heterosexual student organizations had a version of a speakers' bureau to provide personal experiences of individual non-heterosexuals to classes and/or campus housing units. Additionally, most non-heterosexual campus organizations at the Midwestern universities provided at least one form of peer counseling on coming, either over the phone or in person, at private group discussion sessions.

Also during that time, popular and campus press represented gay and lesbian issues more than in the past—and generally in less negative fashions— but the AIDS epidemic became synonymous with gay life and identity. The effect of AIDS on the membership and the efforts of the campus gay and lesbian student organizations was dramatic. AIDS was devastating older alumni; the identity politics of the previous years taught many students that coming out put one at risk of bodily harm; and stories perpetuating the dangerous aspects (or, more judgmentally, consequences) of being young and non-heterosexual as fraught with danger and isolation. Student organizations responded, in part, by initiating campus AIDS education efforts, sponsoring candlelight vigils to raise awareness, and hosting speakers on campus.

In the 1980s, more non-heterosexual students entered into campus leadership and student governance positions. Their activism led them to vary their efforts to shape campus policy and lived experience for non-heterosexual students. Although universities were sometimes slow to allow non-heterosexual students into the structures of campus culture, non-heterosexual student activists found places within the structure from which to attempt to advocate for change to the system.

Conversely, by the late 1980s other non-heterosexual students also enacted a form of organizing that harkened back to the early GLFs on campuses and their tactics of public confrontations. "Queer" started to become used, hesitantly and guardedly at first, to describe collective non-heterosexual identities, as compared to the monolithic norm of hetero-sexual identity. The very notion of a queer identity called into question the power of those allowed to demarcate an identity as normal or abnormal.[21] ACT UP and Queer Nation developed in the United States during the late 1980s, primarily in protest to the lack of public awareness or response to the effect of AIDS in the gay community.

> Queer Nation began in New York in 1990, and almost immediately attracted hundreds of burnt-out ACT UP members, community leaders and self-proclaimed "baby dykes and fags" who wanted to organize around some-thing besides AIDS. To be sure, the emphasis was more on polis than eros, with the group defining itself as a "militant and uncompromising group dedicated to subverting compulsory heterosexism in all its political and cul-tural manifestations through direct public actions which will celebrate and flaunt sexual diversity."[22]

The combined ACT UP/Queer Nation movement briefly flourished on larger campuses in the Midwest (and across the country) in the early 1990s. It was rare for either group to register as official student organiza-tions, in part to allow its members greater freedom to flaunt the rules imposed by the universities.

On colleges, ACT UP generally focused on campus policies regarding HIV-positive students, on-campus medical treatments and insurance, and sexual health education efforts. Its ethos was to prompt the institutions to provide medical and other health-related services on campus, particularly to gay men.

Queer Nation, on the other hand, filled a philosophical void that had resulted when the non-heterosexual student organizations focused on campus reform for inclusion rather than ideological deconstruction of het-eronormative society. As social historian Douglas Sadownick noted,

> Like ACT UP before it, Queer Nation thrived on the politics of panache – fol-lowing one activist's imperative, "Go Out There and Be Fabulous." ... Queer Nation tapped into a growing distrust of polite lobbying, checkbook activism, and electoral campaigns to effect political change when it so militantly sani-tized gay life.... Like in the early days of GLF, rage against the system was often channeled into lots of making out and safer-sex jerk-off sessions.[23]

Queer Nation questioned, in very public and showy ways, why institutions would not provide tangible, codified protections of the rights for non-heterosexuals on campus.

If such protections were in place, Queer Nation would stage demonstrations to highlight the inconsistency either of the implementation of those policies (particularly concerning the discrepancies between the institution having non-discrimination language yet allowing Reserve Officer Training Corps and military activities on campus) or of the remaining social stigma against non-heterosexuals engaging in the embedded, gendered, heteronormative culture on campus (particularly evident when same-gendered students held hands or kissed on campus). Still, even those Queer Nation or ACT UP demonstrations that were publicly confrontational of social mores on campus generally were not disruptive of the educational function of the institutions.

By their very nature, Queer Nation and ACT UP required publicity, much like the early Gay and Lesbian Movement "zaps" or demonstrations. By the 1990s, non-heterosexual college students, like many of their activist peers, had learned how to make use of the press. The media on campus might have been more effective at reaching administrators who implemented policies, while media not focused on campus might be more effective at reaching those who made such policies.[24]

OBSERVATIONS

If it seems from a historical vantage point as if the early Midwestern student organizations kept rehashing the same issues, repeating the same arguments and strategies for themselves and their campuses, I would point out two cautions. The first is that by their very nature, colleges do not typically afford students a long period of time in which to make lasting change in the campus culture; indeed, many of the administrators of the campuses in this study seemed to bank on that.

Still, I am struck by the turnover in all of the positions of leadership or publicity, over the years as well as within them. Is it because of egalitarianism? Is it due to pressures students faced, either in time management or in stress? Is it because of the rush of coming out, which is replaced by the complacency of living out? Yes, probably, to all.

Second, these students had lives and responsibilities on campus beyond their work in the non-heterosexual organizations. It is easy to forget that they were doing all of this activism in addition to going to classes, trying to graduate, dealing with all of the issues inherent in college student development and simply "growing up." There was little to know "generational" transition or training; each successive cohort of non-heterosexual students had to learn on its own. Nonetheless, cohort found its own activism; at the core of whatever form of activism, however, was a desire to be included on campus.

ANALYZING THE ORGANIZATIONS' HISTORIES

I posit two sets of themes that describe the student organizations. They are complementary, even overlapping, but I believe they are distinct. Each set of themes has four components that generally occurred sequentially (although that sequence did not necessarily indicate the completion or end of the earlier component). The first set of themes analyzes the efforts of the organizations for itself, as a collection of individuals, as a group, and as a minority. The second set branches from the first set, and it concerns the efforts of the organization's function within the campus.

Internal Themes

Four broad themes reflect the interpersonal aspects of the early Midwestern non-heterosexual student organizations. Particularly during the early 1970s, fostering the members' development of an identity as "gay" or "lesbian" was paramount to the efforts of the organizations. Over time, the nomenclature and details of such an identity changed, but the core remained the same: distinguished from heterosexual. By the 1990s, as more examples of people holding such identities were more evident in society, developing a non-heterosexual identity was less a major feature of the student organization; nonetheless, many student organizations offered forms of peer counseling that focused on individuals' personal efforts at coming out and coming to accept his/her self.

Recognition For the earliest members of Midwestern non-heterosexual student organizations, fostering ways and means for non-heterosexuals to "come out" as such was vital. Philosophically, it was akin to the consciousness-raising ethos of many of the other "movements" of the times; one had to have, and to proclaim, an awareness of one's true beliefs and self in order to be a fully functioning person.

Practically, the organizers needed membership in their groups, not simply to allow for interpersonal communication but also to be recognized by their universities. A group of students asking for change made more of an impression upon administrators than one or two. In order to have a foothold on campus, the groups needed to be recognized by the institutions, at best in a formal sense but at least unofficially.

Such recognition was key to non-heterosexuals being seen as analogous to ethnic or racial minorities. Legal precedent—and resulting increasing social acceptance, such as it was—allowed minority students a codified status on campus. Long-term social changes for gay and lesbian students would require codification on campus as a minority.

Visibility Recognition by the institution in and of itself would provide a form of visibility for the non-heterosexual organizations on campus; so, too, would regular meetings and events. Visibility was a double-edged sword for the early campus organizations: on the one hand, visibility was vital to informing non-heterosexuals that there was a "place" for them on campus; on the other hand, it also provided those who would harass and discriminate against non-heterosexuals a target upon those who went to that "place." While there was safety in numbers, those who lived in fear realized that at some point, everyone went home alone. By the organizations producing increasingly public and visible activities on campus, however, their members became more adept at feeling comfortable being "out" in public settings.

Vocality For decades, homosexuals had generally been viewed as meek and quiet. Such estimations changed through the actions of the Gay Movement, and they influenced the efforts of the early Midwestern gay and lesbian student organizations. One factor of great importance was the ability to speak one's own truth, to admit one's sexuality and sexual identity; to be able to do so in public, on campus, was a sign of increased personal acceptance. To be able to do so as a representative (officer or member) of a non-heterosexual student organization was a sign of strength, both for the individual and the organization. More voices provided greater evidence of the vitality of the organization as a functioning component of campus life.

Representation The final theme intersecting the interpersonal development of the non-heterosexual student organizations and their members was a summation of the earlier three. How would one represent the totality of herself: her sense of self-recognition, her visibility on campus, her voice in campus and social matters? Consequently, how would the organization represent itself?

This was a shifting representation, as both individuals and their groupings changed over time, in relation to the individuals' lives, the campus environment, and the larger social culture. Still, as historian David Eisenbach noted,

> One of the great achievements of the gay liberation movement was the display of the nonstereotypical, well-adjusted homosexual on the televisions in millions of American living rooms.[25]

Typically after the very early 1970s, the organizations strived to be seen on campus as an "official," representative voice of a particular minority of students on campus, and in this, usually deferred to more "respectable" or "gentile" stances, rather than dramatic or revolutionary stances. By the end of the 1980s, however, non-heterosexual student organizations returned in many instances to public demonstrations. Like those of the 1970s, 1980s demonstrators strove to prompt change—but in policy, rather than in social order or structures. Students used their same-sex sexuality to disrupt campus norms, but only to draw attention to the presumption that non-heterosexuals should not engage in such public activities as kissing or holding hands. Despite their tactics, the demonstrators' goal was to have their actions, their lives, their identities considered "normal"—"just like everyone else."

External Themes

Four broad themes encapsulate the early Midwestern student gay and lesbian (and during the 1970s and 1980s, those were often two distinct groups of students) organizations' efforts on behalf of the students and campus populations. They are outreach, awareness, inclusion, and policy change advocacy.

Outreach Campus gay and lesbian student organizations (and to be clear, those were often two distinct sets of organizations on many Midwestern campuses) had initially been founded at least in part with a mission of outreach to non-heterosexuals on campus and in their surrounding communities. Gay and lesbian students used their campus organizations to provide direct services to non-heterosexual students, including phone peer counseling, in-person peer counseling, social meeting times (including formal meetings, coffeehouse settings, and informal times in office spaces or other "appropriated" space in campus union buildings), and dances on campus. Many of these services, particularly those designed to assist individual students in their self-identification processes, are now typically provided by offices of student affairs at most universities.

Awareness The non-heterosexual campus organizations created opportunities, aimed primarily at straight students but also reaching non-heterosexuals not in the organizations, opportunities that would provide visibility of non-heterosexual issues on campus. These activities included kiss-in, annual "Pride Day" or "Pride Week" activities, annual "Gay and Lesbian Awareness Week" activities, "wear blue jeans if you're gay" events, and, perhaps most important, speakers' bureaus for campus classes and/or organizations. Speakers' bureaus allowed for straight students to hear the stories of, and ask questions of, non-heterosexual peers, but such programs also allowed the students to tell their stories, to find coherence and meaning through composing their narrative.

Inclusion Campus GLB efforts quickly left behind the most confrontational, liberation ideology and became quite assimilationist in their endeavors. The students strove for inclusion in the structures and functions of campus activities; often their rhetoric to justify such inclusion was that non-heterosexual students comprised a unified (or even able to be unified) minority population on campus, akin to racial and ethnic student populations. Publicly identifying non-heterosexual students served in campus governance and leadership, in part to be included but also to help enact policy changes (to ensure funding, for instance, for campus non-heterosexual organizations). Reaching out to recognized minority student populations built alliances and understandings of common experiences of being outside of the majority of students on their campuses.

Despite its earliest credo and models for campus organizing, the GLM on most Midwestern campuses failed to live up to its aspiration of racial minority inclusion. During the period of time for this study, the percentage of students enrolled at Midwestern universities was often in the single digits, perhaps more if all minority students were included. Students who came out as non-heterosexual faced greater alienation, not just from straight communities but from their minority community on campus; they feared having to make a choice that would leave them even more vulnerable in a potentially very hostile campus environment. As one black student at KU told me in 1992, when I asked why he would stop by and visit with members of GLSOK but not attend a Thursday night meeting: "If I go to a meeting on Thursday night, it's going to be all over town by church on Sunday morning."

Policy Changes The fourth theme stems from inclusion. The late 1980s and early 1990s could be termed the "great time of campus climate studies." Such studies were undertaken by a number of postsecondary Midwestern campuses (as well as at postsecondary institutions across the country), usually at the insistence of the student organizations, to limn the opportunities for and preclusion from campus activities experienced by non-heterosexual students (along with faculty and staff).

It was as if each campus administration were echoing University of Michigan President Harold Shapiro, who could not seem to believe that non-heterosexuals felt discrimination or harassment on campus because he had been presented no "hard data." No campus wanted to believe, let alone admit, that it fostered such bigoted or prejudicial sentiments. But, as the campus committees charged with conducting such studies spent months documenting and reporting, no campus was uniquely spared from the negative aspects of heteronormative culture.

CONCLUSIONS

I find three areas in which to understand the nature of LGB organizations on U.S. college campuses over these two decades. First is the focus upon providing opportunities and structures for non-heterosexual students to participate fully on campuses; in this regard, non-heterosexual collegians were making an argument about student rights of access and inclusion that either paralleled earlier ethnic and racial minority students' arguments. Second is a shift in ideology in the campus organizations: the ideology for the majority of the students between the mid-1970s and early 1990s was less revolutionary, more assimilationist, than it had been in the decade preceding it. Further, the activities enacted by the organizations reflected this shift; even those that were publicly confrontational of social mores were disruptive not of the educational function of the institutions.

The earliest, most basic form of activity of the campus gay and lesbian groups was outreach to those who identified (or who would identify) as non-heterosexual. Initially, that outreach was couched in terms and actions familiar to student protesters (street theater, "zaps," etc.), but even those actions were designed in large part to build a campus presence of like-minded gays and lesbians. Outreach, in turn, prompted different and/or greater campus awareness of non-heterosexual people, issues, and politics.

Awareness allowed understanding (and sometimes allegiances) between the non-heterosexual student organizations and organizations composed of or representing other campus minority populations; those understandings influenced strategies to change campus policies to include non-heterosexual populations specifically and/or better. When such strategies were deemed unable to reconcile institutional ideals to specific policies, some students returned to the civil disobedience and public theater, through activities and symbols aligned with the Queer Nation and ACT UP movements.

Is Sexuality Identity?

Recently, seemingly growing numbers of non-heterosexual youth and students have posited that their sexual orientation is but one part of their identity, and not always the most salient part in their self-definitions; some of those youth are even disassociating their identities from their sexual orientation: they are not gay, through action, culture, or identity.[26] They echo Northern Iowa's Adam Buchanan; the sentiment of their statements can be traced back to the 1970s, when campus newspapers featured articles on "the gay lifestyle," as something one lived not something one was. As one Gay Illini member said in 1975,

> A person's sexuality is only a part of his life style... it is not all there is to it. To say that all gay people have a certain life style and other people have another life style just doesn't work.[27]

The term would soon catch on as a condemnation from the conservatives of the 1970s and 1980s, who preached that being non-heterosexual was a choice one made.

Still, to some non-heterosexual campus gay organization members, like the students at the end of the 2010s, sexuality was simply a component of one's self, perhaps not even the defining component. To them, sexual orientation is perhaps nothing notable.

But if sexual orientation is nothing, then sexual orientation has been assimilated into a conceptualization of identity espoused by the assimilationists: being gay is not notable, and performing a "gay" identity is perhaps unnecessary. Perhaps society has been reformed, creating a culture where one could choose not to identify as non-heterosexual (or a particular form or type of non-heterosexual).

Of course, such choices are never made in a social vacuum, nor without consequences: there are still in American society members who discriminate, even to the point of political and personal violence, against those who proclaim themselves (or who are perceived as) non-heterosexual. After completing this project, I am left wondering new questions.

What would the choices of past non-heterosexual college student organizers be today? Would the gay activists of the 1970s be pleased with the extent of the influence of gays and lesbians upon public culture; would they despair at the lack of fundamental change to the social structures that continue to reinforce monetary, social, and political capitalistic stratification and preference? Has, then, as historian Martin Duberman concluded, the GLM failed? After all, the GLF:

> ...saw its mission as challenging and changing mainstream norms, not complying with the.... GLF radicals insisted that gay people were not just like everyone else....[28]

Gay cultural critic Michael Warner bemoaned the acquiescence into the roles in accepted social constructs of marriage; the model of marriage constitutionally eliminates the very ideals that fortified early gay identity.

> Marriage, in short, would make for good gays – the kind who would not challenge the norms of straight culture, who would not flaunt sexuality and who would not insist on living differently from ordinary folk.[29]

On the other hand, might not the next generation of non-heterosexual college students be correct in wanting to be included and unquestioningly accepted as a positive, "good" campus minority population? That might explain their focus, which evolved in the 1980s into arguments for equal benefits and, eventually, rationales for encouraging marriage between non-heterosexuals, as the ultimate demonstration of acceptance.

Would the gay and lesbian college students of the 1980s be satisfied with the current levels or forms of inclusion of campus and social services for non-heterosexuals into most segments of college life, including politics, student affairs, and the canon? Would the activists of the 1980s and early 1990s feel that they were ghettoized in the academy even when their topics, their lives, were being (slightly) included into the general curricula? Perhaps most important: Are student organizations geared toward socialization opportunities for non-heterosexual students even necessary, given social media and the reluctance of many of today's college students to accept, let alone to adopt, a "label" for their sexuality? Has non-heterosexual student assimilation into campus made the point of non-heterosexual student organizations moot?

If non-heterosexuals are "just like everyone else," if their identities are not the central component of their identity, if their identities are parallel to straight identities, then, clearly, the answers to the questions I posed are clear. Non-heterosexuals would need no campus representation, no particularly focused services. Being gay or lesbian would be no big deal, nothing special to note, no different from anyone else. And if being non-heterosexual is nothing "special," then part of the efforts of the early gay and lesbian campus activists would have been pointless.

Initially, "gay" and "lesbian" were not only markers of personal identity but also a cultural marker. The concept of non-heterosexuals being campus minorities was based upon proving coherent, consistent experiences, from which gays and lesbians made sense of their lives. This sense was demonstrated through shared values as much as shared cultural markers such as music, art, and literature. But the cultural distinction seems to have lapsed: few current students seemingly want to focus on "gay" topics or aspects of their identities, let alone to feel delimited in choices of where to live or where to socialize. Have these students so ingrained in the effects of their assimilated socialization that they do not see the extent to which their choices have already been taken from them?

Gay liberationists—and, to a great extent, those who inherited the social and collegiate organizations founded by the gay libbers—were creating a culture one could choose to be in: gay "ghettos" in the cities, gay-identified social spaces in which the norms of the heteronormative world could be ignored, flouted, or flipped. Whether in particular spaces in the Student Union, dances on campus, or even student organization offices, non-heterosexual students would have the freedom to explore their "different" identity without the judgmental norms of heterosexual society, if just for a short while. For many, that experience was more moving, more important, than "fitting in" most of the time.

Notes

1. Jason Etzen, "Sexuality Not a Problem for Northern Iowa Tennis Team," *Northern Iowan*, November 12, 1993, 16.
2. Justin David Suran, "Coming Out Against the War: Antimilitarism and the Politicization of Homosexuality in the Era of Vietnam," *American Quarterly*, 53, No. 3 (September 2001), 452–488, 463.

3. Mary Bernstein, "Identities and Politics: Toward a Historical Understanding of the Lesbian and Gay Movement," *Social Science History*, 26, No. 3 (Fall 2002), 531–581, 545.

4. Bernstein, "Identities and Politics," 545.

5. Bernstein, "Identities and Politics," 552.

6. Tommi Avicolli Mecca (Ed.), *Smash the Church, Smash the State: The Early Years of Gay Liberation* (San Francisco: City Light Books, 2009), p. xii.

7. Brett Beemyn, "The Silence is Broken: A History of the First Lesbian, Gay, and Bisexual College Student Groups." *Journal of the History of Sexuality*, 12, no. 2 (April 2003), 205–223.

8. Jessica Clawson, "Coming Out of the Campus Closet: The Emerging Visibility of Queer Students at the University of Florida, 1970–1982," *Educational Studies*, 50, No. 3 (2014), 209–230; Patrick Dilley, *Queer Man on Campus: A History of Non-Heterosexual Men in College, 1945–2000* (New York: Routledge, 2002).

9. Hal Tarr, "A Consciousness Raised," pp. 22–39 in Tommi Avicolli Mecca, ed., *Smash the Church, Smash the State: The Early Years of Gay Liberation* (San Francisco: City Light Books, 2009), 29.

10. David Eisenbach, *Gay Power: An American Revolution* (New York: Carroll & Graf, 2006); Donn Teal, *The Gay Militants: How Gay Liberation Began in America, 1969–1971* (New York: St. Martin's Press, 1995).

11. See, for example, Frank Browning, *The Culture of Desire: Paradox and Perversity in Gay Lives Today* (New York: Crown Publishers, 1993); Jim Downs, *Stand By Me: The Forgotten History of Gay Liberation* (New York: Basic Books, 2016); and Lillian Faderman and Stuart Timmons, *Gay L.A.: A History of Sexual Outlaws, Power Politics, and Lipstick Lesbians* (New York: Basic Books, 2006).

12. See Vincent Doyle, *Making Out in the Mainstream: GLAAD and the Politics of Respectability* (Montreal: McGill-Queen's University Press, 2016); and Joshua Gamson, *Freaks Talk Back: Tabloid Talk Shows and Gender Nonconformity* (Chicago: University of Chicago Press, 1998).

13. Randy Shilts, "Gay Campus Movement," *The Advocate*, September 8, 1976, 6.

14. See, for instance, Mary Louise Adams, *The Trouble with Normal: Postwar Youth and the Making of Heterosexuality* (Toronto: University of Toronto Press, 1977), pp. 76–80; Maxine Leeds Craig, *Sorry I Don't Dance: Why Men Refuse to Move* (New York: Oxford University Press, 2014); and Mark Kurlasky, *Ready for a Brand New Beat: How "Dancing in the Street" Became an Anthem for Changing America* (New York: Riverhead Books, 2013).

15. See Beth Bailey, *Sex in the Heartland* (Cambridge, MA: Harvard University Press, 1999) and Paula S. Fass, *The Damned and the Beautiful: American Youth in the 1920s* (New York: Oxford University Press, 1977).

16. For more on typical administrative responses to non-heterosexuals dancing on campus earlier in the 20th Century, see William Wright, Harvard's *Secret Court: The Savage 1920 Purge of Campus Homosexuals* (New York: St. Martin's Press, 2005).

17. Ruth Lichtwardt, quoted in Patrick Dilley, *Queer Man on Campus: A History of Non-Heterosexual Men in College, 1945–2000* (New York: Routledge Falmer, 2002), pp. 175–176.

18. Maia Ettinger, "The Pocahontas Paradigm, or Will the Subaltern Please Shut Up?" In *Tilting the Tower: Lesbians Teaching Queer Subjects*, ed. Linda Garber (New York: Routledge, 1994), 51–55.

19. Bernstein, "Identities and Politics," 548.

20. Bernstein, "Identities and Politics," 541.

21. Patrick Dilley, "Queer Theory: Under Construction." *QSE: International Journal of Qualitative Studies in Education*, 50, No. 3 (1999), 209–230; Michael Warner, *The Trouble with Normal: Sex, Politics, and the Ethics of Queer Life* (New York: Free Press, 1999).

22. Douglas Sadownick, *Sex Between Men: An Intimate History of the Sex Lives of Gay Men Postwar to Present* (San Francisco: Harper San Francisco, 1996), 191.

23. Sadownick, *Sex Between Men*, 192.

24. See Robert Rhoads, *Freedom's Web: Student Activism in an Age of Cultural Diversity* (Philadelphia: Johns Hopkins University Press, 1998); Tony Vallela, *New Voices: Student Activism in the '80s and '90s* (Boston: South End Press, 1988).

25. David Eisenbach, *Gay Power: An American Revolution* (New York: Carroll & Graf, 2006), 258.

26. See Lisa M. Diamond, *Sexual Fluidity: Understanding Women's Love and Desire* (Cambridge, MA: Harvard University Press, 2008); Ritch C. Savin-Williams, *Becoming Who I Am: Young Men on Being Gay* (Cambridge, MA: Harvard University Press, 2016); Ritch C. Savin-Williams, *Mostly Straight: Sexual Fluidity Among Men* (Cambridge, MA: Harvard University Press, 2017); and Jane Ward, *Not Gay: Sex Between Straight White Men* (New York: New York University Press, 2015).

27. Judith Agusti, "Gay Illini Discuss Concerns on Weekly Basis," *Daily Illini*, October 29, 1975, 14, 17: 14.

28. Martin Duberman, *Has the Gay Movement Failed?* (Oakland, CA: University of California Press, 2018), 13–14.

29. Warner, *The Trouble With Normal*, 113.

BIBLIOGRAPHY

BOOKS/DISSERTATIONS/THESES

Adams, Mary Louise. *The Trouble with Normal: Postwar Youth and the Making of Heterosexuality.* Toronto, Canada: University of Toronto Press, 1997.

Armstrong, Elizabeth A. *Forging Gay Identities: Organizing Sexuality in San Francisco, 1950–1994.* Chicago: University of Chicago Press, 2002.

Bailey, Beth. *Sex in the Heartland.* Cambridge, MA: Harvard University Press, 1999.

Bell, Arthur. *Dancing the Gay Lib Blues: A Year in the Homosexual Liberation Movement.* New York: Simon & Schuster, 1971.

Browning, Frank. *The Culture of Desire: Paradox and Perversity in Gay Lives Today.* New York: Crown Publishers, 1993.

Carman, Michael. "Not Everything Happens In San Francisco": Creating Sociopolitical Mobilization in Identity-Politics-Era Lansing. Honors thesis: Michigan State University, April 25, 2011.

Carter, David. *Stonewall: The Riots That Sparked the Gay Revolution.* New York: St. Martin's Press, 2004.

Clawson, Jessica. "Queer on Campus: LGBTQ Student Visibility at Three Public Universities in Florida, 1970–1985." Ph.D. Dissertation: University of Florida, 2014.

Clendinen, Dudley, and Adam Nagourney. *Out for Good: The Struggle to Build a Gay Rights Movement in America.* New York: Simon & Schuster, 1999.

Craig, Maxine Leeds. *Sorry I Don't Dance: Why Men Refuse to Move.* New York: Oxford University Press, 2014.

© The Author(s) 2019   253
P. Dilley, *Gay Liberation to Campus Assimilation,*
https://doi.org/10.1007/978-3-030-04645-3

Cruikshank, Margaret. *The Gay and Lesbian Liberation Movement.* New York: Routledge, 1992.

Diamond, Lisa M. *Sexual Fluidity: Understanding Women's Love and Desire.* Cambridge, MA: Harvard University Press, 2008.

Dilley, Patrick. *Queer Man on Campus: A History of Non-Heterosexual Men in College, 1945–2000.* New York: RoutledgeFalmer, 2002.

Downs, Jim. *Stand By Me: The Forgotten History of Gay Liberation.* New York: Basic Books, 2016.

Doyle, Vincent. *Making Out in the Mainstream: GLAAD and the Politics of Respectability.* Montreal, Canada: McGill-Queen's University Press, 2016.

Duberman, Martin. *Stonewall.* New York: Dutton, 1993.

Duberman, Martin. *Has the Gay Movement Failed?* Oakland, CA: University of California Press, 2018.

Eisenbach, David. *Gay Power: An American Revolution.* New York: Carroll & Graf, 2006.

Faderman, Lillian. *The Gay Revolution: The Story of the Struggle.* New York: Simon & Schuster, 2015.

Faderman, Lillian, and Stuart Timmons, *Gay L.A.: A History of Sexual Outlaws, Power Politics, and Lipstick Lesbians.* New York: Basic Books, 2006.

Fass, Paula S. *The Damned and the Beautiful: American Youth in the 1920s.* New York: Oxford University Press, 1977.

Gamson, Joshua. *Freaks Talk Back: Tabloid Talk Shows and Gender Nonconformity.* Chicago: University of Chicago Press, 1998.

Hewetson, Dick. *History of the Gay Movement in Minnesota and the Role of the Minnesota Civil Liberties Union.* Minneapolis, MN: Friends of the Bill of Rights Foundation, 2013.

Horowitz, Helen Lefkowitz. *Campus Life: Undergraduate Cultures from the End of the Eighteenth Century to the Present.* New York: Alfred A. Knopf, 1987.

Jay, Karla. *Tales of the Lavender Menace: A Memoir of Liberation.* New York: Basic Books, 1999.

Jay, Karla, and Allen Young. *Out of the Closet: Voices of Gay Liberation.* New York: Douglas Books, 1972.

Kantrowitz, Arnie. *Under the Rainbow: Growing Up Gay.* New York: William Morrow and Co., 1977.

Katz, Jonathan Ned. *The Invention of Heterosexuality.* New York: Dutton, 1995.

Kurlansky, Mark. *Ready for a Brand New Beat: How "Dancing in the Street" Became an Anthem for a Changing America.* New York: Riverhead Books, 2013.

Lewis, Carolyn Herbst. *Prescription for Heterosexuality: Sexual Citizenship in the Cold War Era.* Chapel Hill, NC: University of North Carolina Press, 2010.

Marcus, Eric. *Making History: The Struggle for Gay and Lesbian Equal Rights, 1945–1990: An Oral History.* New York: Harper Collins, 1992.

Marotta, Toby. *The Politics of Homosexuality.* Boston: Houghton Mifflin, 1981.

McConnell, Michael, with Jack Baker, and Gail Langer Karwoski. *The Wedding Heard 'Round the World: America's First Gay Marriage.* Minneapolis, MN: University of Minnesota Press, 2016.

Mecca, Tommi Avicolli (Ed.). *Smash the Church, Smash the State: The Early Years of Gay Liberation.* San Francisco: City Lights Books, 2009.

Moore, Patrick. *Beyond Shame: Reclaiming the Abandoned History of Radical Gay Sexuality.* Boston: Beacon Press, 2004.

Oberlin College Alumni Office. *Into the Pink: An Oral History of Lesbian, Gay, and Bisexual Students at Oberlin College from 1937 to 1991.* Oberlin, OH: Amherst College Library, 1996.

Rhoads, Robert A. *Freedom's Web: Student Activism in an Age of Cultural Diversity.* Baltimore, MD: Johns Hopkins University Press, 1998.

Sadownick, Douglas. *Sex Between Men: An Intimate History of the Sex Lives of Gay Men Postwar to Present.* San Francisco: Harper San Francisco, 1996.

Savin-Williams, Ritch C. *Becoming Who I Am: Young Men on Being Gay.* Cambridge, MA: Harvard University Press, 2016.

Savin-Williams, Ritch C. *Mostly Straight: Sexual Fluidity Among Men.* Cambridge, MA: Harvard University Press, 2017.

Shilts, Randy. *Conduct Unbecoming: Lesbians and Gays in the U.S. Military, Vietnam to the Persian Gulf.* New York: St. Martin's Press, 1993.

Teal, Donn. *The Gay Militants: How Gay Liberation Began in America, 1969–1971.* New York: St. Martin's Press, 1995.

Vellela, Tony. *New Voices: Student Activism in the '80s and '90s.* Boston: South End Press, 1988.

Ward, Jane. *Not Gay: Sex Between Straight White Men.* New York: New York University Press, 2015.

Warner, Michael. *The Trouble with Normal: Sex, Politics, and the Ethics of Queer Life.* New York: Free Press, 1999.

Wright, William. *Harvard's Secret Court: The Savage 1929 Purge of Campus Homosexuals.* New York: St. Martin's Press, 2005.

Young, Allen. *Left, Gay & Green: A Writer's Life.* North Charleston, SC: CreateSpace, 2018

Chapters/Articles

Altbach, Philip G., and Robert Cohen. "American Student Activism: The Post-Sixties Transformation." *Journal of Higher Education*, 61, No. 1 (January–February, 1990): 32–49.

Beemyn, Brett. "The Silence is Broken: A History of the First Lesbian, Gay, and Bisexual College Student Groups." *Journal of the History of Sexuality*, 12, No. 2 (April, 2003): 205–223.

Bernstein, Mary. "Celebration and Suppression: The Strategic Uses of Identity by the Lesbian and Gay Movement." *American Journal of Sociology*, 103, No. 3 (November, 1997): 531–565.

Bernstein, Mary. "Identities and Politics: Toward a Historical Understanding of the Lesbian and Gay Movement." *Social Science History*, 26, No. 3 (Fall, 2002): 531–581.

Clawson, Jessica. "Coming Out of the Campus Closet: The Emerging Visibility of Queer Students at the University of Florida, 1970–1982." *Educational Studies: Journal of the American Educational Studies Association*, 50, No. 3 (2014): 209–230.

Dilley, Patrick. "Queer Theory: Under Construction." *QSE: International Journal of Qualitative Studies in Education*, 12, No. 5 (1999): 457–472.

Dilley, Patrick. "20th Century Post-secondary Practices and Policies to Control Gay Students." *Review of Higher Education*, 25, No. 4 (2002): 409–431.

Faulkenbury, T. Evan, and Aaron Hayworth. "The Carolina Gay Association, Oral History, and Coming Out at the University of North Carolina." *Oral History Review*, 43, No. 4 (2016): 115–137.

Lewis, Abram J. "'We Are Certain of Our Own Insanity': Antipsychiatry and the Gay Liberation Movement, 1968–1980." *Journal of the History of Sexuality*, 25, No. 1 (January 2016): 83–113.

Meyer, Richard. "*Gay Power* Circa 1970: Visual Strategies for Sexual Revolution." *Gay and Lesbian Quarterly*, 12, No. 3 (2006): 441–464.

Reichard, David A. "'We Can't Hide and They Are Wrong': The Society for Homosexual Freedom and the Struggle for Recognition at Sacramento State College, 1969–1971." *Law and History Review*, 28, No. 3 (August 2010): 629–674.

Reichard, David A. "Behind the Scenes at the Gayzette: The Gay Student Union and Queer World Making at UCLA in the 1970s." *Oral History Review*, 43, No. 1 (2016): 98–114.

Reinhold, Robert, "Thousands of Campus Homosexuals Organize Openly to Win Community Acceptance," *New York Times*, 12/15/71, 1, 2.

Shilts, Randy. "Gay Campus Movement." *The Advocate*, 9/8/76, 6.

Suran, Justin David. "Coming Out Against the War: Antimilitarism and the Politicization of Homosexuality in the Era of Vietnam." *American Quarterly*, 53, No. 3 (September, 2001): 452–488.

Tarr, Hal. "A Consciousness Raised." In Tommi Avicolli Mecca (Ed.), *Smash the Church, Smash the State: The Early Years of Gay Liberation* (San Francisco: City Light Books, 2009), 22–39.

Wrathall, John D. "'What are you after?': A History of Lesbians, Gay Men, Bisexuals and Transgender People at the Twin Cities Campus of the University of Minnesota, 1969–1993." In *Breaking the Silence: Final Report of the Select Committee on Lesbian, Gay, and Bisexual Concerns, University of Minnesota*, November 1, 1993, 48–58.

Index[1]

A

ACT UP, 8, 166, 185, 206, 214, 222, 241, 242, 248
ACT UP KU, 214
Adams, Molly, 128
AIDS, 8, 124, 125, 143, 168, 169, 185, 187, 207, 214, 238, 240, 241
Ambler, David B., 107, 108
Andes, Aaron, 216, 217, 221
Anti-apartheid movement, 175n115
Anti-war movement, 7, 21, 80, 234, 236
Armstrong, Elizabeth, 95

B

Bach, Patricia, 167, 168
Baker, Deane, 162–164, 184–186
Baker, Jack, 1–4, 21–25, 27
Baldwin, Janet, 79
Banning, James, 111
Barker, Frank, 55, 57
Bass, Jeffrey, 187
Bergson, Brian, 199–201

Bernish, Kathryn, 198
Bernstein, Mary, 10n4, 95, 234, 236, 239
Black Men of Today (BMOT) (University of Kansas), 206, 208, 220
Black Power movement, 7, 236
Blake, Michael, 51–53, 142
Boerger, Kristina, 146, 149, 151
Bolin, John, 104
Brock, Mark, 58
Bruce, Aaron, 126, 127, 130
Brumm, Dennis, 103
Buchanan, Adam, 235
Budig, Gene A., 137, 209, 210, 212, 214, 215, 220
Burch, Ken, 52

C

Carman, Michael, 77, 79, 112n1
Cervantes, Angela, 223
Chalmers, E. Laurence, Jr., 104–106

[1]Note: Page numbers followed by 'n' refer to notes.

© The Author(s) 2019
P. Dilley, *Gay Liberation to Campus Assimilation*,
https://doi.org/10.1007/978-3-030-04645-3

Civil rights movement, 21, 58, 91, 95, 121
Clendinen, Dudley, 11n4, 24
Conte, Marc, 169
Cosgrove, Terry, 144, 152, 154
Craig, Chris, 216, 220, 222
Cross-dressing, laws against, 58, 59

D
Dances and dancing, gay, 10, 55
Danos, George, 152, 153
Daughters of Bilitis, 62
Davis, Angela, 216
De Grieck, Jerry, 33, 34, 37–42
Denevan, Suzanne, 202–206
Dilley, Glenda, 110
Duberman, Martin, 3, 11n4, 249
Duderstadt, James, 167, 185
Durrance, Brian, 184

E
Edmiston, Dennis, 55
Eisenbach, David, 11n4, 245
Eisenburg, Elyse, 78, 79
Elliott, Kevin, 131
Ellis, Alan, 149
Ellis, Jonathan, 126
Ettinger, Maia, 238
Everhart, Thomas E., 144–146, 149–154
Eversole, Ann, 215, 216

F
Feminist movement, 21
Fighting Repression of Erotic Expression (FREE), 15–26
Fleming, Robben, 30, 31, 33–35, 38–41, 160, 162–164
Fletcher, Thomas, 169
Foriatt, James, 62
Foubert, Michael, 136, 140, 141

Franko, Joe, 102
Friedman, Mike, 147
Fulcher, Darren, 223

G
Gair, Cynthia, 41
Gaudard, Don, 76
Gay Activists Alliance (GAA), 58–63
Gay Alliance (aka Bisexual Gay and Lesbian Alliance, Ohio State University), 5, 6, 14, 17, 45–47, 57–63, 122, 168–169, 181, 189–198, 212
Gay and Lesbian Association of Students at SIUE (GLASS, GLASSIUE), 198
Gay and Lesbian Awareness Week, 56, 139, 141, 188, 207, 212, 221, 223, 246
Gay identity, 234, 248–250
Gay Illini (aka Gay and Lesbian Illini), 97–101, 119–121, 143, 144, 147, 148, 151–153, 155, 248
Gay Liberation Front (Ames, Iowa State University), 101, 102
Gay Liberation Front (Ann Arbor, University of Michigan), 26, 28–32, 37–39, 124
Gay Liberation Front (Bloomington, Indiana University), 41–49
Gay Liberation Front (Lawrence, University of Kansas), 103–108
Gay Liberation Front (New York City–main), 18, 26, 58, 96
Gay Liberation Front (Ohio State University), 57–63
Gay Liberation Front (University of Illinois), 89–101
Gay Liberation Front (University of Iowa), 49–53
Gay Liberation Front (University of Missouri), 108–111

Gay Liberation Front (University of Pennsylvania), 237
Gay Liberation Movement (Michigan State University), 6, 75–112
Gay Liberation Organization (Southern Illinois University Carbondale), 6, 54–55
Gay Mobilizing Committee (GMC), 94
Gay People's Alliance (Iowa State University), 13
Gay People's Liberation (University of Iowa), 53, 142
Gay People's Union (University of Iowa), 142
Gay Pride Week, 62, 122, 187, 213, 240
Gay Services of Kansas (aka Gay and Lesbian Services of Kansas), 131, 206, 207, 213, 219
Gay Students' Alliance (University of Illinois), 95
Gay-Lesbian Council (aka Lesbian-Gay Council) (Michigan State University), 82–85
Gee, E. Gordon, 197, 198
Gilley, Shirley, 131
Gittings, Barbara, 56
Godre, Cathy, 128, 130
Gordon, Michael, 187
Graff, Leonard, 76, 77, 80, 81
Graham, Phil, 20
Graubart, Jeffrey, 90
Griswold, Wendy, 212

H
Halfhill, Robert, 18, 21–23
Hall, Amie, 212
Hall, William, 192, 193
Hanson, Terry, 20
Hardy, David, 140, 141, 215, 216, 218, 219, 240
Haskell Indian Junior College, 208, 222

Heinfling, Debbie, 79
Higgins, Thom, 23
Human Rights Party (HRP), 41–42
Hutson, Paul, 49

I
Ihrig, Stephen, 15–18, 20, 22–26
Illinois State University, 13
Imber, Steve, 133–139, 141, 142
Indiana Gay Awareness Conferences, 47–49
Indiana University, 6, 41–49, 187–188
Iowa State University, 6, 101–103, 167

J
Jacobson, Robert J., 200, 203, 204
Johnson, Henry, 162, 177n173
Johnson, John, 55
Jones, Dan, 82–89

K
Kaiser, Danny, 215, 216, 218
Kameny, Franklin, 56
Katzman, Andrea, 210
Kincaid, Sharon, 56, 57
Kiss-ins, 149, 167, 188
Knauss, Robert, 40, 41
Knedler, Brian, 169
Kunstler, William, 105
Kurtz, Linda, 166, 168, 185

L
Lange, Kristin, 210, 223
Lenarz, Nick, 20
Lesbian Alliance (Iowa State University), 103
Lesbian Alliance (University of Iowa), 6, 49–53, 142

Lesbian and Gay Rights Organizing
Committee (LaGROC),
124–131, 156–168, 177n173,
183–185
Lesbian Liberation Organization
(Indiana University), 46
Lichtwardt, Ruth, 131–142, 238
Lisowski, Edward, 90
Logan, Albert N., 148, 154
Louden, Alan, 223
Lucksted, Alicia, 159

M
Madamba, Ben, 155
Mallicoat, Jerry, 169
Manning, Scott, 219, 222
Marco, Matthew, 199
Martin, Chris, 155
Matlovich, Leonard, 48, 55
Mattachine Society, 62
Maurer, Patrice, 185
McClure, Marc, 209
McConnell, Michael, 1, 27
McPartalin, David, 200
Mecca, Tommi Avicolli, 236
Michigan State University, 6, 75–112,
182–183
Miller, Lyn, 18, 20, 21
Miller, Patrick, 59, 60
Mitchell, Duncan, 187
Myers, Amy, 213, 214, 222, 239
Myers, Patti, 165
Myers, Skip, 169

N
Nagourney, Adam, 11n4
National Coming Out Day, 167, 168,
186, 240
New Queer Agenda (University of
Michigan), 186
Nordby, Virginia, 159–162, 165

O
Ohio State University, 6, 57–63,
168–169, 189–198

P
Peterson, Tim, 20
Phelps, Koreen, 15–18, 20–25, 63n6
Phillips, Mike, 164
Prados, Joe, 104

Q
Queer Nation, 8, 166, 204–206, 241,
242, 248
Queers Action Committee (QUAC),
125, 128

R
Radical Lesbians (aka Radicalesbians),
37, 38, 40, 61
Reserve Officer Training Corps
(ROTC), 36, 126, 130, 131, 181,
183, 186, 187, 189–191, 197,
199–204, 206, 212–215, 219,
224, 242
Rogers, Howard, 135
Rogers, Mark, 92, 93
Russo, Vito, 48
Ryan, John W., 48

S
Sadownick, Douglas, 241
Sargent, Mary Lee, 145, 147
Satterfield, Arthur, 223
Savage, Dan, 149, 153
Scarce, Michael, 169, 191–193,
197, 198
Schreiner, Michael, 212
Schwaller, Henry, 212, 220
Shanesey, Mary Ellen, 149

Shankel, Delbert, 107, 216, 221–223
Shapiro, Harold, 127, 128, 159,
    162, 247
Shaw, Jack, 59, 60
Shelley, Martha, 62, 144
Sherman, Marcy, 130
Sims, Larry, 169
Smith, Caryl, 209, 218
Smith, Gary, 49, 51
Smith, Robert J., 63
Soldier, Rodney, 222
Southern Illinois University
    Carbondale, 6, 54–55
Southern Illinois University
    Edwardsville, 6, 55–57, 198–199
Stillwell, John Steven, 104
Stock, John, 56
Struble, John, 47
Stubbs, Michael, 104
Students for a Democratic Society (SDS),
    7, 28, 36, 39, 52, 76, 96, 109
Sullivan, Charley, 182
Sullivan, Michael, 223

T
Tarr, Hal, 237
Taylor, John, 54, 55
Templar, George, 105, 106
Tolbert, Liz, 207, 212, 215, 222
Toy, James, 124

U
United Coalition Against Racism
    (UCAR), 158
University of Illinois, 6, 54, 63n1,
    89–100, 119–121, 143–155

University of Iowa, 6, 49–53, 103,
    142–143
University of Kansas, 6, 103–108,
    131–142, 167, 182, 200,
    206–224, 238, 239
University of Michigan, 6, 26–42,
    121–131, 155–168, 184, 186,
    206–224, 247
University of Minnesota–Twin Cities,
    2, 6, 15–25, 27, 204–224
University of Missouri, 6, 108–111
University of Northern Iowa, 6, 233
University of Wisconsin–Madison,
    14–15, 191

V
Van Norman, Allison, 186
Vasbinder, Susan, 60–62
Vogel, Carla, 133, 134

W
Wandel, Rich, 62
Warner, Louis, 90
Warner, Michael, 249
Wayman, Carol, 156, 157, 159–161,
    163, 183
Weaver, Steven, 104
Wechsler, Nancy, 41, 42
Wells, Stanfield, 36, 37, 39, 185
Whitsell, Larry, 56, 57
Withem, Brian, 188

Y
Yapalater, Jeffrey, 61, 62
Young, Allen, 96

CPSIA information can be obtained
at www.ICGtesting.com
Printed in the USA
LVHW081708280219
609071LV00003B/3/P